THE SCHOLASTIC
ART & WRITING AWARDS
PRESENTS

THE BEST TEEN WRITING OF 2013

Edited by
LORETTA LÓPEZ
2010 Scholastic Awards
Gold Medal Portfolio Recipient

Foreword by
TERRANCE HAYES
2010 National Book Award
Recipient in Poetry

**Scholastic
Art & Writing
Awards**

For information or permission, contact:
Alliance for Young Artists & Writers
557 Broadway
New York, NY 10012
www.artandwriting.org

Editor: Loretta López
Senior Manager, Programs: Scott Larner
Managing Editor: Lisa Feder-Feitel
Graphic Designer: Meg Callery
Copy Editor: Ingrid Accardi
Production Assistant: Michael Vinereanu
Cover art: *Bird Man*, Guannan Liu, Grade 11, Age 16,
Chatham, IL. 2013 Gold Medal and American Visions Medal.

Anthology printing, September 2013
ISBN: 978-1492337317
ISBN: 1492337315

DEDICATION

The Best Teen Writing of 2013 is dedicated to the extraordinary team at Scholastic Inc. Corporate Communications and Media Relations: Kyle Good, Cathy Lasiewicz, Morgan Baden, Anne Sparkman, and Lia Zneimer. Their genuine dedication to the students and appreciation for the students' work shines through in everything they do for the Awards and the Alliance for Young Artists & Writers. By raising awareness of the program in national and local media, the team is instrumental in both giving students access to scholarships and helping the Scholastic Art & Writing Awards fulfill its mission.

This committed team works tirelessly to promote the Scholastic Art & Writing Awards. Its many contributions include highlighting students in their hometown newspapers and other local media outlets, approaching national media with trends and themes among Award winners for feature articles, highlighting the National Student Poet Program, spreading the word about Scholastic Awards ceremonies and exhibitions on events pages in print and online, and promoting the visibility of the Awards through social media.

In this 90th Anniversary year, the team's outreach efforts on behalf of the Scholastic Art & Writing Awards proved integral in bringing the program to thousands of new students and teachers. Behind the scenes, Kyle, Cathy, Morgan, Anne, and Lia bring us ever closer to our goal of ensuring that every creative student has the opportunity to submit and be celebrated for their work. Year after year, this amazing group of professionals adds tremendous value to what it means to receive a Scholastic Art & Writing Award.

TABLE OF CONTENTS

ABOUT THE BEST TEEN WRITING OF 2013

The works featured in *The Best Teen Writing of 2013* were selected from National Award–winning written work in this year's Scholastic Art & Writing Awards. The Awards is a national program presented by the Alliance for Young Artists & Writers, which recognizes talented teenagers in the visual and literary arts. Founded in 1923, the program celebrates the accomplishments of creative students and extends opportunities for recognition, exhibition, publication, and scholarships.

This year, 543 teens earned National Scholastic Awards in writing categories. The works selected for this publication represent the diversity of the National Award winners, including age and grade, gender, genre, geography, and subject matter. They also present a spectrum of the insight and creative intellect that inform many award-winning pieces.

A complete listing of National Award winners and online galleries of winning works of art and writing can be found on our website, www.artandwriting.org. Information about how to enter the 2014 Scholastic Art & Writing Awards, a list of our scholarship partners, and ways that you can partner with the Alliance to support young artists and writers in your community are also available.

Some of the writing selections have been excerpted. Go to **www.artandwriting.org/galleries** to read all of the work as it was submitted.

ABOUT THE SCHOLASTIC AWARDS

Started in 1923 by Scholastic founder Maurice R. Robinson, the Awards have grown to become the nation's highest honor and largest source of scholarships for creative teenagers. All students in grades 7–12, whether public, private, or home schooled, are encouraged to apply. Through a nationwide network of more than 115 partnering organizations, the 2013 Awards received more than 230,000 submissions in 28 categories.

Notable Scholastic Awards alumni include Andy Warhol, Richard Avedon, Ken Burns, Truman Capote, Lena Dunham, John Updike, Sylvia Plath, and many more.

RECOGNITION The Alliance and our partners provided regional and national recognition to more than 60,000 teens in 2013. Students earned iconic Gold Key and Silver Key awards, as well as Honorable Mention certificates at the regional level.

The top 15,000 regional winners competed in the national competition—1,700 of whom earned national medals and were celebrated at the annual Awards Ceremony at Carnegie Hall in New York City. Thousands of fellow students, families, and friends celebrated along with those in New York City by tuning in to our 90th Anniversary National Awards Ceremony webcast (**www.artandwriting.org/carnegiewebcast2013**).

EXHIBITION One thousand works were displayed at the ART. WRITE.NOW. National Exhibition at Parsons The New School for Design's Sheila C. Johnson Design Center and Pratt Institute's Pratt Manhattan Gallery in New York City.

The ART.WRITE.NOW. Tour, a traveling exhibition featuring a selection of National Award–winning work, will make stops in Albuquerque, NM; Laramie, WY; Savanah, GA; and

Pittsburgh, PA. The U.S. Department of Education and the President's Committee on the Arts and the Humanities will also host a yearlong exhibition in Washington, D.C.

PUBLICATION This anthology, *The Best Teen Writing of 2013*, features a collection of our students' most exemplary works of writing. The Alliance also features National Award–winning work in our National Catalog and on our website. These publications are distributed free of charge to schools, students, teachers, museums, libraries, and arts organizations.

SCHOLARSHIPS The Alliance distributes nearly $250,000 in direct scholarships annually to National Award–winning students. Seniors also leverage their success in the Awards for funds from a network of 60 partnering universities, colleges, and art schools, which collectively earmark more than $8 million in financial aid and additional scholarships.

NATIONAL STUDENT POETS PROGRAM In 2011, the President's Committee on the Arts and the Humanities and the Institute for Museum and Library Services partnered with the Alliance to create the National Student Poets Program (NSPP), the country's highest honor for youth poets presenting original work. Annually, five high school poets who demonstrate exceptional creativity, dedication to craft, and promise serve for a year as national poetry ambassadors.

National Student Poets are chosen from national medalists in the Scholastic Art & Writing Awards by a jury of literary luminaries and leaders in education and the arts. Student Poets receive college scholarships, opportunities to present their work at writing events, and appear at the National Book Festival in Washington, D.C., in cooperation with the Library of Congress.

THE BEST TEEN WRITING 2013 JURORS

American Voices
Kurt Andersen
Edwidge Danticat
John Darnielle
Kay Parks Haas
Karrie Jacobs
Kamran Pasha
Davy Rothbart
Kerri Schlottman
Ned Vizzini

Best in Grade
Annabeth Bondor-Stone
Carolyn Boriss-Krimsky
Leila Sales
Eliot Schrefer
Lisa Schulman
Laura Tisdel

Creativity and Citizenship
Kevin Bales
John Leland
Margy Rochlin

Dramatic Script
Blair Brown
Joanna Settle
Connor White

Flash Fiction
David Krasnow
Elizabeth Lee Wurtzel
Leigh Stein

Humor
Jesse Andrews
Nate Dern
Chris Kelly
Horatio Sanz

Journalism
Melinda Beck
Thom Duffy
Fred Kaplan

New York Life Award
Nell Beram
Carole Geithner

Personal Essay / Memoir
Esther Allen
Moira Bailey
Negin Farsad

Persuasive Writing
Shelley Coriell
Robin Kawakami
Brenda Natoli

Poetry

Laura Baudo Sillerman

Jen Benka

Aracelis Girmay

Brett Fletcher Laurer

Alice Quinn

Carole Spearin McCauley

Sci-Fi / Fantasy

Naif Al-Mutawa

Peter Beagle

Sarwat Chadda

Hannah Jones

Senior Writing Portfolio

Reza Aslan

Eireann Corrigan

Myla Goldberg

David Shenk

Pete Theroux

Short Story

Tanya Baker

Rebecca Bondor

Jill Eisenstadt

Courtney Eldridge

Carson Moss

Helen Schulman

FOREWORD
Terrance Hayes
2010 National Book Award Recipient in Poetry

A decree went out across the land: The king desired a meeting with the world's single best runner. Candidates began arriving almost instantly, by foot, naturally, but by train too, by buggy and bus, horseback and camel. By sunset the next day, the king's courtyard was filled with runners of every stripe: men, women, children, old and young, short, thin, tall, plump. I know because I was there among them. We stood beholding the king's perplexed brow. He'd expected three or four svelte runners from the corners of the earth, perhaps a woman with wings on her shoes, a man with muscular calf muscles. What he got numbered in the dozens, hundreds. Had his message been confused? (No one had been brave enough to ask him what kind of runner he required or why.) The king summoned the court messenger to his throne for an explanation.

"Well, your Highness," the messenger said nervously. "I called for the one who ran the fastest, but I figured the one who was quickest would probably lack stamina. So I called also for the one who ran the farthest, but I suspected one who could cover the greatest distance would probably be too slow. So I summoned the best in both areas, Sire."

The king nodded. He looked out over the crowd.

"Then I called for the runner who could run up a mountain best," the messenger continued, "and the runner who could run through a dark tangled forest best, and the runner who ran best with no shoes, the runner who ran best wearing armor, the runner who ran best in the rain—"

The king cut him off, frowning. "Was there no single runner superior in all these categories?" The king was thinking back to the myths he read in his youth. Hermes, Nike, Mercury. He'd expected someone who was half man, half god, half cheetah.

"There are runners who do many things well, your Majesty," the messenger said, clearing his throat. "But, in reality, no one is simply the best at all of them."

The king sat stroking his beard for a long moment.

Yes, I was in the crowd too.

I grew up running and was well aware of those who were bigger, faster, stronger. My coach always advised us to race against the clock and our "personal bests." (Maybe this is why runners mostly practice in solitude.) Even in the game, we were advised to focus on our own lane not the lanes around us. Writing too is a matter of solitude and personal bests. But play the running analogy out and you know someone always finishes first and someone always finishes last. Is that synonymous with who is the best? No, no.

I have spent much of these past months reading journals in search of the best poems published this year. I'm editing an annual publication of the best contemporary American poetry and have had a lot of time to think about what "best" means. At the beginning of the process I thought only the poems that made me weep or laugh out loud should qualify as "the best of the best." Then I encountered great narrative poems, great musical poems, great formal poems, great experimental poems, great surprises. Like the messenger, I came to see the difficulties in seeking a singular "best." This is, as you likely know, especially impossible when it comes to art. It seemed better to make "best" a word with lots of room, lots of versatility.

This anthology is a celebration of personal bests. Each of these teen writers is distinguished for originality, craft, and voice. Each is like the serious runner who works on speed as well as endurance. It is also an encouragement for those literary athletes who are not yet here.

Dear Reader, you should not go into this marvelous anthology with a measuring stick. Do not make the king's mistake of narrowing your gaze according to a slim vision of the best. The king! I forgot to finish the story about the king. "When I said best, perhaps what I should have said was excellent." The king said finally. "I would like only those who chase excellence." "That you have, your Highness!" the messenger chirped. A roar burst from the crowd.

There are losses and failures in track and writing that still sting a bit—but let's not get into that. It is ambition enough to race yourself, to try making the next thing you write better than the last thing you wrote. This anthology celebrates excellence, brilliance, and potential. Let us celebrate all that comes after the best.

EDITOR'S INTRODUCTION
Loretta López
2010 Portfolio Gold Medalist
Scholastic Art & Writing Awards

In the year 2013, we are saturated with information. Technology has given us access to an unimaginable number of stories, allowing us to understand our world through a plethora of perspectives. However, the nature of its format—malleable and intangible—allows us to skim through ideas for a millisecond, only to click away. As we become accustomed to the fast pace at which technology permits us to travel, we may also begin to excuse our impatience. While we search through a surplus of information, we might dismiss what does not immediately please us and miss out on a mind-opening experience.

As you read through this anthology, be conscious of your attention span. Indulge in the practice of patience. If a story or poem does not fit into the context of your life and knowledge, I challenge you to stop and listen harder. For these brave writers prove to us that in the midst of daily commotion, there is time to explore unconventional and innovative ideas.

The writers in this anthology address difficult subjects with honesty, inventiveness, and humor. They investigate moments of beauty carefully and recognize the complexity of happiness. As an audience, we are not underestimated. We have been given room to interpret and delve into the multiplicity of meaning. And while everyone in this book is brave, each individual is courageous in a distinct way, in his or her own tone and genre.

Some writers choose to share their opinions in personal memories. They ask us to meditate on challenging questions: What does it mean to be an American citizen? How can we find happiness in adult life? What labels do we place on our sexuality and why? Others, determined to persuade readers, audaciously denounce the practices of multi-billion-dollar corporations. Within these pages, a concerned teenager writes a sincere letter to Wal-Mart and a young man defends the rights of women by advocating funding for Planned Parenthood. Equally daring, fiction writers examine surreal and absurd scenarios—a girl eats her house for dinner, two drunken cowboys converse with violent talking bears, and a doorman discovers the disappointing secret that lies behind the door he has guarded his whole life. As readers we must decipher metaphors, and enjoy finding our own answers to our inquiries. A few writers take us a step deeper into this process. They let go of plots, schemes, and characters and prioritize language, forcing us to be imaginative readers who read stories twice, three times, even more.

Listen to these voices carefully. Turn the pages of this book or scroll down your screen slowly. Agree and disagree.

React.

Be disgusted, angered, confused, excited, pleased, and inspired.

Then, amid the commotion, carve out a moment of time to write your own creative response. Convince yourself to take your writing beyond a first draft. Show your work to others, let your words get criticized, edited, cut. As you are influenced by the work you read here and elsewhere, become an observer of your surroundings. Give yourself time to pay attention. Study the lines of a stranger's expression at a train station. Eavesdrop on passersby on your evening walk. Don't let your surroundings intimidate or bore you. Write and give your imagination permission to exaggerate.

The writers in this book share with us their visions and voices. They have invited us to engage with them. Let's be brave enough to respond.

LEAH BYDALEK, *Limbo*, Grade 12, Age 17. Cypress Falls High School, Houston, TX, Bryan Reese, *Teacher*. 2013 Portfolio Gold Medalist.

PORTFOLIO GOLD MEDALS

Graduating high school seniors may submit a portfolio of three to eight works for review by authors, educators, and literary professionals. Recipients of the Gold Medal Writing Portfolio receive a $10,000 scholarship.

Some of the writing selections have been excerpted. Go to **www.artandwriting.org/galleries** to read all of the work as it was submitted.

Unraveling

KATHLEEN RADIGAN, Grade 12, Age 18. The Prout School,
Wakefield, RI, Marion Wrye, *Teacher*

Take your mouth and sew it over someone else's skin.
You learn a lot about string that way,
and lowering a tongue like a corpse into a casket
can teach you a thing or two
about dying.
I have one breath left and I'm learning how to say it all at once.
In Harlem, men are burning tires.
In suburbs, *Good Housekeeping* magazines lie face-up on
tables.
In Paris, they're learning how to sing—salt and wine and
mayonnaise
swirling in kitchens.
So swing around the next fellow who blusters in and offer him
your arm.
Shine a light on a dog in a thunderstorm.
This is the beginning.
Take the hands of the boy you love and let them go through
you.
Learn about stalling on paper wings.
Blow the bees out their hives.

Thin Ice

ISABELLA GIOVANNINI, Grade 12, Age 18. Writopia Lab,
New York, NY, Rebecca Wallace-Segall, *Teacher*

The first thing you are supposed to do if ice begins to crack is to lie down and be very still. But how do you do that if the ice isn't really ice and the crack isn't really a crack?

We have been best friends for nine years—since kindergarten—but we have had some fragile patches. I remember so clearly the chill sight of her with her arm about another girl's shoulders, walking by laughing. We have been thrown together in circumstances of outstanding pressure and become stuck, like tectonic plates. We've had a couple of major earthquakes.

After every earthquake, there must be one moment when the Earth is perfectly still. Then it slowly begins to slide smoothly again. This New Year's Eve, we were just beginning to slide again. We were relearning the deep connections we had, and reconfiguring how they linked us.

I stepped over the black line where there was no snow and onto the frozen lake. To my surprise, I sank about six inches before hitting hard ice. The wind whipped straight into my face, through the scarf, slamming into my cheeks and hurtling past. It blasted into my eyes at fifty miles per hour and made my eyelashes hum. I hunched over and clutched the rolled rug I was holding even tighter. Each step was a task. First, one silver boot had to be lifted up and up over the snow and prodded forward into the wind. Then it sank down through millions of snowflakes to the ice, which had to be tested before putting weight on it. At negative thirteen degrees, however, we were pretty sure it was solid. Lila's house, now far behind us, cast several faint, glowing rectangles from its windows onto the snow ahead. They seemed a mile away in the inky blackness.

We trudged closer to the lights, left footprints in the cold yellow, and into the dark beyond. Instantly, the wind wheeled the snow over them. For all the ice and snow told, we could have never existed.

We advanced, bodies bent to protect our freezing faces from the assaulting wind. As we struggled to pull farther from the shore, the blanket of snow on the ice thinned out and out until there was no more snow. If it had been possible to see anything besides the stars in the black sky and the even blacker outline of the opposite shore, the warped ice would have reflected us into an infinity of symmetrical worlds.

Lila lurched on the ice behind, and I heard her suck at the air before she righted herself. The ice was totally solid. It did not creak or gurgle or even sigh under our weight. I stopped for a moment to explore the cold seeping in through my boots and three pairs of socks to my toes. I felt the wind weave through the stitches in my knitted black gloves to my fingers. And I experienced the pressure—the weight—of the wind on my face.

Lila caught up to me, slipping again. Instinctively, her hands flailed out and grabbed at my arm. I let her pull herself up. We are continuously testing the friendship: how much pressure it can hold, where we cannot go, how to avoid the slippery patches.

Lila bent over to retrieve the rug she had dropped. I started to speak, but she put out her hand. I could not see it, but I felt it.

"Listen," she said, "listen to that."

She was facing the other way, back toward the shore. I turned to look where she was looking, back at the lighted windows and yearning branches. Facing that way, the wind was to our backs, out of our ears. I thought—or maybe imagined—I could hear the faintest rustle of trees from the shore. The wind still streaked past us, but now it seemed to be flowing around us, not attacking. We stood there and looked back where we had walked. Straight down, at black ice. Farther away, at black snow. Still farther, at less-black snow. Then at golden rectangles of snow, strewn like beads to a broken necklace. Then more black snow. Then the short, steep bank lined with brush, and then we were gazing up at the house. The large front window, so small from here and suffused with golden light. A television screen flashing colors. And I imagined I could see Lila's parents sitting in front of it.

"Do you hear it?"

I remembered to listen then. Again, I thought of rustling trees. But the trees were mere rattling skeletons at this time of year; there were no leaves to rustle. I stood there, balanced on the ice, clutching my rug, with six pairs of pants and eight shirts on.

And then I heard it. It is the purest sound that the Earth has ever heard. It is so clear, but you have to listen so hard to hear it. Once you do, it is the only audible noise. It is utter silence.

Time should exist only when you think about it. It should be something that man has invented. If a person has the courage to lose count of the years, the months, the days, the seconds, then it should stop. When they think to count again, it should start where they left off. Maybe the problem is that there are so many people in the world that not everyone has the courage to lose count at the same time, because then there would be no way to situate oneself after.

Ice is water frozen in time. The ice I was standing on was really water that had simply decided to stop counting and stand still for a bit. Inside it, there were probably little bubbles of air trapped from when it froze. Air that had not changed for days. Friendship has those little bubbles, those little memories that situate it in time. Like everyone, Lila and I have good and bad bubbles.

For a nonexistent amount of time, time did not exist for us. Then we turned back into the wind.

"Here?"

"Here."

I cautiously flung myself down on the ice and lay there, eyes to the stars. The wind at my head whirled snow across me, trying to obliterate me like my footprints. It was so tempting to lie there forever, but we were running out of time. Lila was spreading out her rug, that dark rectangle, on the snow. I sat up, encrusted with white, and unrolled my bundle. Out came a spoon and knife, which I placed on my rug with my knee over them to prevent the wind from carrying them away. From Lila's rug emerged the cylinder of cookie dough. Snowflakes were flying in horizontal stripes between us, and the dough was frozen nearly solid. Clumsily, I wrapped my tingling fingers and glove around the knife and sliced the cookie dough. Snow stuck to it and glazed it over on its journey between the wrapper and my mouth.

Lila was fumbling in her pocket to pull out her watch. The glowing blue face hardly made a dent in the furrows of dark around us, and I could not read the time. She looked up at me, the corners of her eyes crinkling into a grin. We began the countdown into the new year, shouting over the wind, through the snow, across the ice.

Two Pillars of Salt

ANTHONY DESANTIS, Grade 12, Age 17. South Carolina Governor's School of the Arts and Humanities, Greenville, SC, Scott Gould, *Teacher*

Parked out front, I prepare myself for the worst. She eventually emerges from her apartment, clad in the usual T-shirt with flowery print that doesn't match her red shorts. What gets me, though, is the straw hat. It's twice the size of her head and sags down to her hunched-over shoulders. This is my Grandma M&M: exhausted by life, slouching, and unaware that her grandson's about to tell her he's gay. Devout Irish-Italian Catholic families like ours have an abundance of rules, and I've probably broken all of them. She inches toward my car as fast as she can—a snail's pace. It gives me time for one last pep-talk, so I ready myself for when she says something other than "That's okay." That'll be my cue to remind her about how she married Grandpa. Remind her that she's broken the rules too.

Grandpa was the college theology professor with the best lectures, and Grandma M&M was the student who took the best notes. I imagine that Theology 101 class being extremely uncomfortable for the other students, between the batted eyelashes and the lectures on how beautiful—how divine—the Bible terms human reproduction. She was twenty. He was forty-five—and a priest. It's important to understand that the

Catholic Church has never allowed its priests to get married. But with my grandparents, there was, for some reason, an exception to that rule.

Rome granted a dispensation to Grandpa that sanctioned his marriage to Grandma M&M in 1968. It also dictated, however, that nothing about their wedding could become formal. No guests, no reception, not even a certificate. My grandma wore a T-shirt and a pair of shorts to church that day. She and Grandpa, dressed in what he wore to, say, his final mass earlier that morning, waited on the local archbishop for over an hour. When he finally arrived, his breath reeked of coffee and cigarettes. My grandparents didn't have the time to be angry.

The one witness to the secret marriage, the church's cleaning lady, quickly materialized and the archbishop sped through the rites. It was convenient that the cleaning lady spoke almost no English because she mouthed the words *tengan prisa*—hurry up—when Grandma M&M hesitated before saying "I do." The archbishop still managed to pronounce them man and wife in record-breaking time. There were conditions, of course. In exchange for the dispensation, only the closest relatives could know. They also couldn't live anywhere outside of south Florida for the rest of Grandpa's life. He could exercise his powers as an ordained priest only in emergencies and, for some odd reason, on cruise ships. "Best of luck," the archbishop added. Then he left. It's an old story—one I now know by heart, even if it happened twenty-seven years before I was born.

Grandma M&M struggles to open the passenger-side door of my car. I know that she'll get it in a moment, so I do nothing but watch. She creeps into the car seat, takes a moment to buckle up, leans toward me with a melodramatic groan, and waits for a kiss on the cheek. Then she says, "Hullo, Mr. Tony," like she always used to in the front doorway of her old house in Pembroke Pines. I miss that house. Its pearl-colored door-bell still rings in my head. My grandma would greet me with arms full of excessive hugs and my favorite candy. That's why I started to call her Grandma M&M in the first place. She loved it, even if it meant that I'd call her something she wasn't.

I remember Ricky's, the local wing joint where my grandma would let me play shuffleboard after I'd eaten every last chicken tender. She watched all of the Disney movies with me, helped me with hokey art projects, and even taught me to play soli-taire before I learned my multiplication tables. Grandpa was always there too. Age had begun to wear him down, but that didn't stop him from meeting my mom and me for lunch at the Broward County Mall's food court once a week, or pinching my cheeks and saying, "That's the way," whenever I brought home an A on my report card. Then one day, I started to dread the slightest mention of a visit to my grandparents' house. I don't know why. It felt uncomfortable, as if we all knew something but were too afraid to talk about it. Something had changed—or was about to change—or had never changed, and was just on the verge of discovery.

A good strategy, one that I read on a self-help website with obnoxious, bright-pink lettering, is to know in advance the an-swers to the obvious questions about to be asked. How do you know you're gay? Just do. Well, when did you realize it? Not sure. Am I supposed to say that even if my preschool crush was Catalina, I couldn't help but stare at James? I could blame it on my parents. They raised me to respect women, as if having sex with them would be impolite. Maybe I should have prepared a piechart. I try to imagine saying, "Here, Grandma M&M, re-search shows that I experimented with more than seventy per-cent of the boys I ever invited to spend the night at my house."

I never had feelings for any of them. Once, I auditioned for the school musical, *Guys and Dolls*, and had a so-called "one-on-one" with a senior in the boys' dressing room immediately afterward. I got the part of Benny Southstreet. I would sometimes tumble around the cramped backseat of a black F-150, sometimes until three in the morning, with my lab partner from Physical Science once or twice a week for a whole two years. My detachment made it all okay. I was normal. As normal as I had been back when Grandpa was still alive.

He was dead for seven or eight years before I ever had the courage to ask Grandma M&M about their marriage. "You've got to understand that no good Catholic agrees with every rule in the book," she said. I listened, asked questions, listened again. Another time I asked her what she thought about homosexuality. The answer was the same as the Church's: Love and marriage should be reserved for only a man and a woman. Anything else would be against the natural way of things. "But the Church doesn't punish people for homosexual thoughts," she said. Her next words were rushed: "only homosexual actions." I fought back the urge to ask her about the Church's teachings on the celibacy of its priests. The same basic rules apply. To be tempted is forgivable, to act upon is forbidden. Or supposed to be forbidden.

If she asks me whether or not my parents know, I could bring up Connor. He didn't spend the night at my house, didn't tumble around a truck with me, and we didn't have "one-on-ones" in a dressing room—or anywhere. Just feelings. He was the kind of person you think is your first love. Grandma M&M's met him a handful of times—like when the three of us and the rest of my family went out to a barbecue restaurant. She said he was her favorite of my friends after that. Obviously, she didn't see us hold hands under the table. Connor helped me come out to my parents. I remember how I curled up in a corner of my bedroom and tried to stop myself from crying, while he and my mom sat on the bed and laughed at how overdramatic I was being. The next morning, Connor and I made breakfast with my dad. If Grandma M&M considered all of that, then she couldn't hate him, ever. Right?

My grandma asks me how I'm doing, and I lie to her. I say that I've never felt better. She smells like Japanese Cherry Blossom tinged with Bailey's Irish Cream. Part of me wants to stop and reflect on how these smells say something, perhaps the most important thing, about her. Part of me knows she drinks only when she knows something isn't quite right. At least I can feel more like my coming out is expected, a sort of "right on time" kind of thing. Everything around my grandma's apartment complex explodes with color. For the first time in months, the air isn't stifling. I'm comfortable with myself and my surroundings—at last.

The only problem is reality. There is no beautiful day, no decision to tell Grandma M&M I'm gay, no final pep talk, and certainly no comfort in my sexuality. My grandma and I are a pair of rule-breaking blasphemers, both afraid of not being alone. Still, I always want to say, "Look, there's something I have to talk to you about, Grandma M&M." She'd tell me that I could talk to her about anything, because families are supposed to stay together. That's the moment when I'd grab a firm hold of the gear-shift and put the car into drive.

Prostitute Appeals to the Pope

JANAY ALEXANDREA CRANE, Grade 12, Age 17. John Glenn High School, Walkerton, IN, Paul Hernandez, *Teacher*

To the Holy Pope, the Bishop of the Roman Catholic Church of Rome:

Everyone has a past. Mine is more shameful than most, but at least it is mine. School was never really my thing. I laid low throughout most of the ordeal, never making much of a fuss and never responding to glares or the names I was often called. I was busy. I was busy hiding the bruises and burns on my arms, moving my hair part over so slightly to cover that black eye from when Daddy drank a little too much.

I hated it when he hit me, but at least when he hit me, he knew who I was. Most of my dad's time was spent working at the factory. He'd stumble home, already drunk, and on a good day, he'd walk right past me and fall onto the bed that my parents shared. I could hear muffled words and zippers as my mother closed the door behind them. The next morning my father would leave, and my mother would resurrect herself from their bed, bruised and worn down. She would sit in a ball on the couch until dad came home, and we would start all over. You could always tell when it wasn't a good day, because Dad didn't stumble with the keys, he didn't falter in his steps. He would set the keys on the table and in his smooth Italian voice, he'd whisper to me, "Bambina, come here. I have something for you." I would walk over and cautiously take whatever small trinket he would give to me.

"Do you like it?" he would purr gently.

I would nod silently and prepare myself for what I knew was next. He would grab my face and lean in to kiss me. Kiss me like a man would kiss a woman, deep and warm and so very, very wrong. My whole body shuddered, and I was barely able to suppress the screams scratching at the back of my throat. He would lead me by the hand to my room, and I would look to my mother, frozen in fear at her bedroom door, and I could feel the hatred radiating off of her as she disappeared behind my closing door.

For years this was my life. I never knew love to be anything but an empty word, spoken from drunken tongues. I graduated from high school, a miracle in and of itself, and I was left with a choice that I wasn't prepared to make. As I walked across that stage, it dawned on me that I was free. Free to leave this life, these people, this place. I smiled and accepted my diploma, but the diploma in my hand was the next-to-last thing on my mind.

A week after graduation, I stepped off the bus in a state of confusion and excitement. I went around to the side of the bus, and found my one duffel bag, small and blue, almost completely hidden under a mound of other bags. I grabbed it and followed the swarm of people through the terminal doors. The Arizona heat penetrated the inside of the building, suffocating its occupants. I wearily looked around the bus station, watching all the suntanned legs and secretive eyes hidden behind expensive sunglasses. I'm sure I was struck with a little bit of culture shock, having gone from the bleak, depressing streets of Washington to the silent and isolated seats of a Greyhound, into this bright, shining piece of heaven. But I was soon to learn that even heaven has its demons.

* * *

"Hello," Rico chuckled. His voice was deep and could melt even the most respectable girl (which I was not) into butter. "You must be new around here. I'm Rico, and this is Home."

"Uhm, hi. I'm—I'm Sarafina. It's, uh, it's nice to meet you." I stumbled over my words in my usual manner and felt more exposed than ever. Rico smiled what must have been the biggest, warmest, sexiest smile anyone's ever been privileged to see. He turned quietly into the kitchen and looked behind him.

"C'mon, Yankee, I'll show you around."

I followed him into the kitchen, and he disappeared into what looked like the refrigerator. I walked around the room, taking in the grill and three ovens. Two large coffeemakers sat on a barista table toward the front, and there was a small chair in the far corner. I hoisted myself up onto an island in the middle of the room and waited for Rico to return.

When he did, he was carrying two very frosted coffee drinks, one of which I gladly took.

"So, what's a pretty little girl like you doing in a big old place like this?"

I could feel the blood rush to my face, as Rico placed himself on the counter next to me. "Uh, well I, I just thought it'd be nice. To get away from all the rain."

"Well, there's no rain here, so you got that part right. Where are you from, anyway?"

"I'm from Washington. The state, not the capital."

"Ah, that explains a lot." I looked at him inquisitively. "Well, first of all, you're terribly pale. It looks like you haven't had proper sunlight a day in your life. Second, you've got an accent, and it's awfully cute." I was sure that if I wasn't blushing before, I most certainly was now.

"Oh, I hadn't noticed."

Rico's laugh reverberated off the walls and bounced back to his suntanned face.

"Course you didn't, Sarafina. You didn't know to notice. Tell you what, since this is such a special day, you coming to town and all, I'm going to close down shop in a minute, and you can stay with me. It's a big city, and you'll need someone to protect you."

And that's exactly what he did. Rico and I carried on great for a very long time. He showed me the city, taught me how to work the espresso machine and coax street vendors into giving me the best produce. He showed me how to grate cheese and how to keep from sweating to death in the Arizona heat. He also showed me other things. Things that had seemed so wrong before, things that had seemed so distant. With Rico, everything felt right and good, and I felt as though nothing could hurt me.

I was so in love with him, that I didn't care when he would give me things I couldn't name. I never blinked to swallow a pill or inhale any number of white lines for him. Rico was my world. I moved out of my small room, into a large apartment with my newfound love. I was so caught up in Rico's sweet words and the soothing ocean green of his eyes, that I didn't notice myself spiraling downwards. Soon, he was inviting men over, letting them watch me undress, and making me do things with them that I knew I shouldn't have. But I would never have questioned Rico, not for a second, because I loved him. And I thought he loved me. He bought me clothes and flowers and chocolates, everything I could ever dream. He called me his Sarafina, his own little angel.

The drugs soon became a staple in our house. The drugs, the men, the lies, all became things Rico force-fed me, like some demented game of house. At first, the things I did didn't bother me. I was well taken care of and I was "loved." But soon, the flowers stopped coming. I would have strangers in my bed more often than Rico, who started coming home less and less. When Rico was home, he was angry and impatient with me, asking what I had made today, if there had been any "walk-ins." This should have been a red flag, but to me, I just thought that if I worked harder, Rico would cast his favor my way. I began to walk streets, looking for any poor sap I could pick up out of the gutter. All he really needed was a checkbook. All of this, I did for Rico.

It had been some months after my arrival, months of working and stress when Rico first started his little deception. He hadn't been around in weeks, and I stopped waiting up for him. What came next was nothing less then divine intervention.

I had been turning tricks all night, every night, and what happened wasn't surprising since I had never been careful. I was pregnant. There was no way to deny it. I think I must have taken at least five tests, all saying the same thing:

Positive.

Positive.

Positive.

The irony of that word struck me as I read a note Rico left on the nightstand when he abandoned me: "If you can't work, you can't stay."

Positive.

Not likely. This baby had ruined my life, and it wasn't even here yet, or so I thought.

I looked into every possible avenue. I talked to adoption agencies that said they would be happy to take my baby. Places that offered to take my baby and give her to a good home. I even went to an abortion clinic, where they explained how they could "neutralize my situation." I walked out of that place within ten minutes of going in. I sat crying on the front steps of that damned clinic for hours before I knew. This baby was mine. No matter what, this child inside of me was my responsibility. It wasn't someone else's to have, and it wasn't my life to take.

It was December, and it was cool outside. All the stars came out especially early and lined the Arizona sky with countless lights. I walked along the streets until I came to a church. I had seen it before, and I vaguely recalled being approached once by one of the deacons. I worked that night, and he came up to me and gave me a small bible, which is somewhere in a small bag of things in my car. The church was quiet, but the sign out front said, "Come, ye who seek rest." It was fitting, so I entered. I walked to the back of the cathedral and saw a wooden box. I had seen such confession boxes in enough movies that I knew what to do. I drew the curtain and sat down.

"Speak my child," a calming voice said behind the curtain in front of me. To this day, I have not heard a more gentle voice. That voice saved me, and I told it everything. I told that priest every disgusting, vulgar, horrendous thing I had ever done. And the voice told me that God loved me, and not like my father loved me or like Rico loved me. God was not someone to stand in silent rage as I was hurt, like my mother. God wanted to hold me, to protect me from all the things in life that had made me the person I was. The voice said that Jesus died for me. He gave up everything to save me, that it was his own personal prerogative to save me, to be reunited with me. This voice gave me hope. And every day for the past four years, I have listened to that voice. Every Sunday, Father Chris holds mass, and every Sunday, I am in the front row. My little Noel and I, dressed in our Sunday best, watch and pray and listen to the Father.

I have done what I can to raise Noel in a good, Catholic home. I am now an accountant, and we live not a block from the church. Noel goes to the school there, and she loves God just as much as I do. I thank our Holy Mother that I found faith when I did. Noel deserves so much better than the life I was living before. I would actually like to commit my life to the service of God. I want to become a priestess and save the women I once knew. I want to help girls like me, girls who have no hope, no love, joy or peace, and bring them into the arms of the Lord. I have talked to Father Chris about my passion many times, and he is all for it. I would like to begin training, but there is a problem. The rules state that I must be pure, a virgin. And that, as you well know, is not the case. I am far from innocent, which is why I am writing you.

Your holy gracious lord, I know what the laws of the Church are. They state that you have to be pure, righteous, and holy to serve God. You must set an example for the people you wish to lead. I understand the stigma of having a woman like me preach at a pulpit. But sir, I am pure, for God can wash away all sin, and he has set me free of my past transgressions. I am no longer the woman who did those things. I am new and reborn.

The Holy Mother smiles on me and my daughter, and all I want to do is share that light. So, if you could possibly reevaluate my case, allow a waiver of some kind so I can carry out the work the Lord sent me to do. You will not be ashamed, for what better example for lost women is there than a woman who has been found?

With love and God's will,
Sarafina Manicotti

Cycles

ANNA XIE, Grade 12, Age 18. John D. O'Bryan School of Math &
Science, Roxbury, MA, Monica Edwards, *Teacher*

I. (Summer)

Sleepless city mornings and seaside nights, it was the season of pouring rain, 2008. That summer you charted the way the rain fell from smoky skies, preserving voyages of tiny commas in disconnected, incoherent scribbles on your windowpane. You were thirteen and tan, willow tree limbs and skinned knees wired to a tiny frame, heartstrings stitched with good intentions. (Sunshine child)

It must have been the way the rain called your name, stringing it delicately like the Christmas lights your father never took down from the walls. It sang into your chestnut nest of hair (Why is it so brown? your mother once remarked with laced fingers: ivory, feathered brass) and explored the threads of your baggy T-shirt with fascination and watered your bones like they were flowers. The air was warm, and the roofs of the houses you could never draw when you were eight smiled as the strange, elusive sun peeked through walls of gray.

You were thirteen and tan, willow tree limbs and skinned knees wired to a tiny frame, heartstrings stitched with good intentions. Seventy-nine never haunted your thoughts, the scales never frightened you, and the doctor never assumed you were a seven-lettered "b" word.

(Once, on the playground, Ray picked you up and threw you into the air like a handful of flames in autumn and everything was a blur: September hid behind the trees with a shy smile.)

Four years from now, when you turn seventeen, you will learn about the logistics of free fall in your Physics class and realize that summer 2008 was the season of weightlessness.

II. (Autumn)

Coffee-stained eyes and matchstick legs, I am more than just a faint memory in the recesses of your mind. I thought I saw you in the mass of bodies trudging through the rain today, but you were asleep in Connecticut, 102 miles away. Everyone is starting to look like you, and I feel out of control.

My autumn foliage hair has seen two winters, it dreams along my vertebrae like russet vines on a Victorian house. Under the sun, it is fifty shades of red and brown meticulously pieced together, draping over my Indian-summered arms and bird-boned shoulders like spools of fine thread. Everyone tells me I am small, and Mother says I should look my age.

I cling to the ghosts of my past and lament over the tragic stitching of my wavering emotional state. We wish to be magnificent.

We are not magnificent.

III. (Winter)

Hollow nights and empty hands, my friends are either occupied or slipping away. I feel the indifference seeping into my bones, and I am increasingly aware of wilting roses. Loneliness is a terrible thing, but we all have expiration dates.

People are seasons, and they never stop changing, I tell myself this now in the bathtub. With shaking, uncertain fingers I carve distances out of granite rocks and painstakingly detach myself from everything that reminds me of the past. Like roses, we bruise too easily. My friends are glass people with machine hearts. I forge my chin up and sometimes I forget how to breathe.

Remind me how to breathe.

IV. (Spring)

The sky is crying, and I am drowning in the city, half moons carved underneath my eyes. Rain is falling on the apartments erected from stories of Renaissance, Italianate, Greek, Victorian, and French dreams, 1830. The trees were on fire last month, and winter snuffed them out with her grandiose arrival, temperatures bowed their heads in modesty.

When a strange boy paints my dreams at night, I feel hollowly empty the next morning, husks and shells. The human heart is frightening. Sometimes I like to believe that he does exist in this world, breathing fragments of himself into the air. I think I was born to travel. On some days my mind is elsewhere: backpacking across the Carolinas, scaling the fiery skies of France, dancing along Melbourne coastlines, wildfires in a secluded forest. Possibilities are frightening.

I fall too deep too easily with strangers in the city and in bookstores and the way the lights remind me of Times Square, New York. On some nights, my skies are dreamless. Once I saw something orange in the obscured folds of a starless evening canvas, and to this day I tell people about how I saw the planet Jupiter. Self-destruction is when Zachary sings, planting flames in my aching heart. That is the cycle of life, death, and revival.

I am suffocating.

V. (Summer)

I destroy beautiful things.

Sometimes the wiring of my bones shake, and I want to desperately fold into myself, to become something less, but I am afraid there is nothing left. People play dress up with evergreen trees, and I am spindrift thoughts and amaranthine veins in a terribly gray winter. I tangle stars in my tawny hair so I can be reminded of a flaxen summer with ginger eyes when I cannot sleep at night.

A muted watercolor on a virgin canvas, I am falling away from everyone and the indifference echoes in my lungs. She blows out her birthday candles in a dimmed room, surrounded by the resplendent company of old and new friends. To become nothing is a frighteningly silent process.

I am convinced that I can save you somehow, with my willow tree arms and ivory bones. Your cinnamon-colored skin looked lovely amidst the city lights and everyone drowned in Saturday air. My heart was silent, but I was content. Sometimes I want to leave. Incompatibility has torn the stitching of a family and we hide behind closed bathroom doors and bedrooms where we scream. It makes me nauseous, and I have learned how to be silent with my hollow tears. You tell me get away from you as far as possible. This was never supposed to happen.

Some things, I will never let go of. Some things, they will never change.

I am flawed and free.

VI. (Autumn)

My soul is an overgrown garden, and I am lost.

I stumble on the entirety of things, clumsily, with thin ankles of a ballerina. Before I had a machine heart, you used to call at one in the morning and I was always asleep. It is December, and I am wide awake when the sun breaks through the ashen clouds like combustible stars. Daylight is always too fleeting.

You tangle yourself in between the lines of my notebook and guitar strings, demanding for a love poem. I am capturing slivers of my life in expired film canisters, sharpie scrawlings documenting twenty-four brittle births of exposures in chronological order. Sometimes the city swallows the weekday sunsets with bright lights, and I feel the need to reinvent my name. We are just breathing underwater and—

I have yet to savor the sound of your voice at 1:00 a.m.

Habibi

SAMANTHA WEST, Grade 12, Age 17. Capitol High School, Boise, ID,
Carla Zumwalt, *Teacher*

In 1948, my grandmother was chased out of Palestine when
she was nine years old. She fled to Syria, where she eventually
raised my mother. She was not religious, only loosely following
Islam. However, when my mother came to America, she could
not escape the actions of her people, and neither could I.

I was too young to understand at the time. I knew Mom was
from Syria, and she painted it like a magical land, full of ornate
Aladdin-like buildings. It had to be beautiful. When my kindergarten teacher learned this, she asked if my mom would speak
to the class. I was overjoyed when Mom agreed. My classmates
would get the honor of hearing about her (and my) fascinating
history. How cool would I be, once I was the Arabic girl?

My classmates found Mom . . . funny. They were stupid
and cruel. "Hey, is your mom from Cereal?" they used to ask
laughing, mocking her accent. I was hurt. I hated them. I complained, and Mom said, "Don't worry, habibi. They will stop."

Habibi was Mom's nickname for me. She said it meant "my
love."

The teasing did stop. Children have blissfully short memories.
Adults, however, do not.

Mom loved being involved. She started teaching Sunday

school at our church—our Christian church. The young ones adored her. She treated them with care and love, like they were her own.

Then it was 9/11. Suddenly there were rumors that a *Muslim* was being allowed to teach the children. I didn't know what a Muslim was, only that the news said it was bad. It never occurred to me they meant my *mom*.

We stopped attending church. I was so upset, leaving friends whose parents were suddenly herding them away from me. I didn't understand. It wasn't like I was a Muslim or anything.

I blamed the Muslims. It was their fault we'd had to leave. I told Mom I hated the Muslims. She asked if I had ever met one.

I hesitated. No, I had not.

I remember Mom sighing. She took off her glasses and kissed me on the head. "Time for bed, ya habibi."

It wasn't until much later that I understood all of this. I had been subjected to racism, to the stereotype of Arabs and Muslims that my mother unfortunately portrayed with her accent and heritage. Looking back, I can't believe people were this cruel. To alienate an entire family . . . it's disgusting. The moment I understood what happened to me, I grew as a person. No longer am I judging or childish about what I see. I know how bad it hurts to be singled out for something uncontrollable, and that the actions of a few are not the ones of many.

My mother is the strongest person I know. To have put up with all these people, and me, insulting her . . . It still mystifies me. She is not a terrorist. She is not Muslim. She is my mother, and that is all she ever need be.

Brasília

LUISA BANCHOFF, Grade 12, Age 17. Washington Lee High School, Arlington, VA, Sarah Congable, *Teacher*

Nobody in this street but the salt.

Three more feet of snow in Manitoba but here just the empty rasp
of sodium, licking absently at the wind, filling cracks that lace
the lanes like stretch marks or border control. Salt signaling through the

fog, settling in the caruncula of morning as it blinks, aftertaste
of seaside on skin from where it once curved the bends of bodies.
Salt grains on a father's receding hairline sweating themselves into

a daughter's wedding pearls. Salty mouths swathed in jerky walking
out from the corner 7-Eleven, spitting more salt into the curbside.
Where was this salt three weeks ago when she

trudged out under burgeoning flurries and shoved
the roll of stolen quarters into the payphone there—
see how the one she dropped begins to crystallize—

and punched in a foreign line that ends in Brasília because
he is there, covering the leathery women in blankets and rebuilding

the shanty schools, salting the earth, stitching up spines,
handing out heartbeats?

When he picks up, she wants to run her tongue over the
receiver but licks her
lips instead, recracking their knitwork, and he can feel the
brackish
on her breath like the county council calling for more salt

to beat the snow to the streets. "An abortion," she says.
My mind is made up, hums the wind, but you had a right,
clicks the phone cord stretching an equator between

them. Brasília is silent. The southern hemisphere holding
its breath. Soon they hear a click. Quarters running out.
Bridges being christened. Salt running her eyes through.

Afterward, she spreads herself out on the street. Face
down, the snow on her teeth could almost be mistaken
for scripture. The flakes on her coat, the salt falling off

heavenly loaves as they are broken.

GOLD, SILVER, AMERICAN VOICES, AND CREATIVE CONCEPT AWARDS

Students in grades 7–12 may submit works in 11 writing categories. This year more than 2,900 Regional Award–winning writing submissions were reviewed by authors, educators, and literary professionals. Gold, Silver, and American Voices medals were awarded to works that demonstrated originality, technical skill, and emergence of a personal voice.

Creative Concept Awards recognized works that dealt with grieving and loss (The New York Life Award) and voting rights (Creativity & Citizenship).

Some of the writing selections have been excerpted. Go to **www.artandwriting.org/galleries** to read all of the work as it was submitted.

KEVIN ARAGON, *Suburban Astronaut*, Grade 12, Age 18. Pine Creek High School, Colorado Springs, CO, Lindsay Williams, *Teacher*.

Reflections

REBECCA SCURLOCK, Grade 8, Age 14. Lakeside School, Seattle, WA,
Susan Mortensen, *Teacher*

1. *My Name*

Rebecca Scurlock. Rebecca is Jewish, and I'm Christian. Scurlock is Welsh, and I'm Irish.

Papa tells me it came from the old man who traveled to America four hundred years ago. It survived through the founding of our nation; through the Civil War; through generations of fathers, husbands, and grandsons. It finally came to a girl: an only child, who was named Rebecca for no real reason at all.

I grew into the name Rebecca. It became me; I became it. But Rebecca turned into Becky, which turned into Beckers, Becksy, Beck-Beck, B-Dawg. It was like a native wetland turning into a towering skyscraper: It was from soft lavender to imposing magenta, from a flowing stream to a steel metallic box, from subtle olive oil to designer perfume. It was from water to ice, from me to not me.

But Becky is now my name. When people say it, it sounds like they're biting down on a frozen McDonald's cheeseburger: the "be" slow and luxurious but the "cky" fast and sharp. If they add my last name, it sounds like a creaking teeter-totter. Be-cky Scurlock, Be-cky Scurlock, Be-cky Scurlock.

I was once told what my real name means. According to the

Torah, Isaac was tied to a mountain as a sacrifice to God. As Isaac's unfortunate wife's name, Rebecca means to tie, or to bond.

I've since wondered what this means for me. Of course Rebecca's husband was tied up, but what does it mean if your name means to tie?

Maybe it means to make mischief, like tying knots in the rope of life. Maybe it means to connect, like bonding with friends or family. Maybe it means to love, like Rebecca loved her husband.

Maybe I'll decide what it means. One day, I'll be sitting in my bathtub, and I'll have an epiphany, and I'll run out into the streets naked, shouting, "Eureka! Eureka! I know my name!" just like Archimedes. Yes, that's my plan. What fun it will be! For now, though, I guess I'll just have to wait.

2. Thanksgiving

Thanksgiving is my favorite day of the year, except for Christmas and Halloween and my birthday, which is sometimes on Thanksgiving anyways. We always take a ride in the big Ferry Boat to visit all my aunts and uncles and cousins in Coupeville. If it's my birthday, they give me lots of presents, and I even get two whole days of no school.

When we get to Uncle Johnny's house, their doggy Fido always jumps up on us and we pet him until he jumps back down again. Then we walk inside, and we all smell Aunty Sarah's warm buttermilk biscuits and scrumptious pumpkin pie. And if Uncle Henry's already there, we smell his sweet-potato and marshmallow crisp, which is like a big crunchy cloud on top of a sticky orange sky.

The adults always tell us kids to go down in the basement so we won't bother them with all our noise. So Ethan, Olivia,

Paige, Anthony, Christian, and I all go downstairs to play, but sometimes Christian stays upstairs, because he's 15 and he thinks he's too old for us.

We play hide-and-seek and catch-the-dog and tackle-Christian-because-he's-evil if Christian comes down with us. We jump on Olivia's bed and play on the funny exercise machine that makes your feet go up and down and up again until you fall off. We even play Wii once in a while, but that's never any fun because Anthony always hogs the remote.

Sometimes at night after our yummy dinner, we sneak all the cookies we can fit under our shirts and then we go outside and make grass angels. It's not all bright and shiny like in the city, so we can see all the tiny little holes in the sky. Cousin Ethan knows all the constellations, so he points out Cassiopeia, Scorpio, Ursa Major, Pegasus, Taurus, and Orion until we forget about the cookies and fall asleep under the big, big moon.

3. Raindrops

Everything was wrong when I woke up this morning. The house was all silent, and the birds weren't chirping, and all I could hear was the pitter-patter of the autumn raindrops tickling the windows. No slam of Mitsubishi doors, no hum of the ancient microwave, not even the neighbors' wind chime that tinkles in the breeze.

When I pounded downstairs to fill the silence, I found Mama grasping the phone in her quivering hand and weeping. She was staring out the window at the gray rain. Papa was holding her hand and crooning, "It's okay, it's okay, don't cry," like she was a baby. Her other hand was drooped around little puppy Tippit, who was staring out the window too. I'd read a book in which the characters cried in their hearts, so I leaned over to her and whispered that my heart was crying too.

I've always thought people regretted things they'd done. But now I regretted the things I hadn't done. Because when Mama choked out between gasps like she was drowning that her mother died today, just like that, she sank away into the earth like raindrops in a mud puddle. I wanted to cry, I wanted to cry so bad, but I couldn't.

I wanted to cry for all my memories of Grandma. I wanted to cry for her soft lilting Boston accent, for the nostalgic stories of childhood that she'd tell me over and over, for the way she'd wave away the compliments on her famous apple pie and say it was nothing. I wanted to cry and cry and cry with Mama until my nose ran and my eyes stung.

But I'd never heard her accent or listened to her stories or eaten her apple pie. I'd never known her because she lived far away, and when we saw her at Christmas, I'd always forget to say hi and how are you and what's new. And she was gone now, and I never knew her, I'll never know her because every day I thought she'd be there tomorrow.

After Mama told me, it was all silent except for Grandma's rain. Mama and Papa and little puppy Tippit were all staring out the window, and I was staring at them, and I wished I could be there too, I wished I were the raindrops trickling out of the gutter.

4. Papa Who

Papa who smiles like warm honey
and asks how are you sweetie
who is fried eggs and overcooked pasta
who is sailboats and bicycles
who is rain and rainbows
who laughs like Santa Claus, heavy
who waits every morning to eat breakfast with me

who spouts chemistry lectures at dinner
who knocks on my door to say good-night
is the first star I see tonight
who grins and chuckles at my lame jokes
whose thick gray hair is turning white
who forgets what I told him yesterday
and says my heart is in the right place
even if my mind isn't
who counts his days like pennies
who counts his blessings like diamonds
is the flicker of the embers in the hearth
is the shimmer of the evening sunset
is the haze of the midnight moon
that slowly trickles away
as morning nears again

5. *Something I Love*

I'm just a naïve teenager who doesn't think about anything other than clothes and makeup and boys.

That's what Mrs. Rodriguez down the street told me on my thirteenth birthday.

Maybe she's right. I do love to flip through *Seventeen* magazine, which is exclusively about clothes and makeup and boys. And once in a while I like to experiment with Mom's lipstick and indigo eyeliner too.

I guess I'm too pretentious to admit that I'm living up to her expectations. I like to think that I'm just as mature as that old lady; that I've been through every walk of life like she has. But of course I haven't.

Mrs. Rodriguez says she knows everything there is to know. Whenever it so happens that I pass by her house at the same moment she looks up from her crocheting, she calls down to me and says, "Becky Scurlock, what brings you here?" and begins to recount the extensive story of her life without waiting for an answer.

Once, she paused to ask me what I thought of her new dahlias. I made the mistake of telling her that I loved how beautiful they were.

"Kids these days!" she shouted. "Going around talking about love like it's a toy! Don't say that word, Miss, because you don't understand anything you're saying."

Somewhere inside I know she's right: When I grow old like her, I'll see that I didn't really love anything I think I love now. I'm just being a teenager.

But if only she could see me run, maybe she'd see the love in my soul—no matter how young and callow. She might see me inspired: running with long, graceful strides down the sidewalk and a wacky smile plastered over my face. Maybe she'd see me sad: running all slow with my head in the trees. She'd laugh if she saw me confused: running with stiff legs and fuzzy eyes; my head in the moon.

Maybe then she'd see my love. Maybe she'd see that even if I'm just a teenager, my love for running is as pure as crisp air on an autumn morning.

Maybe she'd see that it doesn't really matter whether it's teenager love or real love. Because when you give something your love, you set your heart free, and you can go up to the moon and back down again, without ever leaving the ground.

6. Smiles

He thought I was pretty. He thought ten other girls were pretty too. He liked my smile. When he told me so, I covered my mouth, but he still knew I was smiling. He said I was the only girl tall enough for him because he's 5'9" and I'm 5'6".

Everywhere I turned, he was there. Walking to class, in the lunch line, in my dorm room . . . he was always there and I would always smile, even though I hoped and hoped and hoped he would just go away.

I told him I was short compared to him and that there were plenty of girls who were taller. I told him I was ugly because I am, but then I smiled and he just looked at me all funny because he thought I was joking. I told him to go away, but he didn't because I smiled, and so instead he just moved in closer.

He moved in closer, he moved in closer. He moved in closer, and I couldn't wipe the stupid smile off my face, and he moved in closer. "Go away, go away!" I wanted to scream, but I couldn't, and his hot breath was on my neck and he moved in closer.

I wish I could forget everything. I wish I could tuck the memories away in a little locked box and lose the key. I wish I could forget what he did to me.

But that night he walked away in the rain, no jacket, just robin's-egg polo and strong arms fading away under the streetlamp, and I watched him, I watched him from the window, the tears streamed down my cheeks, it wasn't his fault. It wasn't his fault, because I'm the one who smiled.

7. Dreams

Everyone seems to have a dream. Mama dreams of having a perfect family. Papa dreams of being a virtuoso on the cello. Little Zoë across the street dreams of riding to the sun and back on her stuffed unicorn Sally, which has a light-up horn and a sparkly tail.

I have dreams too. At night I dream about the sky, about never-ending paradises and rainbow lollipops. I dream about new beginnings, about starting over again and no regrets. I dream about flying away on midnight's wings, up, up, up, never to return again.

Sometimes I wonder if there's someone out there who doesn't dream. Who spends their days with their head in the clouds, their body in the sky, spirit in the stars. Who knows love and happiness like their own reflection; whose life is as clear as the glimmering ocean below them. Who can't dream because there's nothing left to dream for.

Maybe someday I'll find that person. I'll ask them, what is life without dreams? What's it like without a goal, without a purpose? Isn't it a shame never to feel pain, or hunger, or regret? Because in my experience, you can't appreciate happiness without pain, fulfillment without hunger, satisfaction without regret. It's the moments of imperfection that give meaning to life, the moments of melancholy that kindle dreams.

I'm not sure how they'd respond. I don't know if they'd see what I see.

But I do know that somewhere beneath all their ignorance, they'd understand something it's taken me fourteen years to discover: that a life without dreams is sun without sunshine, rain without raindrops, a heart without a soul.

The Pink Sari

POOJA CHANDRASHEKAR, Grade 10, Age 15. Thomas Jefferson
High School of Science and Technology, Alexandria, VA,
Jennifer Seavey, *Teacher*

When I slowly flip through the faded pages of the albums enclosing the old photographs of my first visits to India, almost all of the pictures have Ajji in them. My grandmother always looks so regal, holding her head high like a queen, and her sari wraps perfectly around her body while her blouse peeks out on top. I love those saris, the way they shimmer and catch the light when the morning sun spills through the windows. She'd sweep her hair back, a raven's color dusted with white powder, and tuck the corner of the sari to her waist as she goes to buy vegetables.

The vendors' voices soar through the crisp morning air, lilting and twirling amidst the towering oaks that line the streets. I wake up to these voices every morning. To the neighbors, it's not a fresh sound. But to the little girl from America, where the storekeepers don't sing, the sounds fill my body like warm sticky honey. The wind moves quietly among the trees, the curtains in the open windows embrace the rustling leaves, and the euphonious bird calls. The gentle music offsets the brilliant blue hue that paints the sky and the green that tints the foliage.

As I peek through the little wooden window of Ajji's house, her firm voice cuts through the air. She always bargains with the vendors. Her glasses frame her face, the creamy chocolate skin just beginning to wrinkle. Her face reflects her emotions. But sometimes she's good at hiding her feelings as well. She'll drape her feelings with a mask, and layer them over and over with happiness. She drapes her sari the same way, first tucking one side to her waist, then making tiny precise folds until the whole cloth covers her body, hidden away beneath the innumerable folds, just like the wrinkles on her face hide her emotions.

In the corner of Ajji's bedroom is an old weathered chest, one with faded and cracked leather skin. The sides are lined with nicks, and the top is half caved in. I run my hand along its surface, feeling the grooves and indentations. It reminds me of those magical wooden cupboards hidden away in the dark cobweb-filled corners of castles in Ajji's folktales. "Can I open this?" I ask. "Not now," she replies. I pout, exaggerating my childish discontent at not being able to get what I want and know what everyone else knows. She laughs. I strain my eyes and catch a fleeting glimpse of something pink. But, soon after, the splash of color is but a blurry streak in my overwrought memory. I can only guess and wait. Ancestral jewelry encrusted with diamonds and glittering gems, a dark family secret? They are all intertwined in my web of fantasy.

She walks out onto the crowded Indian streets, holding me by the hand. The shops tower up on either side of us, their bright-colored advertisement boards catawampus and frayed on the edges. Children run barefoot on the stone-lined roads, and the smell of freshly cooked sweets and snacks drifts among the carts and painted bangles that sparkle as they catch the light. Stray animals freely roam the streets, silently napping in the middle of the sidewalks. I clutch Ajji's hand tighter as one of the dogs watches me with piercing eyes. She drapes a thin veil of her sari around me, as if the mere cloth can protect me, and I squeeze my eyes shut. "Nothing will happen," she says. But my mouth is closed tight in case the fear spills out.

We enter a sari shop, cloaked in gorgeous hues of silk and hand-embroidered cloth. There is a characteristic smell to Indian saris, one that creeps through the shops and hides amongst the fabric. It is a tablespoon of musk sautéed with a pinch of fresh tropical breeze and finally garnished with the affection of a warm hug. It's one of those unforgettable smells in my memory of Ajji.

As I grow older, perhaps getting a bit more mature and less wide-eyed than I was back then, my perspectives also change. The Indian culture that had so influenced each of my decisions and actions no longer tethers me to my native country. As I became assimilated into Western culture my grip on my Indian heritage slowly loosens. The stories of the maharajahs and maharanis that had haunted my imagination seem to fade away.

I see my grandmother only once every two or three years, and the time in between waters down my memories so that they shimmer then dissolve. Last year, when I visited Ajji in India, she was very sick. She looked frail and weak, and her voice shook when she spoke. She didn't speak much, and our conversation was limited to cordialities and a quick hug here and there. When normally I had to force myself to slow the tumbling cascade of words, I had to search for what to say and think about how to build the sentences. The days rolled by, and it was soon the morning of our departure. As I was preparing to leave, Ajji motioned for me to sit next to her. I look up at her, and for the first time, I realize how much different she looks. Her face is lined with wrinkles, and her hair is dusted with snowflakes, more white than raven. As I look at her with a questioning gaze, I am suddenly drawn back into my whimsical childhood days. Resting in her wrinkled palms is the weathered leather box, the box that had evoked such flights of fantasy when I was but a little girl trying to search the world for answers to my endless questions.

"This is for you," she says, handing me the chest. Slowly, I lift the lid, not knowing what to expect. There is only an old burlap cloth wrapped around something very thin and fine. I separate the pieces of the fabric and draw in my breath sharply. My mind flashes back to my childhood days, when the weathered chest had evoked such fantastical musings. The surreal splash of pink that had faded away from my memory many years ago is suddenly part of something enchantingly real.

"Yes, this is my wedding sari. For you." The stunning shade of pink is lined with gold embroidery that etches out symbols of Indian culture and beliefs. The soft colors dance before me, the dappled light casting chocolate shadows on the walls.

I take the shimmering fabric and touch it to my face. Its memories evoke much more than what picture frames enclosing black-and-white photographs can do. The sari now lies tucked away in my hardwood armoire, quietly sleeping, waiting. Sometimes, I'll take the cloth down from the shelf and wrap it around me. This tangy-smelling pink sari lined with peacocks fosters dreams painted in color. And, as all inanimate objects close to the heart have an invigorating spirit of life, I have given the pink sari a name—Nidhi, meaning treasure.

Sometimes I wonder, if I were to have a daughter, what would happen to her? How would I instill in her an appreciation of her Indian heritage? How would I tell the magical stories without Ajji's guidance and magic? At least I know I can give her the old weathered box and watch her animated face as her hand runs along the golden borders and delights in the stories and memories woven amongst the fabric. And I hope my Nidhi will be her treasure too.

Fish Skin

ELIZABETH HEYM, Grade 12, Age 16. Bexley High School, Bexley, OH, Chad Hemmelgam, *Teacher*

When I was little, the most common question people asked me was "What's wrong with your face?"

It's not a particularly polite question, but looking back, I can't blame them. It's not every day that a kid sees someone with a face that looks like it has been plastered with papier-mâché in a kindergarten art project.

Everywhere I went, kids would ogle at me from a distance, clutching their mothers' pants legs. Parents would scold their children for asking such insensitive questions, while they themselves peered curiously at my marled skin. The bars of deformity isolated me, relegating me to be like a spectacle: an animal in a zoo. The dry lacy web of skin sprawled across my face must have been for everyone else like a haunting painting. People couldn't tear their eyes away from my skin, bound by some strange fascination with the unusual and terrible. Like passersby riveted morbidly to a car crash, they couldn't look away.

Ichthyosis, it is called. I can remember how the word scraped over the doctor's tongue, hanging about awkwardly in the room like an unwanted intruder. They told me it was also called "Fish Skin Disease," but I wish they hadn't. It made me feel dehumanized, and from that moment I became a helpless child trapped in the skin of a fish.

I began kindergarten trying desperately to make friends. But every time I would try to speak to someone, they asked me the same question about my face. I would try to explain. I would say it was "no big deal," but my response became forced, because I had begun to believe that it was a big deal.

I was relieved when my classmates stopped asking what was wrong with me. I was convinced that I would soon be able to play four square with them and join them in running around pretending to be horses. But soon after, word spread around the school that my skin condition was contagious. My classmates became convinced that touching my papery, cracked surface would send an itchy dryness creeping up their little fingers. No use of my limited knowledge of medical terms could break through the plague of fear.

Eventually I gave up trying to make them understand, and I crafted a masterful story. To me, it was devious and genius. I decided that if I couldn't escape being a pariah, I might as well take advantage of this strange, terrible power of fear my skin gave me. I knew that the rumor would eagerly spread like an infectious disease. I told everyone that I was an alien, a Martian sent to corrupt the world and turn every little kid into a Martian with demented skin just like mine.

They no longer ogled from a distance; they fled. I had a strange, wicked power that I hadn't known before. I would chase them around the playground and through the jungle gym, shrieking and threatening to curse them with the same fate I had been given. I truly came to feel like an alien, and I even came to wish that my disease were contagious. All I wanted was a companion on my pedestal of shame, while the crowd fearfully watched from afar.

A few long years later, I found the companion I had been searching for. To my infinite delight, there was another "fish skin kid" in my gymnastics class in the fourth grade. As soon as I saw his peeling, flyaway skin and he saw mine, we were instantly bound by our common place. Our unique sphere of existence on the margin of society bound us in a secret pact.

We rarely talked, but we would often catch each other's eyes in silent solidarity; we had an understanding that didn't need to be spoken because we already knew all that needed to be known.

Strangely, though, I soon came to learn that he had many friends. People listened to him, not out of fear but respect. Slowly, I began to see that his skin didn't define him. He could tell people that his skin was "no big deal" and people believed because he believed it himself.

One day, flushed with excitement, my gymnastics class bustled into the gym. But as I cautiously looked around, I noticed some kids staring at me. He noticed too, and his normally cheery face clouded.

All he said was, "Hey, knock it off! Mind your own business!" They uncomfortably looked away and walked past us to find some other way to occupy themselves.

"Thank you," I said. Those were the only words I ever spoke to him and the only words I ever needed to say.

That was the first time someone truly stood up for me.

I don't know what it means to feel comfortable in my own skin. In fact, I'm not really sure what it means to feel normal. But I learned that day the one thing that I can be sure of in life, no matter what.

I am human.

That Girl a Table to My Right

ALEXANDER NGUYEN, Grade 10, Age 15. Klein Forest High School,
Houston, TX, Stephanie Vaughan, *Teacher*

My sister dresses me, peppy-striped, argyle sweater, a neon array of graphic T's, with high-waist saffron shorts pulled past the knees, Neurotmesis-inducing jeans, a straw fedora. She says, "A splash of color, that's what gets the people's attention!" I get attention. I get questions.

I'm not gay.

There's that girl a table to my right. She sits like a ballerina, legs crossed and a foot into relevé. *The Adventures of Tom Sawyer*, my favorite, splayed out before her.

I have a small larynx. When the telephone rings, my hello is responded to with ma'am or some form of second-person female pronouns. Puberty failed me. I've been told that I sound like my mother, not my father, not even my brother. My mouth rambles alongside my mind, my thin vocal folds fluctuate with my emotion, accenting and stylizing every word with a distinctive prosody. I overuse "like."

I'm not gay.

Her hair fell from her pinna, cascading a waterfall of black silk down her profile. That girl a table to my right catches it before it obscures her entire face; her paper hands push it gracefully back into place, like picking up water and bringing it back to the sky. She flips to the next page.

I tried to catch a football. Once. It broke through my fingers and fractured my pinkie. I told everyone I fell down the stairs. Apparently, it was more believable than me playing football. Some guys joked about the Dallas Cowboys and called them the Dallas Cowgirls. At that moment in my life, however, I adamantly acknowledged the existence of the Cowgirls. I don't watch sports.

I'm not gay.

That girl a table to my right masks her nose and mouth in expectancy of a sneeze. Her eyes squint shut, she leans in my direction and offers a kitten sneeze, the kind that would rack up millions of views on YouTube. There arose the rare moment in human society where communication across social barriers was acceptable. "Bless y—" It came out as a whisper and died into a regrettable silence somewhere along the way.

All of my friends are girls. I guess we share a similar state of maturity, initiative, and docile behavior. Boys are more aggressive. A few punches of acceptance into the threshold of masculine psychology were not worth it. I bruise easily. I don't hit back. I laugh with the girls. The boys snicker at me.

I'm not gay.

Paper hands still clasped to her face, her eyes opened as faded denim blue, but their roundness and size compensated for a startling effect. That girl a table to my right heard me. "Thank you," ever so eloquently.

The boys hungry for social attention "come out." It causes ripples in gossip pools as he dives under girls' radars. Then he scoops one up. Now they are dating. Mark Simpson coined it "metrosexuality." I can't swim. I'm not metrosexual.

I'm not gay.

That girl a table to my right is back into *Tom Sawyer*. Her face is akin to a Barbie doll's. Not the new, cat-eyed ones. Like the prettier ones from the '90s. She flips another page.

I notice how dangerously short her shorts are, up-cutting the end of her paper thighs and outlining what little butt she had perfectly.

I'm not gay.

I notice how her loose, crochet top left a large opening from the neck hole to her modest cleavage and how the smaller holes in her shirt compose a mosaic of the shape of her body underneath. Another page.

I'm not gay.

I notice how his sun-kissed arms grip her around her thin waist, how every muscle catches the light when he spins her around. How his muscle shirt traces the shape of his squared pegs and presses against his abs so neatly that the shadows illustrate his body on a cotton canvas. How his broad shoulders caress her head and his sonorous laughter contests his strength. When his Colgate smile shrinks into slightly pursed lips as that girl a table to my right leans in and makes contact. He catches me in his peripheral and breaks from her. His eyes an old, floorboard hazel, sunken deep into his chiseled face pierced like a belligerent shark as it tapered down to his permanent flirtatious lips and a cleft chin that accented his face. The dark, clean arches of his eyebrows enunciated his eyes and his hair, starting with a baby widow's peak, stuck up in a sharp, athlete cut. Like black velvet crowning his handsome bronze face.

I'm not.

As I Hear It

EMMA HATHAWAY, Grade 12, Age 18. Bergen Academies, Hackensack, NJ, William Hathaway, *Teacher*

From the instant I yelped into this world, ready to make my presence known, he was there. It was the quickest friendship I have ever made, and, all things permitting, the longest friendship I will ever have. I think I love him.

The beauty of our relationship lies in the balanced give-and-take. As I hum, as I speak, as I sing, as I drum the table with my fingertips, it is all for him. And when I hear the twinkle of a human voice, the creak of a floorboard, or the satisfying crinkle of a potato chip bag, I like to think that it is all for me.

Yes, sound and I, we are old friends, and I could not ask for a more loyal companion.

There has never been a time, in my conscious memory, when I have been unaware of sound's presence. The music of Janine's giggle on the trampoline after a long day at kindergarten; the joyous cacophony of middle school marching band; the animated wave of conversation in the high school cafeteria. Sound is ubiquitous and constant, comforting and secure. For awhile, he was all I knew.

But sound has a partner, and her name is silence.

Enter fifth grade. Enter a new middle school building and a new teacher and new kids and the stress of kickball teams and

John, who says it is weird that my shoes are green.

Enter silence.

From the instant I was thrown into this new, preteen, alternative world, so ready to make my presence known but not knowing how, silence was there. It was the quickest acquaintance I have ever made, and I prayed it would be short-lived. I thought I loathed her.

In that new middle school world, in a constant effort to find my place, make good impressions, and form fast friendships, I feared judgment at every turn. And as I became more acutely aware of sound, I became more acutely aware of those moments when sound was missing.

Frankly, they terrified me.

Awareness of silence and fear of silence were one and the same to my eleven-year-old self. Sound encompassed everything I associated with good. Sound was an indicator of laughter, of chatter, of the people around me having a great time because I was fun and we were friends. It was a tangible indicator of connection.

In its absence, what was left?

Jenny and I were on the bus coming back from a field trip, and I was so focused on thinking of something fantastic to say that, as is the contrary tendency when we think too consciously about anything, it was becoming impossible for me to think of anything to say at all.

Silence.

"You're boring, Emma," Jenny casually observed.

Silence was an omen of all things disastrous. She was an indicator of dullness, of boredom, of having a terribly lame time. Silence was an indicator of distance. And all I wanted was connection.

My path became clear. I was ready to fight silence at all costs. Prepared to babble on about nonsensical trivialities for the sake of sound, forgetting entirely that the beauty of sound lies in the listening.

Whenever I read *Waiting for Godot,* I am touched to remember this rather crazy fifth-grade version of myself. It is not a far stretch to say that at age eleven, I was purposefully living out my own theater of the absurd.

I resorted to the monologue. I would go home each night and think of little anecdotes to tell my friends or family the next day so as to make sure that silence had no chance to show herself. It was exhausting, and to what purpose?

I was stuck. Here I was, speaking, and thinking about speaking, more than I ever had before, yet still feeling as though I had nothing to say and as though I could hardly connect with anyone. I missed being ten years old. Everything is easier when you can count your entire age on your own two hands.

Moms make things better too.

Mom and I were driving back from a ballet rehearsal one night, and after about 15 minutes, I realized that neither of us had been speaking. What's more, I realized that I felt no obligation to be speaking. And a small voice in the back of my head seemed to whisper, "Perhaps this contented silence is an indication of just how strong your relationship really is."

Mom was, after all, the only one I felt like I was still able to talk to throughout the entirety of this mini communication crisis.

The wheels began to turn, but it took some time for me to really see—to really see that relationships are defined not by the tangible sound between two people, but by an intangible, silent understanding, an understanding that is always present, regardless of what the other person does or does not say. An understanding that this relationship is a balanced give-and-take, that it is mutually beneficial, and that you are there for, and because of, each other.

I would see my parents sitting at the table, not saying a word, and I would realize that this was entirely all right. I would see two best friends in school walking down the hallway in silence, and I would realize that they were still best friends even though neither of the two was speaking at that exact moment.

With these realizations came the understanding that my fight should not be one against silence herself, but against my fear.

Seven years have passed, and I am still fighting that battle. But it has gotten easier. My awareness of silence has grown into understanding, and this understanding into a form of appreciation that is constantly growing. Granted, I still feel much more comfortable when sound is around, but that is just because I have known him longer.

Sound and silence coexisting—that is the key to this communication business as I hear it. Sound gives us the chance to express and to share, to fill the empty spaces with emotion and life. Silence gives us the chance to process and to tune into the sound of ourselves, so often drowned out in the sounds of the external world. Silence gives sound a rest, so that when sound does decide to come back in, it is a meaningful entrance.

Silence and I, we are slowly building the foundations of a lasting friendship. I am sure of it. The beauty of our relationship lies in the balanced give-and-take—the silent understanding. She makes sure that I have rest, and that I take time to think and reflect instead of jumping ahead to the next verbal train of thought. And though it takes effort, I try to give her my utmost attention whenever she's around. I'm beginning to think that I can oftentimes hear a lot more in silence than I can in sound.

I think I love her.

Honorifics

MICHAEL SUN, Grade 9, Age 14. Seoul International School, Seongnam, South Korea, Melanie Kempe, *Teacher*

When bowing to your elders, "yo" must be added to the end of a sentence, just as older siblings and upperclassmen are to be called "hyung" for boys and "noona" for girls. These are just a few of the linguistic tips that one must follow to avoid verbal, and sometimes physical, confrontation with your "sunbaes" (elders) at school.

When opening my mouth, I must always assess beforehand whether the person I am speaking to is older than me. This is an idiosyncrasy that many Westerners cannot comprehend. Yet for those who have been raised like me, in Korean culture, paying attention to such details can make a world of difference in whether we are able to navigate smoothly in this sea of social hierarchy. When a single syllable can make your entire remark sound like it is coming from an uneducated brute, when a few key words can please the ears of a teacher enough to overlook your folly, you learn to take great care in what falls from your tongue. Living in the Republic of Korea is an experience in the traditions of Confucianism, where respect for one's elders supersedes respect for an individual's cultivated virtues.

Although this custom is practiced throughout the Korean peninsula, it is especially intense in schools, where bullies can easily take advantage of this rule without necessarily having cultivated the wisdom and compassion that age is supposed to bestow. As a younger student, I must confess that even I am scared of the stereotypical bully who chews gum like an angry cow while swaggering around campus sporting a loose necktie and a malicious grin. To avoid getting beat up, or made fun of, we students have learned to keep our heads bowed low, to avoid eye contact, and to speak only when spoken to. This is the abiding law of the land.

The irony of all of this is that the rule of showing respect to our elders stemmed from the Confucian idea that, by having more life experience than us, our elders had the ability to guide and protect us from the mistakes that they made themselves. In this way, the older generation becomes the steward of the younger generation, while the younger generations support the efforts of the older. Yet in all my years at school, I have rarely seen my teachers intercede on the behalf of lowerclassmen when these Confucian values are used and abused by bullies. Instead of being a tool that helps to unite us into a stronger family, these values have divided us and made us like hens within a pecking order; each individual pecking and being pecked on in turn, with everyone aspiring to become a senior so they can live out the maxim that "absolute power corrupts absolutely."

Exacerbating an already serious problem is the confusion brought on by rank versus age. In school, an upperclassman is not always older than you in years. Do you then speak to them with the honorific "yo," or should you expect it from them? This problem is amplified even further in the mandatory military service that every Korean male is expected to undertake for two years. Since men can enter into the military anytime between the ages of twenty and thirty, it is not uncommon for individuals to encounter younger officers who are of higher rank than you or older officers who are of lower rank. As one can imagine, in a culture that places such emphasis on age and hierarchy, it is just too easy for an older, but lower-ranked, soldier to resent being treated like an underling by a younger, but higher-ranked, officer. Equally complicated is the temptation by the younger, higher-ranked officer to take retribution on the older, lower-ranked soldier because of all the ridicule he may be suffering from those who are even older or higher-ranked than himself. In the end, everyone feels emasculated rather than empowered. I cannot see how such a system can continue without further weakening the culture in which it currently thrives.

For as monolithic and immutable as this outdated custom is, a part of me still holds on to the spirit behind this law, created so long ago: stewardship of the younger generation. I have often asked myself how it might be possible to guide us back to Confucius's true intentions, without chaffing too hard against the grain. The answer I have come up with is this: One day, I, too, will be a senior, a highly ranked officer, or even a teacher and role model. When these times come, I will not only restrain myself from bullying, but I will also set an example for others by truly mentoring those who are younger than me. I will use firm but gentle ways to dissuade the reckless abuse of power. I will show the world the spirit of solidarity that this law can manifest when it is followed with integrity. In this way, perhaps I can illustrate to others the difference between power and force. In this way, perhaps I can finally become the change I wish to see in this world I am a part of.

Dip Into Happiness

HANA ZERIC, Grade 10, Age 15. St. Stephen's School, Rome, Italy,
Tamzen Flanders, *Teacher*

The sound of a wave more powerful than the others reawakens me from my daydream. At once excitement flows through my veins. I realize where I am. I stand in front of the grand sea, motionless, feigning a calm that I do not own. Joy in its pure shape. Here, basking in the light of this spot, I can feel my true self, the one that does not need people's company, people's help, and people's approval. I am alone with the waves. Somewhere behind me, however, I perceive the laughter of my brother, the voices of my parents, and I feel warmed by their protection. Ahead there is just a vast valley of sapphire water. I breathe in the pure marine aromas.

Behind the gentle curve of the promontory that the beach follows, I feel the presence of my true home, Makarska. Home sweet home.

 From miles above, the heavenly azure sky surmounts my smallness. At the horizon, it is covered with a single scarf of soft clouds, like fluctuating snow. The sea is sparkling with all the colors of the rainbow. The white, hard, perfectly shaped pebbles leave uneven and strange marks on the soles of my feet.

One wave after another crashes incessantly against the shore.

The burning rays of the sun, whose undying light shines

through even when I close my eyes, illuminate the perfection of this moment.

I look up toward the faraway islands. My gaze expands in every possible direction, without boundaries or obstacles. My thoughts fly high in the sky and deep in the sea, escaping from human sight. I am at the portal to an unidentified world.

I move the first paces into the cool and transparent water. A shiver of pleasure runs up my spine. I am about to dip and disappear into the purity of water that washes away sorrows and joys, leaving me in a state of ideal nothing, where even the thoughts trapped in my mind will be wiped away by the water passed through my ears, and where I just swim, moving forward. I am about to, but I do not entirely dare. The cold makes me shiver, and yet I do not move from this point, vacillating with indecision. I am in between water and land, in the cold. Half of my body is immersed, and the other half is dry. Whether I come out of the water or I plunge myself into the depths of the sea, I will sense the tender heat of the sun, or I will be so cooled down by the crystal water that I will feel almost warm again. My hands run to the goggles stretched on my forehead, and I pull them downwards, to cover my eyes.

Another year has passed, and my soul has been shaped by tears, sudden joys, my parents kissing me on the cheeks in the morning before I leave, long walks hand-in-hand with my brother, friends greeting me every morning and embracing me with their affection, the first acknowledged encounters with injustice and death, newfound knowledge, and love above all, but the sea is untouched in its mystery.

I feel a deep, pleasant pain in my chest. My heart is overwhelmed by the grandeur of this sight, and I feel smaller than a drop in the ocean.

Then a wave of daring overcomes my fear, and I let my limbs follow my feet, which seem more in charge than my brain. Finally, I plunge my head into the water.

The only functioning sense is now sight. My ears fill with a soft noise, an echo of centuries of existence. The salt suffuses my lips, making them sour and yet somehow alive.

The rays penetrating into this reality kiss my peachy cheeks and are absorbed by the halo of slow-moving hair that surrounds my eyes like fair tentacles. Myriad diamonds of light shine around my body. I look at my hands, and they are strangers to me, coming from another planet.

I go back up, with my hair pulling downwards, and I breathe in. This is the only prosaic interruption I allow myself. My journey into the depths does not admit hiatuses. I take another stroke, and more blue embraces my glowing body. The shapes of the sea urchins, which are unaware of their fate as future ornaments on my shelves, come into sight on the seabed. They will soon have contact with air, but for the moment I just look at their still, simple nobility.

I swim until my lungs urge me to return to the outside world. While I allow the force of the sea to slowly eject me, I return my immersed body to the surface. I see the border of the two entities that live side by side and never disturb each other. Air and water. I see the world outside, the dollhouses on the shore, the palms and the mountains, and I feel the sky and the sun.

My mouth involuntarily curves up into a large smile.

As my face breaks the perfection of this boundary, I perceive the infinity of beauty an instant can embrace.

A Passenger to the Infinite

RICHA BIJLANI, Grade 12, Age 17. Detroit Country Day Upper School, Beverly Hills, MI, Matthew Sadler, *Teacher*

My grandfather speaks in haikus. He sees from behind thick and cracked rose-colored glasses. And he listens as if he will hear God one day. He rises at 4:00 a.m. to walk beside wild dogs and lazy pigs on the beaten paths in front of his home before the moon has been swallowed by the sun. The air in Ajmer is brisk and cold this early in the morning, even during hot Indian summers, when the temperature soars above 40° Celsius well before noon. He walks when the thermometer reads five degrees. Sometimes I tell him, "Nana, you're crazy," but he laughs and doesn't understand. Last Christmas, we bought him a thick cap to protect his ears from the chill and to shield his thoughts from being blown away with the wind, and gloves to keep his weathered hands warm and ready to write when he returns. Most people are waiting for something to happen, but my grandfather is not one of those people. He walks in search of something. I cannot say exactly what that something is, and I don't think he can explain it either. Even though I am seventeen and he is seventy-seven, we are on the same odyssey, a pilgrim's progress toward something. Perhaps it is completeness of the soul.

With the exception of a few puttering cars whose drivers are still wiping the sleep from their bloodshot eyes, and a poverty-stricken wanderer who has lost his sense of time, my grandfather walks alone through the narrow drives of his colony. In the darkness, he thinks of his childhood, of the partition of India. He thinks of his parents, and the village where he was born. When he was my age, my nana had already been an adult for many years; terror, violence, and death made him old before his time. Now time has caught up to him and has taken his thick hair, his hearing, and his health. In the dim glow of dawn, he walks beyond the crumbling home where he raised two children. He turned an abandoned dentist's office with a leaky ceiling and steel pots on the dirt floor that overflowed into puddles during the wet monsoon season into a home for his family. Tugging at his cap, he tries to hide his memories under the knitted wool until he is back in his study. He keeps his journals on a modest wooden desk where he writes. I imagine he must have hundreds of journals, piled as high as the Himalayas along the edge of the table. From the desk, he can see his garden through a large paned window adorned by heavy curtains that have never been drawn closed. But right now it is dark, and the flowers seem to be sleeping under a blanket of dew. In the day, the jasmine and lilies will dance to remind my nana that he is surrounded by life.

In the pool of light from a single lamp, he slowly peels off his cap and gloves and smooths his wispy, white hair with his frail and wrinkled hands. With an ink-dipped fountain pen in his grasp, he scribbles quickly and the words spill onto a new page of an old journal. In his poetry he escapes reality, or rather, transcends reality. My grandfather publishes his work in both English and Hindi, but today he writes in Hindi. I cannot read all of the Devanagari script that looks more like pictures than letters, yet I can almost hear him reciting the poem in his tender voice and heavy accent. The verse is complex and wise, but raw and savage at the same time. The words burn my ears with dark intensity like a branding iron on calf hide, and I see his pursed lips scowling as he reads.

But as the sun seduces the sky with its warm and orange touch, I know my nana is smiling. These days he is always smiling. On the same desk where his yellowing journals sit, he has set up a computer and a web camera. He grins and claps his stained hands when we video chat. I am still adjusting my eyes to the light as my grandfather returns from work at the Sewa Mandir, a nonprofit hospital he runs with the help of my grandmother. It is 8:00 a.m. in Michigan and 6:30 p.m. in Ajmer, but his home and my home have never seemed so close. Today, though, I have trouble looking into his eyes, and I stare down at my sweating palms. He knows that I haven't been able to get out of bed for days, that I've been missing too much school, and that I've been overwhelmed by anxiety. I wait for him to ask me if I'm sick or if I need help, but instead he promises that I will be okay. He tells me that he and my grandmother got a new puppy: a tiny retriever named Goldie. He tells me Goldie hides in his shoes and nips at his ankles on the cold marble floors. He tells me, "Goldie is very smart. He likes to play on the stairs. He climbs one step, and jumps down. He climbs two steps, and jumps down. He climbs up to the third step, but he knows it is too high, and he does not jump down. Even Goldie knows his limits." My grandfather learns from everything around him. He wants to help everything around him. "Break the shackles," he says. Then he tells me a story that I don't understand: "There were two buckets. One was golden and proud, and the other was of humble tin. A thirsty traveler asked for water. Both buckets ran to drench him, but you know the water was the same."

I have been told that I am a lot like my nana. I think that we both depend on the power of words to help us break free from the shackles that restrain us. Sometimes I feel like an old soul, tired from struggling under the weight of the chains, like I am seventy-seven and not seventeen. I wonder if he is tired too: tired of walking, tired of searching. I envision my grandfather on the streets of Ajmer, with his hands clasped behind his back and the soles of his shoes marking his path behind him. He is not tired. Nor should I be. This is more than an odyssey; this is evolution.

Arresting Development

NACHIKETA BARU, Grade 12, Age 17. Canyon Crest Academy,
San Diego, CA, Christopher Black, *Teacher*

It has always struck me as a bit of an oddity that *Peter Pan,* that
charming story of a swashbuckling young lad who refuses to
become an adult, is targeted to the exact audience (say, four-to-
nine-year-olds) least able to sympathize with its central prem-
ise. Talk to any young child, and they will almost universally
express their eagerness to "grow up." It is a reaction that is
inexorably ingrained into the bright-faced innocents by classical conditioning. From their tentative first steps to their first
bowel movement successfully executed while seated on a toilet
to their first day braving the wilds of kindergarten, children
are reinforced by parents, teachers, and other assorted author-
ity figures who praise them as inchoate big boys/girls.

I have been pondering this phenomenon more and more
recently, a function of the fact that, as a high school senior,
I am surrounded by kids eagerly counting down the days to
when they can finally claim for themselves the mystical title of
"adults." Most of them will, in some nine months' time, move
on to whatever institute of higher learning will have them,
where they will presumably blossom into full maturity amidst
ramen-noodle dinners and alcohol-saturated fraternity parties. However, not for me this increasingly feverish tizzy over

the prospect of impending adulthood; simply put, I'm afraid of growing up.

Much of my apprehension stems from the fact that, from what I have been able to observe through my life in a middle-class suburban enclave, even adults don't seem to enjoy adulthood all that much. Life as a grown-up seems to consist largely of rushing between appointments, deadlines, and meetings, stressors blunted only by a customary evening-time alcoholic beverage and a couple of hours flipping through cable network, before passing out during a late-night talk-show host's monologue. As a naturally shy and annoyingly pensive individual, I am not necessarily enamored with the hormonal ooze of high school life either, but even then, a dry two-hour chemistry lecture seems to be infinitely preferable to paying the heating bills or contesting charges with unresponsive credit-card-company answering machines.

And I don't think that I speculate about this disheartening drudgery with no foundation. As teenagers, we have gotten used to the sermonizing of teachers and others who ask us to prepare ourselves for the vagaries of the so-called "real world," which is apparently populated by hyenas and vultures just waiting for us to stumble so they can swoop down, pluck out our eyeballs, and feast heartily on our entrails. The central theme of these tough-love speeches, these grim hybrids of boot-camp pep talks and video Pilates-instructor directives, is that, to paraphrase Uncle Ben from the first Spiderman movie, with the great power and independence afforded to us by "adult life," we must also take on great responsibility.

Perhaps, but then again, many of these obligations seem thrust upon us as a result of the curious machinations of entirely artificial constructs of human thought. I mean, what is an "economy" anyway, and what is it about a confident interviewing manner and well-formatted résumés that will somehow give us the privilege of being able to "contribute" to it in a positive manner? And what makes us obligated to show great loyalty to bosses and companies that would gladly throw their employees out on the street if they found they could move their operations to Thailand or Guatemala?

To be clear, I don't mean for this to devolve into a foot-stamping rant against the Western capitalism that has bestowed upon us such wonders as automobiles, skyscrapers, and the self-lubricating catheter. It is simply an expression of frustration at the fact that adult life seems doomed to be nothing more than one long anxiety attack over how to allot the rectangular pieces of green paper that seem to be the defining barometer of self-worth in our society.

It also stems from worry over the idea that I may very well be in the process of missing my prime. I had always heard that high school was supposed to be the best time of one's life, but as someone who was (is) chronically unable to indulge in the dates and parties that are supposedly the hallmark of the teenage years, I feel that that train has already left the station. Some have attempted to remedy such despair on my part by saying that, in fact, it is one's college years that are the apex.

I suppose that gives me some more time to work on my social shortcomings. But does that mean that, in roughly five to six years, I can prepare for one long downward slide, at least until I retire and spend my days shunting a croquet ball around a retirement-home lawn? Or will I find that my frontal cortex eventually reaches full development, and one day in my mid-twenties I'll wake up with an overwhelming urge to put on a suit and tie and go provide for my progeny? Either way, I'd like to take this chance to make a tentative reservation for one to Neverland.

Kitchen Lights

ANISHA DATTA, Grade 11, Age 16. Glencoe High School, Hillsboro, OR, Bill Huntzinger, *Teacher*

I like kitchen lights. I like kitchen lights because they're warm, like little upside-down puddles of gold, tinting everything they touch with this sort of waxy coating of familiarity. They bronze the skins of bell peppers and tomatoes like the bare-backed models on those glossy tanning-salon ads. Food is more appetizing under these lights.

I also like these lights because of the things they do to my father's eyes. And mine, for that matter, since our eyes are essentially the same. I can see his eyes as he cooks, even though he doesn't look at me when he talks, in case he forgets to add a pinch of this or a dash of that. Even after a life of a coffee addict (roughly three cups a day, strong enough to dissolve the spoon as my grandmother says), the whites of his eyes are still clear as an egg. And the browns of his irises are different too. Notice I said browns. Most people have flat eyes, eyes that are only one color, like everything's already been stirred together in their depths to make a uniform hue. But not my father. His eyes are darker, more enigmatic, and under the kitchen lights you can see the strings of amber traveling outward from his pupils, even though I'm sitting ten feet away.

He's talking to me about solipsism or religion or something abstract like that. He likes to talk about these things, especially with me. My mother is as intelligent as he is, but in a much more pragmatic sense; just like my brother. I like listening to him and watching him cook. His hands only add to his speech, as he times his points to coordinate with his cuts and sprinkles. It's a very holistic experience, really.

"Dad? Who taught you to cook?"

"My mom." He stirs something. "I grew up in a very traditional village. Women were not allowed to clean or go out of the house or cook when they were on their period. I was the only one at home. So I learned to cook, so that we would have something to eat then."

I've heard this explanation a lot. It's as far as he's comfortable going.

"What was your mom like?"

"Motherly."

"Go figure," I say before I can think. He stirs the pot again, chuckling thoughtfully. He can take a joke, but I figure I had been too harsh. "But really, Dad. What was she like?"

"Kind. Nice. Cooked good food. Made sure we all went to school. You know."

I don't know. But I need to be delicate with these kinds of things.

"No. I mean, apart from being a mom. What did she like to do?"

"I don't know."

"Of course you do. She was your mom!"

He adds a dash of cumin with uncharacteristic vigor. It means he's trying to forget something.

"She liked to sing."

"What did she like to sing?"

"Songs." He hesitated a moment. "Classical music, mostly. Songs that were popular back then."

"Did she sing to you?"

"Hm!" He exclaimed, which is his way of saying "yes." It's hard to describe, but there's a lot of force behind the word, as the pitch increases at least three notes. "Mothers like to sing to their kids."

"Was she a good singer?"

He paused. It was a mental pause; his hands were still moving, the food was still being cooked, but his thoughts stalled in his eyes. "Yes. She was good."

"Very good?"

"Very good."

"How good?"

"She was so good that she used to sing at anti-British rallies. People would call her to sing, in front of thousands of people. She was in sixth, seventh grade."

I've never heard him brag about his mother. Himself? All the time. But never his mother. He mostly just tries to forget her. He gives the pot one final stir and sits down in a lawn chair that has found its way into our kitchen. He moves slowly, deliberately. Part of this is because of his back, which has curled into a hunchback that makes him stand slightly shorter than me.

"And Mom used to sing and sing until the soldiers would come and fire their guns, and everyone would run away as far as they could."

"Mom?" I asked, trying to picture my mother that old.

"No. My mom."

I don't think I can effectively explain to you the significance of this. Everyone in our house calls my mother Mom. Including my dad. He refers to his mother as "my mom." This switch was

. . . powerful. I think he recognized his unconscious slip too. We were both silent for a moment. The pot bubbled contently behind us.

"Did you like it when she sang to you?"

He nodded as much as he could. "Yes, I asked her to sing for me."

"Do you remember any of her songs? Can you sing one?"

"Now?"

"Now."

He breathes deeply, trying to gather the lyrics. I remember my mom telling me that when they were young, my dad would ask her to sing for him. Every day. She has a beautiful voice too. I guess my dad had a soft spot for good singers.

To be honest, I didn't expect much when he sang. Both my brother and I have played the piano for most of our lives, and have bent over backward trying to get him to recognize simple things in music, like major or minor scales, or hitting a note. It's been exasperating, to say the least.

But he had a decent voice. More than decent, actually. A good voice. It was warm and rich, like his eyes and the kitchen lights. All these things melted together to form this wonderful perfection in our kitchen, with his voice and the smells and the bronzy shades dappled around us.

It took me a few bars to recognize the song. He used to sing it to me when I was little and couldn't fall asleep. He aborted the song after a few verses, saying that it was distracting him from his cooking, and shuffled in the hobbitesque way that he has back to the pot. And I let him, mostly because my dad hates it when other people see him cry.

When the Gods Leave

AKSHAN DEALWIS, Grade 11, Age 16. Noble and Greenough School, Dedham, MA, Richard Baker, *Teacher*

When my mother called from Boston to tell Aththamma that I was a boy, it was too late. Aththamma had already packed her bags and ordered the pinhead-size diamond earrings and gold bracelets for the granddaughter she thought was on the way. The doll-size bangles are still in a box with the faded blue velvet on my mother's dresser, along with the picture of a tiny brown sleeping baby who looks nothing like me. In the same box is the sacred white thread that now looks like rusted wire with the five gold charms to battle the evil eye that harms the newborn. My mother never slipped the bangles through my chubby fingers and, afraid that I would swallow the charms, never hung them around my neck. The earrings went back to Sri Lanka to a six-year-old granddaughter with eyes like black diamonds.

For months before I came to the world, Aththamma offered milk rice and jasmines to the gods under the Sal tree in her garden, hoping that I would be healthy. She would wash the old silver bowl with the carvings of the intertwined dragons and fill it with the steaming milk rice the cook would bring to her. The maids would pluck the jasmine still heavy with dew and string miniature garlands to be hung on the branches. Aththamma would not allow the gardener to cut a single branch, for fear the gods would leave the tree. So the tree grew throttling the overripe jack fruit trees and the musky araliya bushes. My grandfather watched in bewilderment as the branches choked the gutters and clawed their way up to the wrought-iron balconies, spilling coral-colored flowers swollen with yellow stamen on the bedsheets hung out to dry. "Do not touch the baby's tree," my grandmother would warn him severely.

For fourteen years, every summer, I would arrive sleepy and nauseated after eating the egg sandwiches that were sent to the airport with the driver and my grandfather, who came to pick me up on the 3:00 a.m. flight to Colombo. Aththamma would be waiting to greet me on the red-tiled veranda with the sari drawn tightly across her so-thin shoulders like a shroud. Flecks of lights would sparkle from inside the house, and outside on the Sal tree circled flickering clay lamps. Nestled in the branches was the small shrine with statues mildewed and decayed. The shrine is heavy with the heady smell of the slowly budding Sal flowers and the swiftly dying jasmines offered the previous morning.

When Aththamma fell ill last year, there was no one to offer milk rice at the shrine and light a lamp for her health. Her maids had left her, unable to take care of a woman who no longer could eat without help. The nursing aides would not pluck flowers in the morning. That was not their job. Still, Aththamma would not allow the branches of the Sal tree to be cut. The gardener would come twice a week to cut the grass and sweep away the purple bougainvillea flowers scattered like thousands of crumpled tissue papers on the lawns but he did not touch the baby's tree. The old stone statues green with moss had long slipped off the tree and cracked into myriad delicate lines. Without the jasmines garlanding the tree, there were no bees with their mechanical murmurs buzzing around the tree. The squirrels had built a nest in the hollowed-out bodhiya, and because the branches were reaching into the house, my grandfather's office room often had a green lizard on the windowsill, watching beady-eyed during the siesta hour.

The last time I saw Aththamma, she was so tiny that I could barely hold her papery hand. When I bowed to touch her feet in worship, my fingers touched little misshapen bones sticking out in different directions. Before I left, I sorted through her old books, where silverfish had bored through filigree, like holes. "To little Sarojini on her eighth birthday" is written on a worn copy of *Little Women*. Years later, my mother had written her own name on the inside cover in a thick red crayon. Her handwriting, like a child's, is exaggerated with an elaborate flourish to the R. A copy of Pushkin's poetry is underlined meticulously with a ruler. A tiny black-and-white photo falls out of it. There are three children sitting on the steps of Aththamma's garden. The photo is so gray that the girl's billowy skirt melts into the blackness. Her long hair is tied in a ribbon, and she wears no shoes. The two boys have curly hair and look like me. I put the photo in my pocket. "To Dearest Sarojini," my grandfather's unruly handwriting is on the covers of the *Complete Works of Shakespeare*, "on our engagement." Then there is the book Aththamma gave to my grandfather, a leather-bound copy of *War and Peace*, inscribed in her elegant curling writing, "All my love, on our engagement." I pick them up to take back to Boston, but then put them back again side by side, pushed far back on the bookshelf so no one would see them and separate them. I wondered why my grandmother gave her new husband a copy of *War and Peace*. On the Shakespeare volume, I could still carve out the embossed faces of comedy and tragedy. I put in my backpack the Rubaiyat given to Aththamma by her grandfather. There are no terms of endearment written on that book: "To Sarojini from your grandfather on the day you leave for university." The Rubaiyat is broken halfway down the spine and held together carefully with yellowed, wrinkled Scotch tape and the last pages are missing from it.

Behind the books is an old box of Monopoly covered in dust and stains. I had never seen a Monopoly board with Piccadilly Circus and Kensington Gardens on it. On a balled-up piece of paper three children had drawn crooked columns under their names and totted up the amounts they had made in real estate. The houses red, blue, and yellow are still arranged in unsteady rows, as if after the game was over the children played with the miniature plastic houses on a foreign land that they called their monopoly. What did they think about building houses on unfamiliar lands? How did they build houses on land that had no araliya trees with sticky oozing milk or wild bougainvillea spilling off of tiled roofs? How could those children born where gods lived in every tree build their homes in strange lands without those gods?

"What will you do with the house?" my father asks my mother tentatively, almost afraid to say the words. Neither speaks about what has happened, what is yet to happen. My mother slowly removes the papers that look like old deeds from a file tied with string and hands it to him. The string looks twisted and discolored on Aththamma's saris that my mother has laid out on her bed. Pink and green and saffron and ochre with a faint smell of incense burnt to keep out the mosquitoes still clinging to them, the saris are like waves of undulating color. I remember how they would flutter like a giant kite when Aththamma ran behind me on her driveway while I shouted, "Run, run as fast as you can, you can't catch me, I am the gingerbread boy." When she would catch up with me, she would hold me tight, her bangles bruising my cheek and her hair smelling of sandalwood. "I don't know," my mother says. "There are lots of things to do before we decide any of that. I am told that the Sal tree must be cut before the roots crack the foundation. We have to save the house." No one asks me what I think, because this is an adults' conversation. But I want to shout, "Don't! This is not Monopoly. The gods will leave if you do that." But I am worried that it may be already too late, that the gods may have already left us.

Magnolias

LYDIA SUTTLE, Grade 8, Age 14. Grassland Middle School,
Franklin, TN, Lilly Leffler and Cindy Pons, *Teachers*

Everyone has a wall, she said. Everyone. She made it seem so
normal and absolute that I believed in it.

. . .

Listen to me.

Listen to me.

. . . Everyone's got a secret.

Everyone.

. . .

Remember that day? The one in March when we were pen-
guins. When the air was sticky and warm and filled to the brim
with a scent of magnolias. When the taste of artificial strawberry became my favorite and now sometimes tastes so bitter
that I make a face. You looked good.

S-o

good.

And sometimes I relive that day in my dreams. And the air is
still sticky and warm and you still look

s-o

good.

   But at some point, the magnolias turn into stars and, oh,
they're so pretty and clear. And I wish on them, over and over

until my head is full of them and I am laughing about how many there are. Laughing, laughing, laughing.

I hold onto this day until I can't stand it anymore. Until I cry over it, though the reason eludes me. But the air is still warm, you still look s-o good, and the stars are magnolias, but wait—isn't it supposed to be the magnolias that are stars and, oh, the wishes are beautiful and perfect and flawless, and I am still laughing, laughing, laughing.

. . .

She calls up to me, "I'll be done in ten minutes," and I tell her okay, but she tells me that I won't get it done. Nothing gets done in this house, though.

I hang on to the banister and let my back arch, arch, arch until my head is lolled back too, upside down. And I smile, because it feels good to me. I can feel my hip bones press into the jeans that I had wanted for so long, and I hold on to the bones, because they're so beautiful to me. I can feel my hair swinging and dusting my lower back, and I laugh, because I feel beautiful.

I let my eyes open, and I see the lights and, oh, they're so pretty and clear like the magnolias, and I laugh because everything seems so beautiful and perfect and flawless. So much that I want to cry. And I almost do.

And I think of you. And I think of mango tea and of bittersweet strawberries and magnolias and stars. And I think of that linen-grass-woods smell that I'd know anywhere. And of a warm touch on my back, shoulder, and hand. And of the time when you wrapped me in your arms as I shook like an earthquake, and all I could think was "Oh, God, he's staying." And I think of the two weeks where I saw so much but heard so little . . .

I think of many things, and my hip bones still press, my hair still swings, and my back still arches, and I can still see the lights that are stars that are magnolias that are still so beautiful-perfect-flawless.

And then I feel it. Something lifting, stretching, and expanding like a balloon. I get excited because I only feel this every other Monday, I was due for this tomorrow but now it's early.

And my hips are still pressing and my back is still arching and my hair is still swinging and, oh, the lights that are stars that are magnolias still are so beautiful-perfect-flawless but I feel even more so.

Something's lifting. And I realize that, yes! It is my wall that's lifting, lifting, lifting, and I am laughing, laughing, laughing, and I feel the girl that rarely comes out, taking a tentative step into this unfamiliar world, and she is beautiful-perfect-flawless too. Like the magnolias. And it feels good. It feels so good. Like breathing after being underwater for a very long time.

And then, I notice that I didn't need anyone for this lifting. I am just hanging from our banister and I am free.

My sister had long since finished, but I didn't care. Nothing got done in this house anyways. My hips were still pressing, my back still arching, and my hair still swinging and, oh, the lights that are stars that are magnolias are still so beautiful-perfect-flawless, and I wish on them until it dizzies and dazzles me over and over, an explosion that I will never understand.

And I laugh. I laugh because I feel beautiful-perfect-flawless, and I truly know the reason of happiness and why others are so addicted to this feeling, to the point that they do ridiculous things to achieve it, yet I had all of the answers in the lights that are stars that are magnolias and, oh, wasn't it funny that it was here all along? And I know you are trying to talk to me, but I'm sorry, I'm too busy being free and allowing this girl to breathe fresh air instead of remaining in her prison for so long, and how odd, I think, that I have no name for a girl I know so well yet so little.

And suddenly, it doesn't matter so much, because we are laughing, me and this mystery girl. And I am suddenly soaring and arching up, up, up like my own back, and I am above the Earth just soaring past everyone and everything. Past the planets until I touch the lights that are stars that are magnolias, and I cry because they are so beautiful-perfect-flawless. But I laugh because I feel free. So I laugh with tears on my cheeks but I feel happy. I feel like flying. And I stretch out among the magnolias and touch them because, oh, I have loved them for so long and how splendid it is to get to see them, finally.

And my hips are still pressing, my back is still arching, and my hair is still swinging and, oh, the lights that are stars that are magnolias are so beautiful-perfect-flawless . . . and I am free.

Stock of the Season

LUKE HAAS, Grade 8, Age 13. John F. Kennedy Middle School, Florence, MA, Holly Graham, *Teacher*

May 7th, Entry 1: Not even a light bulb painter.

Right off the bat, I'd like to throw out a tip to anyone who cares to pay attention: DO NOT move to Rhode Island. Just don't do it. I could list several reasons why, but I don't feel like writing an essay. I've written enough essays to get into Brown University, so I think I'm done. Not that it was rewarding, anyway. I got my master's in business during April, which apparently wasn't good enough to get a spot in General Electric. They wouldn't even let me in as a light bulb painter. For full effect, I'll repeat that sentence for you: They wouldn't even let me in as a light bulb painter. What is a light bulb painter, you ask? That is precisely my point. Sure, I have a criminal record. I can understand how that would bring me down, but really? Not even a light bulb painter.

Now, don't think I'm some scumbag who tries to steal cars but always forgets that breaking the window will set off an alarm. I'm not a burglar, a robber, a vandal, or a criminal in any way, shape, or form. I got into Brown from a public school in Windham, Connecticut, and Windham is a lot less awesome than Providence. On a scale of one to ten, Windham would get a three. You get my point. Anyway, it's obvious I'm no dope. So what did I do? I ran someone over. To be more specific, I ran the mayor of Windham over.

Okay, I know that sounds pretty bad, but before you judge, you should know that the mayor of Windham at the time was quite short. He also happened to be dressed in an orange sweater with white stripes that day, which made him look basically identical to a street cone. Actually, that probably made you judge me considerably more, so why don't we just forget I said that? It's not like I'm writing this journal to let whoever reads this in a few years judge me. Matter of fact, I didn't want to write this at all. But my uncle made me. He's a professor at Brown (which is how my "incident" got overlooked in my application), and he's also my former, and only, legal guardian.

I never did know my mom and dad. Only Uncle Roland and Aunt Mary, but she passed away when I was six. Go ahead, pity me, boo-hoo, all that crap, but I don't remember any of it vividly. If you're going to pity anyone, pity my uncle. He's the one who went through all of the deaths. It's kind of ironic, because my uncle is always so happy. He brings so much life into the world, just to see it disappear. Now that I think about it, irony is my family curse. My aunt died of cancer after it was caught too late. She was an oncologist. A building collapsed on my dad during a business trip in western California. He was an architect. My mom died of Lyme disease, a result of a tick bite. She was an entomologist, one who studies insects and arachnids.

I'll probably die like that too. The victim of irony, the target of misfortune. Maybe I'll become a chef and starve to death. Maybe I'll be working for a car company, only to be run over by its most recent brand. Maybe I'll be a daredevil who dies of something lame, like old age. I doubt any of those will happen though. It's not like I've got much of a future ahead of me if I can't even be a light bulb painter for the General Electric headquarters. Not even a light bulb painter . . .

May 23rd, Entry 2: The street cone.

Ever since I got denied that application to GE, I've kind of been lying low. By lying low, I mean hollowing out my uncle's fridge and playing *Call of Duty.* I'm casually looking at different companies and corporations, but I'm filled with despair as I read requirements of character and application formats, because I know a light bulb painter at the GE headquarters has a better chance of making it into any large business. Maybe I'll go into banking, you know? They do all kinds of illegal crap that the government doesn't care about, so I'd probably fit in pretty nicely. Nah, who am I kidding. There's no way to be successful with a record . . .

Hold up, I never really expanded on that story about me running over the mayor of Windham, did I? Let me be clear. I never intended to do such a thing. He was opening up some highway apparently, and I could only see the back of him. My uncle told me that this highway was opening at 9:00 a.m. over the phone, and I mistook that for 8:00 a.m. So I drive over, arriving at 8:30, and see nothing but the highway, a just-snapped red ribbon, and an authoritative street cone. Remember, there are no people standing and watching, because let's be honest: it's Windham. No one goes to public events in this town. I simply figured the highway was open, and I was the first one there. I barreled through, eager to visit New London (my friend moved there, and the highway was a direct route) and then the street cone that I ever-so-carelessly knocked into rolled over the hood of my Honda Civic, screaming like a human. Like an angry mayor type of human.

Listen, I've said this before, and I'll say it again: I'm not a dope. I got into an Ivy League university. So what if my uncle teaches Literature there? With my record, it kind of cancels out. So don't think I wasn't shocked when I realized I was responsible for several broken bones in our "treasured" mayor. That was one of the stupidest things I've ever done in my life. But to be honest, it was pretty hilarious a couple days after. You know, after all the legal stuff was worked out. I was probably cracking up the whole day, which is weird, because I don't "crack up." It kind of sucks that running over short people was the thing that got me, though. But the whole situation was so . . . ironic. Yeah. I think that family curse is catching up to me. But really, the mayor getting run over right after he opens a highway to the public? That's good stuff.

Now that I think about it, the only person in my family who hasn't experienced a lot of irony is my Uncle Roland. Which is ironic because he teaches ironic pieces in his classes for a good part of each year. So is that ironic? Is it ironic that I'm confused about irony when I may be part of one of the most ironic families on earth? Is it ironic that I've used the word "ironic" or "irony" about eight times in this paragraph alone? The world may never know. Let's just leave it at that, I suppose. I've overworked my brain enough today.

Anyway, I guess what I'll try to do is start my own business. I'll probably have to start off small, though. I think I'm just going to work up some money being a cashier or something like that, then use the money I've saved up to get the wheels turning for my business. My theory for business is specialization and uniqueness; you've got to specialize in one thing in particular, and make sure you don't have much competition. Even if it's something random, like, I don't know, spoons. But you've got to make the best spoons out there, put them up for a reasonable price, and you've got business. Yeah, spoons. That sounds pretty good, actually. I'm gonna write that down. Spoons.

June 19th, Entry 3: A meaningful "Nice to meet you."
It's been more than a month since I started this journal, and I believe you've been in the dark about one crucial detail: my identity. Additionally, my gender. Maybe you assume I'm a man because of my talk of business and whatnot, in which case I'd have the right to call you sexist. However, I am indeed male, so I can't do that. If only, if only. Anyway, I think it's about time you know my name. Hello, my name is David Luther. Nice to meet you.

Now that we've cleared that up, I think it's necessary to say I've found my low-key business to work in. Before I say what it is, I hope you acknowledge that I've been looking everywhere for the right job since I wrote my second entry. I started working at some fast-food restaurants, but that was too demeaning. I can enjoy a Big Mac every once and a while, but not one that's been made by a co-worker. Aside from McDonald's and KFC, I worked at a frozen yogurt place called "Cream-Haven." I got out of there pretty quickly for two important reasons: One, Rhode Island frozen yogurt doesn't make money, because Rhode Island frozen yogurt stinks. Two, I may be liberal, but the owners wanted to set me up with their dog. No, thanks.

Finally, I ended up where I think I'll be for a good amount of time. It's a convenience store in downtown Providence called "Stock of the Season." Staying true to its name, it sells all different types of convenience-store appliances according to the season. For example, over the summer we sell blow-up kiddie pools, suntan lotion, and those foam noodles that embarrassing uncles of teenagers bring into public pool areas. Especially eccentric uncles named Roland who work at Brown University and wear full wetsuits . . . for the shallow end. God, that was a disaster.

On my first day, everyone was quite friendly. I'm a cashier

along with two other people, a short blonde girl currently attending Brown University (she must be alright if she's going to a college like that) named Carol Ackerman, and an African-American seventeen-year-old named James Graham, but he said I could just call him Jim. It was sort of awkward considering the fact that I'm several years older than both of them, but like I said, they were very grateful to see a new face. At least that's the vibe they gave off.

"You're gonna start a business?" Jim said when I told him my long-term plan. "How are you supposed to do that without a loan?"

"I don't trust banks. I barely trust them with my account," I said truthfully.

"Well said, David. Well said."

I've got to say though, the application interview was the most awkward part. The owner, George Robin, was like eighty-something, and he sometimes just paused before asking a question, which made a really awkward silence. I kind of felt bad for him, though. He never got married or had any kids, so he's pretty much running this store until the day he retires, which he should have done a couple of decades ago. I guess he must be really committed to that place. The end of the interview was him telling me how I was a "leader type" with "fresh ideas" and "a good sense of character," which is really nice considering the fact that I had to confess that I ran over the mayor of Windham. Nevertheless, he likes me, I appreciate him, and we respect each other behind the register. This is my kind of business.

The most interesting part was the greetings. Anywhere you work, people say "hello" and "nice to meet you," but they don't really care. They just want to go home and relax at the end of the day. But at Stock of the Season, it felt like they meant it. In any workplace, you'll make friends who you weren't friendly with in the beginning, but here, stage one of friendship turns into stage two. So, if I know anything about logical progressions, stage two will become stage three, and stage three . . .

Stage three is like having a second family.

July 4th, Entry 4: The curse has arrived.

Screw irony.

I hate it! It's stupid, counterproductive, and unfair. Especially today, because today it's double irony. Today is supposed to be the day of America, the country of business, the country of success, and I get more death. And more responsibility.

Of course, the moment I feel comfortable in my workplace, another irony-bomb drops. Of course! What would the son of Kim and Thomas Luther be without irony. I don't know if I've even written this down yet, but my whole life has been irony. In third grade I got into trains. Trains, trains, trains. It was all about trains. And the day I bought that gigantic train set, that's the day my dog got run over. By a train. I used to be really into nature in the fifth grade. I was out in the woods almost every day. The animals, the trees, the grass, the leaves. And the day before I go out to camp, I break my leg. By falling out of a tree. I've got dozens more examples, but you get my point. But this . . . this is the worst of all.

Goddammit, so much for getting on my feet, huh? I joined Stock of the Season because it was a decent salary that could help me start a business, but no. My plans never work out. Never have, never will. You think I wanted to get bailed out by my uncle after an hour of jail time and get a twice-as-long lecture from the police and my uncle the day I ran over that authoritative street cone? No, I was planning to see my buddy, Nick. We were gonna spend the day together, catch up. But I forgot that nothing works out for David Luther, never!

And now it's the last straw. I can't take it anymore! The irony, the death, the lost dreams, I've had enough. But it isn't really my choice, I suppose. I guess I just thought things would work out for once, that I could get a big break with one good idea, but that was stupid of me. I should have known what I was getting into.

You know what? I think he meant to do it, the old coot! All that talk about me being a leader type . . . it was so obvious what he was doing! He finally had a chance to relax, with me coming along. He had no more responsibilities with a "leader type," so why wouldn't he take a break. He could chill for the first time, and that's what killed him. Not old age.

And you know how it's ironic? Let me give you a bulleted list:

• I'm the newest employee at Stock of the Season; I've only been working here for half a month.

• It's the Fourth of July, Independence Day, the day we get to make our own choices.

Although there are only two details that make this occurrence ironic, they're big ones. Very big ones. Matter of fact, I think I'm going to need to reintroduce myself: Hello, my name is David Luther. Nice to meet you. I am now, by right of will, the new owner of Stock of the Season.

Creative Napping 101

KATELYN DAVIS, Grade 11, Age 16. Mississippi School for the Arts, Brookhaven, MS, Jeanne Lebow, *Teacher*

8:43 a.m.

She draped her black pea coat over the back of her chair and straightened out her sweater in the reflection of her computer screen. Seventeen minutes, she noted as she rolled her Pilot Bottle-2-Pen between her fingers. Promptly two minutes later, she paced to the door, opening it, just before a handful of students piled in. She cantered back over to her desk, sitting upon it, waiting in silence for the room to fill.

When it did, she adjusted her thick-rimmed, cat-eyed glasses and spoke. "My name is Dr. Mary Lee. You will address me as Dr. Lee and only that." She stared out at the paled faces. "You will need paper, pens, creativity, determination, and a sense for dry humor. If you have come to class without any of these materials, the door is to your right. Please do not close it behind you, as I'm sure there will be more to follow."

She looked up as one young girl shamefully walked to the door, and then continued.

"In addition, good grammar, a compelling love for strong English tea, a high tolerance for confessional poetry, and excellent comprehension of overcharacterized metaphors will prove itself useful in this course. You may want to invest in a high-capacity mobile filing cabinet as well." She gave her audience a blank expression, counted one . . . two . . . three . . . four, until another portion of her class had exited.

"If you're looking for an easy A, I would suggest you leave now in order to make it to home economics on time. If you're here because you think you're a good writer, you should probably start searching for a gullible publishing company, and it wouldn't be a bad idea to pick up some food-court applications on your way out."

Two more students disappeared.

"If you're here because you thought this was an English class, reread your class descriptions and find your way to admissions." Three more students disappeared into the hallway.

Dr. Lee turned toward her white board and wrote "Creative Writing 101" and then turned back to her quickly dissipating class just as a latecomer staggered in at exactly 9:08.

"If you cannot be here five minutes early, this isn't the class for you." She watched him stop mid-trek, turn, and walk back out.

"If you have ever in your life referred to a grocery basket as a "buggy" or a Pepsi as a "Coke," I suggest you switch to an English class and consider taking this class next year." Dr. Lee paced to the back of her classroom and removed a stack of worn, heavily-used composition books from the closet. Returning to the front of the room, she let the stack of books land solidly on a student's desk.

"You will need an unlimited supply of composition books and a bottomless pit of ink in multiple colors. Inspiration will be key in this course. If you do not have inspirational surroundings, I suggest you indulge in some type of tragedy. Murder has proven to be great inspiration for me in the past."

At that instant the entire second and third row of her class headed for the door. Dr. Lee simply stared at them blankly as they left her classroom behind.

"In conclusion, you will need an infinite amount of passion for your writing to survive my course. If you are still here, you must think you have what it takes." She said as her last two students peered at her over a stack of outlandish supplies. They said nothing.

"So?" Dr. Lee raised an eyebrow at the smallest girl. She rose to her feet and exploded into tiny tears of intimidation and fled from the classroom, leaving her filing cabinet behind. Dr. Lee turned to the only remaining student. After a good thirty seconds of an intense staring contest, she retreated back to her desk drawer and pulled out a mass of papers, neatly lined and bound with a binder clip.

The stack of papers landed neatly on the last student's desk along with the words "This is your syllabus for the first grading period." Before Dr. Lee could enjoy the anticipated look of fear in his eyes, the last student had her back turned on Creative Writing 101 and was through the door.

Dr. Lee glanced at her watch. 9:22 a.m.

"That took five minutes longer than last year," she announced to an empty class as she pulled a blanket from under her desk and nestled into her chair for her first nap of the year.

#InternetProbz

DYLAN MAGRUDER, Grade 12, Age 17. South Carolina Governor's School for the Arts and Humanities, Greenville, SC, Scott Gould, *Teacher*

Of the 7 billion people in the world, about 140 million of them have Twitter, and I admit, I am one of them. We are the writers of 140-character commentaries on life, the narcissists, the obsessively realtime. We are the two percent. And some of us, the ones who registered our usernames in the early years—2008 and before—we've watched while our Rome has burned at the hands of undereducated or apathetic users. We've seen our timelines fill with the noise of millions—tens of millions—of users more interested in vapid, low-culture topics than they are in anything that actually matters. The Trending Topics—which once reflected important world news and broke stories the media hadn't picked up—filled up with things like #YourSexLifeInASingleImage, #10Ways YouKnowYourSonIsGay, "Ecuador loves Britney!", #20Million-Beliebers. When the Frankenstorm (or Frankenstorm's Monster, for the anal retentive literature geeks of the world) devastated New York City, my timeline didn't flood with tweets of support for the city's stranded citizens or commentary on FEMA's response or even videos of Bloomberg's hilarious sign-language interpreter. Instead, I had to scroll through dozens of people, some of them New Yorkers, tweeting pictures of vodka bottles with the caption "all I need to survive the hurricane" (@annepat and important reminders that "the gay sex is not canceled" (@alexdimitrov).

I'm not saying that I've never done anything wrong or that all of the tweets I've sent have been valid and intelligent. I went through a dark time in my life like everyone else. In my rebellious years, I decided that there was no purpose to commas, periods, or vowels. In the darkest times of my life, I was known to tweet nonsense at celebrities, like @ladygaga, hoping that they might see my posts and tweet back at me. This approach worked only once, when I asked the director of *Scott Pilgrim vs. the World* his opinion of the movie *Avatar*. When he responded, I was excited, but only for a few minutes. Then emptiness consumed me once again as I realized I had added nothing valuable to the world.

In 2009, the Twitterverse grew twelve hundred percent, and I started to notice the asinine direction in which tweets were moving. I could see myself in Twitter's millions of new users. I had a realization: We early users, we were on the front lines of a kind of war, and if I was going to help in that fight, I'd have to clean up my feed, use some real English words (proper spelling and everything), learn enough about politics to separate myself from the likes of Nicki Minaj (who tweeted a video of herself rapping support for Mitt Romney).

I saw the first signs that the fight was over and intelligence had lost the battle for Twitter's soul back in 2010, when the company's executives announced that three percent of their servers constantly deliver tweets about Justin Bieber, that year's "King of Twitter," which, scary in itself, implies something much darker. Of the half a billion tweets per day, fifteen million of them are about America's favorite Canadian. Fifteen million times per day, someone feels compelled to stop thinking and actually write about a prepubescent, hair-twirling pop sensation. That's 174 times every second that @sswwaaggyy-biber feels the need to tell Justin "just ignore the h8ers" or @ hipstermermaid compels himself to insult the Bieb's new haircut (and let's be honest, it looks terrible). Like I said, I've sent my share of horrible tweets, but I'd never lower myself to begging for attention from Justin Bieber, no matter how many times he posts pictures of himself shirtless. But damn, he looks good.

At the time, I think the ninety-seven percent of us who weren't tweeting about Justin just held on to the hope that the stupidity would contain itself to Biebermania, and as long as we avoided following members of that three percent (three percent of the two percent I mentioned before, which I guess is more like .06 percent), our baby social network could avoid a horrible, vapid death. This was *Star Wars*, and we thought we were the Empire. We weren't. We were a collective Obi wan Kenobi.

Since 2010, Twitter's crown has passed to Lady Gaga. I'm not surprised, considering her millions of fans are so obsessed with the "high fashion" popstar that they call her "Mother Monster" and have even termed themselves her "Little Monsters," implying that all thirty million of them burst forth from Gaga's swollen uterus, hair dyed pink, screaming the lyrics to "Born This Way." Bieber represented the worst of social networking in the first decade of this century, but Lady Gaga and her Monsters take viral stupidity to a whole new level. Every few weeks, they flood the Twitter Trending Topics with hashtags begging for the star's attention. #JakartaNeedsTheBornThisWayBall, #AnotherMillionMonsters, and #MadonnaCanSuckGagasTit are actual honest-to-God hashtags that made the Trending Topics, but without a doubt, the worst trend inspired by the pop icon has to be #IWorshipLadyGodga. "Godga." It's kind of like a worst nightmare.

What I'm saying is this: I know that Twitter is just a tool for attention whores to satisfy their needs—if you've paid enough attention, it's common knowledge, and that doesn't piss me off enough to write an essay about it. What pisses me off—let's call it the fall of Twitter—is the propensity of Internet users to take something fantastic and turn it into a technically advanced pile of radioactive, methane-breathing shit that cares more about #ObamaRyanGayFic than it does Hurricane Sandy or an upcoming presidential election. Twitter isn't the only social network to suffer this way—Reddit, Digg, 4chan, Tumblr, Flickr, YouTube, Vimeo, Foursquare, Instagram, and Goodreads have also gone bad. I'm not saying people can't have fun, but if they're going to spend their limited time and energy in this life writing short-burst messages about their favorite celebrity or how their coffee is too hot (I know, @curlykrysten, it's a hard life), then I'd ask them to please pull themselves together and post that crap somewhere else. I hear MySpace is looking for users.

I've made an effort over the years to make my Twitter something respectable, and I've encouraged other people to do the same. To people outside of the Twitterverse, I probably come on a little strong. I might seem obsessive. But I've spent the past five years cultivating my (tiny) following and building up my Klout score from a lowly ten to a little over fifty, which puts me above ninety-five percent of Internet users. If I can put work into making sure my Twitter feed is (usually) grammatically correct and my tweets are about things that matter, why can't @annepat or @connorhoward95? And how is it fair that Lady Gaga and Justin Bieber have tens of millions of followers even though all of her tweets are written while she's drunk or high and his consist of bad Instagram pictures of his (admittedly well-shaped) body? Some of us, what seems like the minority, are trying to post content that's funny or interesting or just well written, but we'll always lose out to celebrity selfies and drunk tweets from college students.

Wedding Feast

HOLLY RICE, Grade 11, Age 16. North East School of the Arts,
San Antonio, TX, Amy Stengel, *Teacher*

The small town of Castle Marks (one might not really call it a town since only 193 people actually lived there), was known for rules. It seemed the conservative community had a law for anything that could appear before the pathway of the foolish, and many appreciated this, for it gave the people delight in knowing what they could and could not do. The constrictions felt freeing in a way that was grounding to know that you would never have to doubt the right versus the wrong. Everything you could need to understand was all there before you. At least, that's how Emma felt.

Emma had been pleased to find out her cousin had chosen to be married in the Town Hall she had grown up in. The girl had been afraid her cousin's eccentric fiancé would have an influence over his bride; and he did, to some degree.

The dresses were less than chaste in her opinion, but the color was nice. The town members often wore royal blue during such events, so Emma was not used to much else, but the lilac color chosen looked pleasant against her gray skin, and the flower-adorned hat covered a section of the exposed brain peeking out from her skull. She could not decide whether she liked covering this or not. She had been told women should cover their assets in order not to cause temptation in the male species. Emma never found her exposed cranium particularly sexy, but supposed it was better safe than sorry, and she reminded herself to let her mother know she would need more of the flower hats for the Sunday service.

"Emma dear, could you bring me my purse? I believe one of my fingers is loose, and I don't wish for it to fall off during the ceremony."

Emma turned from organizing the white rose bouquets and looked at her Aunt Virginia. The middle-aged woman wore a shawl over her hunched shoulders. She chuckled slightly under a velvet-laced veil, and dry flakes of decayed flesh sprinkled onto the carpeted floor. Her niece complied dutifully as she picked the small, plum-colored bag and fetched a needle and thread from its organized contents. Emma did not like the feel of the much-used kit in her hands, but she could never explain why. It was very helpful to her family, and she was certain as time went on it would serve her as well. Still, she had never felt content around needles, no matter how wonderful they could be.

"Thanks, darling."

Virginia smiled, her brown-and-red gums showing underneath her cracked lips. With a shaking left hand, the woman pulled out a silver needle with a lilac thread, to match the colors of the wedding party, and started looping it through a thin layer of skin covering her middle finger.

"This whole day has my stitches coming undone. Margret hasn't had a craving for brains in two weeks, and her skin is starting to pinken! I swear, if she wasn't my daughter . . ."

The woman shook her head, securing the thread with a knot. She dropped the needle and kit back into the plum purse and placed it by her ankles.

"Well, nothing I can do now. At least I have another go with you."

Emma nodded, hoping to look as if she was paying attention. She loved her aunt, but her insistence on controlling her upbringing could be quite exasperating. At that moment, Margret, dressed in a white-lace gown, entered the holding room with a cluster of her bridesmaids. Emma recognized two of them; her cousins Eden and Charity were glancing down nervously at their spaghetti-strap dresses while talking idly with one another. The twins smiled their hellos at Emma and Virginia as they filed into the powder room.

The other two girls were obviously from the groom's side of the family. Their skin had a yellowy glow to it, and they had long, flowing hair that looked too shiny to be a wig. Emma tried to smile at them, but they hastily turned away.

Giving her niece a small hug, Margret let out a nervous laugh. Emma noticed her skin was softer than it had been before and had a rosy tone to it. The girl didn't comment though; her aunt's frown was enough to conclude that it was not her imagination.

"Let's hurry up then," Virginia said as she picked herself up from a lounge chair, her bones crackling like wood as she stood.

The group of girls met the rest of the wedding party outside the chapel doors. Margret had decided on using the newer, smaller building as opposed to the larger auditorium used during services and town meetings. She had also insisted on having her future husband's pastor lead their service instead of Mayor James, who often was very involved in anything occurring in his town. Virginia was against this but finally relented after having her daughter promise to invite the family friend to the service.

Emma's Uncle Bill let out a scratchy moan as his daughter approached him. His left eye dangled next to his open mouth as he embraced Margret. His rotting, gangly fingers touched her shoulders for a moment, before intertwining her arm with his in preparation to march down the aisle.

Virginia lined up the girls in front of the bride. The grooms-men stood next to the bridesmaids. The man of honor tugged at his dress collar nervously as Eden, the twin who had always been a tad closer to Margret, came to stand next to him with her bouquet of long, white roses.

Emma took her place next to a boy in his early twenties, trying very hard to conceal her mottled pale blush. She had never found men with such clear skin attractive before, except for Mayor James, but that was when she was much younger. With this boy she found herself wondering what the folds of his brain looked like, and how he would look if his finger were to loosen. Of course, Emma chided herself for thinking such dirty things, but she couldn't help but wonder.

The wooden doors of the small building opened as the organ began to play. As they had rehearsed, the wedding party walked down the aisle slowly and carefully. Virginia, Eden, and Charity had all made sure their legs and ankles were properly attached and stitched; it was always better to be safe than sorry.

Emma noticed Mayor James smiling at her from the second row of benches, his strawberry blonde hair combed back and his porcelain skin glowing in the reflection of the stained-glass windows. He winked a hazel eye at her, and Emma couldn't help but shiver slightly. She never knew why she was so jittery around the mayor. He had practically raised her, but she never could get the cold feeling out of her stomach when he was around. Her mother and aunt reassured her that these feelings went away with time, and that as long as she did what he said, everything would be fine.

The guests stood as Margret walked next to her father. The girl had a wide smile on her face, showcasing two teeth poking out from pale gums. Emma wondered if she would look that happy when she was getting married, and decided she probably wouldn't. Her parents, who were sitting stoically in the fifth row, never recalled their wedding day to be particularly joyful, nor did her aunt or uncle.

The ceremony was short, and Emma was glad. Even though she did not require stitches yet, her bones were becoming weak, and standing for too long made her feel faint.

When the preacher announced that the groom could now kiss his bride, Emma watched with a questioning gaze. Her cousin's lips, which were now touching her groom's, became a pink color, and her patches of dark brown hair seemed to become glossy and longer against her flesh. Emma had heard of people kissing like this, but she never thought it was true. She had not seen much affectionate contact in her life, except when she had once accidently walked in on her parents rubbing brains. That was a moment, though, she would have liked to forget.

On the bride's side, a clunk was heard as Emma's Uncle Bill's head rolled across the wooden floor. There were a couple of gasps and wide-eyed looks from the groom's side of the room, but her Aunt Virginia ignored them as she discreetly scooped up her husband's detached brain-pan and held it in her arm as she returned back to her place.

As the guests filed out of the room, some ogling at the head-less body still by the altar, Aunt Virginia dutifully passed the head to Mayor James, whose lips curled happily in response. Bill's left eye still dangled from its socket, but the right one had now closed. Emma frowned when she noticed the hungry look her family held as their eyes rested on Bill's exposed brain. She wondered for some reason if Margret, who surely had noticed her father's fate, was sad about what was to come. This bothered her, for she felt as if she should be sad too, but wasn't able to make sense of the reasoning. Instead, she helped guide her uncle's body to the storage closet, in case it started to move around while unattended, and headed out the oak doors down to the reception area.

Emma sat beside Charity as Margret and her new husband twirled across the small wooden floor. The building had no rooms made for dancing, so the wedding guests had pushed back the white, cloth-covered tables to create a small dance floor for the bride and groom. Emma saw her Aunt Virginia staring disapprovingly at her daughter and as some of the groom's family made to join them. Mayor James never liked dancing, so the town did not like dancing either.

Chicken and salads had been passed out, and the smooth-skinned, full-haired guests ate with eager bites. They looked at the occupants of the town oddly as their china remained empty. It was obvious to Emma that they were not aware of the change in menu for the bride's guests.

Margret let out a laugh as the man holding her hand spun her around, her dress flowing elegantly by her ankles. She didn't seem to notice when Mayor James, who had disappeared after the ceremony, entered the reception area's door, a lid-covered tray held in his hands.

He smiled a row of pearl-like teeth as his followers started to approach him, plates at the ready. Emma stood with Charity and Eden, her own plate gripped tightly in her hands. She, personally, could not smell what was under the silver cover but could tell by the longing looks in her family's clouded eyes that they all could smell it perfectly.

Mayor James chuckled, amused.

"I know you all have been waiting," he said, his eyes flickering to the tray, "but what better way to celebrate such a beautiful occasion?"

With a lavish movement, Mayor James grabbed the handle of the lid, and pulled it away. Emma could faintly smell something that reminded her of meatloaf. Her cousin Eden's shriveled tongue poked out of her lips, and Emma could see her father's mouth let out a moan. Mayor James smiled.

"Dig in."

Filed in a perfect line, one by one the guests held their plates up to the mayor, not waiting long before digging their teeth, or gums in most cases, into the rubbery substance. Emma was close in line, and the food on the tray could still be recognized as a brain.

Emma sat back down, having received her portion. Her piece was smaller than most of the other guests', seeing as she was younger and did not need as much to behave properly. She bowed her head.

Thank you, Uncle Bill, for your contribution, Emma thought.

And with that, Emma took her fork and dug in.

Don't Be Afraid of the Dark

GLORIA MARTINEZ, Grade 8, Age 13. BASIS Oro Valley,
Oro Valley, AZ, Heather Nagami, *Teacher*

My older brother Tynan always tells me not to be afraid of the dark, but it's a hard thing to do.

I clutch the edge of my quilted blanket tighter as I wait for the small sliver of blue light to stretch throughout the room and chase away the darkness. The tiny light that is a sign of the dawn that is to come has just appeared on the dark wooden floor from the frost-covered window above me. It lies in front of the white bedroom door, and I blink quickly to see if it will change, but it doesn't.

"Come on, little light," I whisper on the cold breath of winter air that escapes my lips. "Please make the darkness go away."

The light doesn't seem to hear me, for it ignores my request.

From the bed beside me, I hear Tynan yawn before his bare feet hit the floor with a thump. I listen to Tynan's footsteps as he walks around his bed until he stops to lean down beside the little light.

"Ara," Tynan says without looking at me. "Don't be afraid of the dark."

"But Ty," I whine while pushing my blankets off my body stubbornly. I immediately regret the action, as a blast of cold air causes a shiver to run across my spine. "I c-can't st-stop being afraid-d of the d-d-dark," I stutter as my teeth chatter.

Tynan doesn't reply as he walks over to the head of my bed and kneels down, so his face is close to mine. His dark gray eyes with a blue undertone that's the same color as the little blue light on the floor reminds me of a piece of stone slate submerged in a river.

"Ara," he says but pauses as his eyes shift downward. "Can I ask why you were talking to the light?"

I bite my lip and look down, so my hair can cover the blushing skin of my freckled face. "I don't know," I mumble. "I just wanted the light to make the dark go away."

Tynan lets out a deep sigh, and I look up just as he stands and holds out a hand for me to take. I place my hand in his, and Tynan pulls me from the bed. The floor feels cool from the coldness of the air, and I listen to the soft pitter-patter of our feet as Tynan leads me out the door.

Just before we disappear around the corner, I look back to see that the little blue light is a tiny bit bigger than the last time I looked at it, and I let a smile twitch my lips upward for just a second before Tynan leads me away from the cold darkness.

* * *

I'm sitting outside with my hands clasped around my knees as I watch my origami paper bird fly around my head. It lands on my shoulder and begins to peck at my hair, and with a brush of my hand, the bird becomes nothing more than a piece of folded paper on my shoulder. I take the bird and place it in my lap just as I hear footsteps approach me.

"Ara, I thought I told you not to play with these silly things," I hear Tynan say at the same time I hear a crushing sound. When I look up, I see that Tynan has killed a little origami hummingbird that I had brought to life.

"You didn't have to crush it," I say bitterly as Tynan hands me the dead paper bird. "They have feelings too, you know."

Tynan groans as he plops down on the ground with me. "Ara," Tynan says as he shakes his head. "What am I going to do with you?"

Looking down, I let my fingers fumble with the piece of paper within their grasp. I don't answer because I'm sure that whatever I say will only make Tynan angry.

I unfold the lifeless paper bird in front of me and refold it, so it looks like a fox. Then I touch the tip of its nose, and with a shiver of movement, the fox springs to life. The fox regards Tynan cautiously before it curls up into a ball, tucking its head underneath its body.

I hear Tynan shift the contents in his bag as he looks for something, and I turn my head to watch as he pulls a document from the bag.

"This is what I'm going to do with you," Tynan says while looking down at the document, but his words are more to himself than they are to me.

I take the piece of paper out of his hand and look it over. It's an application for Miss Pegg's boarding school, and I notice that quite a few of the questions look like they belong on an exam to check people's mental health.

"Ty," I whisper, my voice shaking as I look up at my older brother, "are you sending me away?"

"It's for your own good," Tynan replies tightly, but he doesn't meet my eyes when he speaks. "Miss Pegg is a woman who knows how to deal with . . . unusual cases. She can help you."

"Help me with what?" I ask while fingering the paper fox's ear. It seems to purr at my touch, and I can't help but smile down at the little creature.

Tynan makes a sound in the back of his throat, and I look up only to notice that his face has tightened into a look of rage.

Without any warning, Tynan reaches forward and snatches the paper fox by the scruff of its neck.

"Hey!" I exclaim, reaching up to take the fox away from Tynan, but Tynan holds it out of my reach. "Tynan, you're hurting it! Let it go!"

"You want to know what Miss Pegg can help you with," Tynan growls over the sound of my anguished cries and the fox's howls of rage and terror. "This is what she's going to help you with!" Tynan says while shaking the fox in front of my face. "This curse of yours!"

The fox growls fiercely at Tynan's words, and it twists around violently as it tries to bite the flesh of Tynan's hand. The snap of its jaws as it closes around empty air is an unpleasant sound that reminds me of shattering bones. With a loud howl, I watch as the fox makes one last effort to reach Tynan's hand and manages to snap its jaws around Tynan's pinkie.

Tynan cries out in surprise and pain as he drops the paper fox to clutch his bleeding pinkie. Tynan glares at the fox, and it hisses angrily in reply before jumping back into my lap.

I touch the fox, turning it back into a lifeless origami fox before I speak. "It's not a curse," I say firmly, although to the best of my knowledge, Tynan could be right. "But if you really want me to go, then I will. But don't you ever call my gift a curse again."

And true to his word, Tynan has me packed and sent off to Miss Pegg's boarding school within a week.

The moment of goodbye is tense as Tynan shifts between showing affection toward me and not, and even though I'm still mad at Tynan, I'm glad when he finally decides on giving me a kiss on my forehead before wishing me off.

Behind me, the huge oak door closes shut with the sound of finality as I'm left to look upon the spanning dark hallway that

I swear hums with the mutterings of a mad man, taunting me to step forward.

"Don't be afraid of the dark, Ara," I mutter to myself while twisting the hem of my dress within my fingers.

"Little girl?" someone calls out in question from behind me, and I twirl around to see a plump woman with a purple hue to her pale skin. "Are you lost?' she asks me in a voice of slow rhythm and thick diction.

To my surprise, the sounds of hissing have ceased from the darkness and instead the hallway is filled with a silence that settles like thick smoke in a muggy room.

I nod in reply to the woman's question, and her lips pull upward in a smile that reminds me of comfort in its purest form. "You must be Ara then. I'm Miss Pegg, and we are all so happy you've come to join our little family. Please, let me show you to your room."

Miss Pegg walks over to the wall and flips a switch, causing the lights in the hallway to turn on, banishing the blackness from the hall. We then walk down the hallway as if there were never any darkness residing in its walls at all.

Halfway down the hall, Miss Pegg opens a door and tells me that this is the room in which I will be staying. I thank her for her hospitality, and she leaves me with a polite gesture of parting.

Entering the room, I tug my suitcase in after me and examine my surroundings for a few seconds, taking the overall velvet appearance of the room. Then I set my suitcase upon my bed and flick the switch open to reveal all of my belongings. Humming a small tune that Tynan taught me, I begin to place my clothing in the drawers and my books upon the bottom shelves of the bookcase that rests against a wall of the room.

After a few minutes, the door opens, and a girl of my age

enters without asking for permission. "Hello," the girl says politely. "I'm Rawnie, your roommate."

"I'm Ara," I reply, holding my hand out for her to shake.

Rawnie steps forward and grabs my hand, entwining our fingers together. We shake, but when I move to let go, Rawnie grabs my hand tighter and pulls me toward her.

"Your face is round," Rawnie says as she gazes into my eyes. "Moon-shaped perhaps. Your eyes are like down feathers you would find on a pigeon or a dove, and your auburn hair is really long." Rawnie concludes that last part with a chuckle as she takes in the ends of my hair that sway around my waist.

Then she lets go of my hand, and I stumble backward a step, caught off guard by Rawnie's abrupt change in behavior from polite to something more aggressive. I watch as Rawnie stands still for a few seconds before her cheeks flush red, and she quickly retreats to her bed. Pulling her knees up to her chest, she apologizes, explaining that she has a disorder that causes her to act a little strange at times.

"Disorder?" I question, the word catching my attention. "Is your disorder something similar to this?" I pull out my origami fox from my suitcase and touch its nose, bringing it to life.

Rawnie's eyes widen as she takes in the moving paper fox as it leaps down from my bedspread and begins to sniff around the room. "It's moving!" Rawnie cries out in surprise. Then she looks at me and smiles, saying, "My disorder is not really similar to that unless you count the fact that my disorder can't be explained by reality, much like yours."

"Can you show me?" I ask, clasping my hands together in a pleading gesture.

Rawnie nods and takes a deep breath before closing the palm of her hand. When she opens her fist, I see blue wisps of light swirl into a shape upon her skin. With a hoot, an owl appears out of the blue light and begins to take a 3-D form, much like my origami fox.

Laughing, I say, "That's no disorder, Rawnie. That's a gift."

The girl blushes before closing her hand again, making the owl disappear. "If it's a gift," Rawnie whispers with what seems to be the appearance of tears in her eyes. "Then why did my family send me here?"

A silence passes over us as tears slide down Rawnie's face. I feel guilty for not saying anything, but there simply isn't an answer to her question that would make her feel better.

"Don't be afraid of the dark, Ara," I mutter to myself bitterly as memories of Tynan just dropping me off here spring to mind. "Why shouldn't I be afraid of the dark?"

"Because there are worse things waiting in the light," Rawnie whispers from her place on her bed, and I'm so shocked by her response that it takes me a few seconds to form a coherent thought.

"What?" I manage to choke out in question.

"Don't be afraid of the dark, because there are worse things waiting in the light," Rawnie repeats slowly, but upon seeing my confused face, she continues her explanation. "The dark contains all of our fears that come from stories, such as ghosts and the boogeyman. The light holds the fears that are contained in reality, such as people with guns and knives. You can't be afraid of children's stories when the world itself is a horror film."

I open my mouth to reply, but I can't seem to find the right words to say. Rawnie nods solemnly before she gets up from her bed and walks out of the room, leaving me to ponder over this newfound knowledge.

Later that evening, when the sun has set and both Rawnie and I lay in our beds waiting for sleep to come, I notice a little blue light in the corner of the room. It might just be my imagination, but it looks like the little blue light from the bedroom Tynan and I shared.

"I'm not afraid of the dark," I tell the little blue light quietly. "Because there are worse things waiting in the light."

I close my eyes and wrap my blankets tighter around my body, feeling sleep slowly sink into my bones. And just before I drift into a dreamless slumber, I hear a tiny voice whisper a response into my ear.

That's what I've been trying to tell you all along.

The Fortune Teller

ROBYN MATTHEWS, Grade 12, Age 17. Home School, Las Vegas, NV,
Lisa Matthews, *Teacher*

"It was him," the boy said. "He read my fortune."

A man of middling height, without much hair, stepped forward. "Sir, will you come with us?"

I leaned on my staff. "Of course." Cooperation was the only reasonable course of action when dealing with Caisterlens.

They began to walk away, without waiting for a response. I followed, taking small steps and counting on my long robes to hide my limp. I couldn't show them any weakness.

The three adult men walked with confidence born of power, the step of men who were used to respect. The boy trotted at their heels. They were walking at a quick pace, and did not seem inclined to slow down to accommodate me. That was fine. I wasn't inclined to speed up to accommodate them. Perhaps they would forget I was there and leave me behind in peace.

One of the men turned, the tallest one. "Hurry up," he ordered me. There was no anger in that voice, but no caring, either. It was blank. Flat. It scared me more than any order that held emotion ever could.

I increased my pace, my left foot shuffle-dragging against the cobblestones. The men didn't notice it.

The tents of the Caisterlen camp stood out starkly against the night. The coarse fabric was white as the priest's clothes, and their harsh angles jabbed at the sky. The camp was empty. Evidently, the other priests had retired for the night.

"This way." The shortest man gestured to a tent. The man of middle height held open the flap. I entered.

The interior of the tent was just as stark as the exterior. No blankets. No rugs to lie on. There was only the dirt floor and the bag. I sat down, laying my staff over my lap. In a pinch, the staff could be used as a weapon, though I harbored no illusions about my chances of survival if the Caisterlens attacked. I was heavily outnumbered, and the Caisterlens weren't just well-trained; they were fanatically devoted to the removal of "sin" from the world. I had little training, and the only thing I was fanatically devoted to was staying alive. That wouldn't be enough to save me.

Still, I could probably give a few of them broken kneecaps before I died.

The three men joined me in the tent, while the boy remained outside. There was hardly enough room for the four of us in the cramped space, probably because I was doing my best to keep my staff between myself and the priests.

"The boy says you read his fortune," said the shortest one.

"Yes, sir." I made sure to keep my voice low.

"And you were able to determine from it that he would face a dragon?"

"Yes, sir."

"He doesn't dress like one of us, and he says he made no mention of his identity before you told him of the dragon."

"Yes, sir."

"So your gift is a real one, not a parlor trick."

"You could say that, yes, sir."

"We could use someone with your talent."

The shadows on the men's faces hollowed their eye sockets, leaving glaring, empty chasms. Their shadow-eyes stared at me, unblinking. I became acutely aware of my own pulse, pounding inside my head. "I'm not sure you want me, sir."

"Because of your skin color?" the shortest one interjected bluntly. "We have seen dark-skinned savages like you before. As long as it's clear that you serve us, you'll have no trouble."

I did not allow them to see me react to that comment. "No. Because I don't understand how my gift could be useful to you." I did understand, far too well. I just hoped that they didn't.

"If you can read someone's purpose as well as their life, then you can help us discover those who will best serve our cause, and help us discover enemies."

Damn. "Enemies?"

"Yes. Sinful people who hide their true identities. The diseased, the liars, the lechers, the homosexuals, the cross-dressers . . . you could tell if someone belonged to one of those groups with your gift, couldn't you?"

My pulse became so rapid that I imagined my heart had moved to between my ears, beating out its frantic pace in an attempt to drown out the Caisterlen. I swallowed. "I—"

"Could you?" asked the tallest man, in the same flat voice he had used before.

Fear froze my mind. If I lied, he would know. I was sure of it. The only thing I could do was tell the truth. "Yes, I could."

"Then you see how you could be useful to us."

"Yes, sir."

"I hope you'll consider it. We would be able to house you and feed you, in addition to paying you for your services."

I looked down at my hands, silent. "If your . . . your holinesses would allow me, I would like to go back to my room in the inn so I may consider your offer."

The three men nodded in unison. A shiver that had nothing to do with the night air ran through me as I left the tent. The boy had fallen asleep, dozing with his ear resting near the door flap. I wished I had never said anything at all about that damned dragon. The tremors continued as I walked back to the outpost.

I wanted nothing more than to get away from the camp, with its stark tents and stark people. But I could not let them know they had frightened me, and my limp kept me from running, anyway. I was forced to exit at a torturously slow pace.

They were offering me a job. One with pay that was not dependent upon the whims of strangers. Room, board, and pay. It was an offer that many would kill for. It was an offer that I would kill for, if it had been extended by anyone else.

It would take me years to be able to afford another house. I was barely making enough to pay for my room at the inn and two meals a day. What the Caisterlens offered me was more than tempting. If I thought of it in terms of money and nothing else, the choice was clear.

But it wasn't just money. There was a job attached to that food and that room, and I couldn't forget it. To use my gift to seek out the kind of people that Caisterlens judged to be sinners . . . They were right. I would be very useful to them. But that didn't change my belief that they didn't want me working for them.

Then again, maybe it would give them even more pleasure to own me if they knew all of who I was. Maybe it would amuse them to force a sinner to seek out others of his kind.

There was no one in the entryway of the inn except for a single guard, who didn't even look up as I passed. By the time I reached my room, the tremors were so severe that it took me four tries to insert my key into the lock, and my leg felt like it was in danger of collapsing under me.

When I chose to hide in plain sight, maybe I should have considered the attention my disguise would attract.

I could refuse the job. But the Caisterlens might question why I would turn down an offer as wonderful as theirs. Once Caisterlens decided they wanted something, they would not back down. If a Caisterlen priest grew to manhood, it meant he had fought a dragon and won. I could not scare them off, and I could not force them to let me go.

Running wasn't an option. I could not escape on foot. I didn't have a horse, and even if I stole one, my leg still impeded my ability to ride. Then I would have the horse's original owner after me as well as the Caisterlens, and there was nowhere I could hide. The outpost was in the plains. My trail would be laughably easy to follow.

Which left me with taking the job.

I began removing my robes. Even in the summer, I always wore at least three layers. With every bit of clothing removed, the hated shape of my body became more defined. But I couldn't sleep in my robes, and so I had to look upon myself every night before going to bed.

I had never been what anyone would call curvy. But even the smallest curve was too much of one for me, forcing me to remember what I had been born as. The slight swell of my breasts pushed against the fabric of my undershirt.

No, the Caisterlens did not want me. They had no idea how much they did not want me.

I couldn't disclose my identity to them in order to avoid taking the job. In their minds, I was a cross-dresser. Not a man born into the wrong body, but a girl who was living in sin. I would be tortured, forced to confess, and then executed.

I was already doing everything possible to hide who I was. The affected voice, the layers of clothing, shading my face beneath my hood . . . it was all to deflect attention from myself. And since they were all obvious attempts to deflect attention from myself, they led people to all the wrong conclusions. To the people of the outpost and the town, I was a fortune-teller with delusions of grandeur, trying to make myself seem more mysterious. But if the Caisterlens saw through the persona created from my disguise . . .

Everything led back to accepting the job. If I accepted, they wouldn't look too hard or too long at me. They would think of me as a stray mongrel that, since they fed and housed him, could be expected to attack on command. All it would take for me to keep their suspicions away from me would be to turn in others of my kind.

For all of their talk of learning about true believers and men they could recruit, I knew that they were really interested in using me to find sinners. That was the real allure of my gift.

Hiding in plain sight hadn't been enough. I rested my elbows on my knees and my face in my hands. I might as well slit my own throat, and save the Caisterlens the trouble. I sighed, and my breasts brushed against my arms.

Slowly, I sat up.

Maybe . . . just maybe . . .

There was another way out.

Three men dressed all in white walked up to the inn the next day, a boy following them. People stared as they passed, but the men paid them no mind. "Where is the fortune-teller?" the one of middling height asked the innkeeper.

"He left last night," the innkeeper replied.

"Where did he go?"

"Dunno."

The tallest man turned his eyes to the innkeeper. They were blank eyes, eyes without a hint of wit, warmth, or soul. "Are you sure?" the tall man asked, his voice bland.

The innkeeper swallowed. "Yessir."

The short man stalked out of the inn, followed by his companions. He caught sight of a beggar sitting on the cobblestones by the side of the inn. "You! Stand up!"

The beggar began to rise, but wasn't quick enough about it for the man's liking. He grabbed the beggar and wrenched upwards. With a cry, the beggar stood, revealing her feminine figure. "Have you seen a man in robes, carrying a staff, with beads around his neck?"

"The fortune-teller, sir?"

"Yes, him."

"No, sir, not since yesterday."

"Are you sure?"

The man of middling height put his hand on the short man's shoulder. "Brother, look at her. Don't you think she's had enough misfortune in her life?"

The short man looked and saw that the girl's left leg was twisted. Some kind of birth deformity, probably. He bowed. "My apologies, miss. It was not my intent to scare you."

"It's all right, sir. Luck to your search, sir," the girl said in a voice barely above a whisper.

The boy was staring at her, as though he saw something familiar in her face. But then he shook his head and followed the men, who were already walking off to interrogate someone else. The fortune-teller leaned heavily on the wall, and thanked all that ever was for the ability to hide in plain sight.

The Lions' Den

MARY ELIZABETH DUBOIS, Grade 12, Age 17. Port Neches-Groves High School, Port Neches, TX, Nancy Daigrepont, *Teacher*

Walking was such a treacherous thing.

She had been walking and walking and walking since she was a small child. Barely breathing, they taught her to walk. Before she learned how to eat or say her name, she was taught to walk.

Always walking.

Treacherous, treacherous walking.

Danny was her best friend. He always walked next to her, ever since she could remember. Why was it she had never walked next to anyone else since her Maker left her side? She couldn't remember the faces of anyone else besides her Maker and the people who walked in front and behind her.

And Danny.

The earliest memory 14 had was holding the hand of her Maker, sweat dripping down the left side of her face like a small rain.

They were in the desert.

It was the first time 14 had ever walked through the desert, though it wouldn't be her last. She remembered her Maker speaking to her softly, though she couldn't recall what was said. She could only see the sun, the sand, and the endless lines of children in front of her.

They marched on.

It was two years later that Danny would finally appear.

14 was walking through a seemingly endless prairie at this point in her Walk. He came walking toward her horizontally, perfectly in step with her. He moved sideways while still moving forward, never breaking the rhythm of the synchronized steps in which everyone walked. His Maker was directly behind him.

Though they were moving rather slowly at that point in time, he walked purposefully; a gentleman's stride.

"Hello," he said. He had reached 14. He no longer walked horizontally, but instead moved only forward now.

14 would always remember that he had spoken first.

They were five years old.

A major concern for the next five years of the Walk was why Danny's name sounded so different than the rest. Everyone else in front and behind of their line were called by number, or so their Makers had told them.

Danny did not sound like the rest. His name was short and rhythmic, and this puzzled the other children in the lines nearest to 14.

"Danny," they would say. "Dannnnny."

Then their Maker's would shush them and take their hands, all the while making sure they were perfectly in sync with the rhythm of the endless steps.

"Are we not so lucky to be preserved?" their Makers would say.

And so the children recited with the voices of a thousand angelic bells, "We are fortunate to be preserved." And the mantra was repeated daily and nightly.

14 noticed that Danny always stumbled over the word "fortunate."

Bread was always passed from the front of the lines to the back. They would each get small, single pieces, and it was lovely, because they didn't know any better. The breadbaskets came twice a day.

"Bread," the children would chant, once their Makers taught them the word. "Bread. Bread. Bread."

One day, as the children were chanting, and the breadbaskets were nearing their own lines, Danny whispered something under his breath.

"But Daniel resolved not to defile himself with the king's food or wine . . . "

When 14 asked him what he meant, Danny just looked away toward the far hills and took her hand in his own.

The day came when it was time for their Makers to leave them.

"You'll see us soon," the Makers said, comforting the children with little pats on their heads. "We won't be far."

They made the children promise to never stop chanting the mantra both daily and nightly, and to always keep in time with the steps in front and behind them.

"Will the breadbaskets still come?" the girl directly in front of 14 in line said tearfully. "Will we still get droplets of water?"

The Makers assured them nothing would change.

14 remembered when her Maker finally let go of her hand and disappeared into the forest along with the others.

She remembered that she cried.

Danny walked on, barely blinking; a face of stone.

He gripped 14's hand tightly.

They grew up slowly and effortlessly, marching toward the unforeseeable future in their structured and never-ending lines. Some children became irritable, others silent. Danny and

14 rarely spoke to the other children once they reached a certain age. They needed only each other.

"The sky is the only thing that remains the same," Danny mused one day when they were twelve, marching through a cold plain covered with snow. "The sun comes and goes, but the sky is always there."

14 tilted her own head back and looked up at the vast, gray sky. Her hair had grown long, and it flew behind her in auburn waves. She smiled up at the gray sky.

"What are you smiling about?" Danny asked. He soon received his answer as small, white flakes of snow came floating down from the sky.

"Oh," he said.

Danny did most of the talking those days.

They never talked about where Danny was from.

14 respected this fact and never brought it up. The older they got, the less she remembered that Danny was not born here, in line, next to her. They never spoke of his arrival and 14 never questioned it.

Besides, what could there be out there besides these lines and the endless plain they walked upon?

Each night a drum would echo throughout the lines, and everyone would halt.

This was sleeping hour.

They would close their eyes, as their Makers had taught them, and sleep.

"Goodnight, 14," Danny would say, squeezing her hand and closing his eyes.

Sometimes 14 didn't close her eyes right away. Sometimes, she would look up at the moon and wonder if children were marching there too.

"I think we've been here before," Danny said one sunny day, when they were seventeen. They were marching through a cornfield. "Doesn't this look familiar, 14?"

14 did not think it looked very familiar. But she didn't say so. "Maybe," she said instead.

"You're very vague, 14," Danny said, smiling. Danny found it awfully funny how indifferent she could be. Danny had always been the talker; 14 was the listener.

Danny always said 14 was the most peaceful and quiet girl he had ever met.

"I don't think I have much competition for that title," 14 said one day, as Danny repeated this statement. The girls in front and behind their line were awfully loud and chatty.

Danny laughed harder than he ever had before.

14 thought it was the most beautiful sound she had ever heard.

Danny started singing when they were about twenty-five.

He would make up lyrics and melodies, and sing them to 14. He often sang songs about 14: her auburn waves, her deep eyes, her quiet disposition. Sometimes the songs would be about the scenery they were currently passing through, such as the mountains, or the rainforests. Occasionally, Danny's songs would have deeper meanings that 14 would recognize as different, but could never grasp what they meant.

"I'm captured by these lines," Danny sang one day, "I want to be swallowed in the sky."

14 asked what this meant. Danny simply gazed at her and then looked away.

14 never grew frustrated by these silences, but instead embraced them. She knew something was different about Danny, and she cherished it. One day she would know, she told herself. One day she would see her Maker again, and know.

They grew older.

They recognized this, and understood they were no longer children. As they passed their thirties, and then forties, Danny began to become more demanding of answers.

"Where are we going?" he said one day, as if the idea had just sprung up on him.

"I think I see a valley ahead," 14 said, squinting beyond the endless lines of people in front of her and into the distance.

"No, no. I mean, where are we going?" Danny said it with such emphasis, 14 was alarmed. "Do we ever stop? Do we ever reach a destination?"

14 had never thought of this before. This was what they did, what they were taught to do. They marched.

It was dusk and was growing time for their nightly mantra.

"We are fortunate to be preserved," they said, the endless lines of people, marching toward whatever lay in front of them.

Danny didn't say a word.

14 was getting tired.

Walking was treacherous, treacherous. She walked every day, every sunlit moment. The sleeping hour became 14's most precious time, and she became obsessed with the thought of closing her eyes, even for a short while.

Her auburn hair was turning gray, like the skies before the thunder came, and Danny found this amusing. He would make up new songs about 14's hair changing colors, and then go back to squinting up at the sky and making statements that 14 didn't always understand.

14 also noticed that Danny's face was changing. It had changed over the years, of course, but this time, it was getting softer. The sharp lines that had once defined his cheekbones and jawline were ceasing to exist, instead replaced by wrinkles.

They were fifty years old.

In their early seventies, a remarkable thing happened that had never occurred for any of them before as they were walking through a desert.

The drum sounded and they halted in the middle of the day.

This came as much relief for most of them, and they steadied their breathing and smiled amongst each other. 14 actually shared a few words with the others around her, which was not a frequent activity.

Danny was not smiling, however.

After a few minutes, the drum sounded and they began marching again. But they received another break about fifteen minutes later. Then they marched again. And then another break.

"I don't like this," Danny said, during their fourth break. His eyes were scanning over the lines in front of them with careful eyes.

"Why?" a girl behind him asked, her voice pinched and annoyed. "We're resting."

14 was studying Danny carefully, however. She trusted him, like she always had, and knew he knew something more.

"What is it?" she asked quietly, touching his hand softly.

"It's not right," Danny said, frowning. "It's not right."

The resting in between marching occurred for two whole days.

On the third day, they began to see something in the distance. It was nothing like anything they had ever seen before, and it excited them.

It was a massive blackness.

Danny and 14 watched closely as the others around them spoke excitedly of the upcoming blackness. They watched the lines in the distance during a break. 14 could see the very first line, which had halted right before the black void, and watched carefully when the drum sounded again and they began to march.

The first line marched right into the blackness and disappeared.

14 could tell that Danny had realized something important.

They were nearing the blackness by the second. Unfamiliar men began to become visible. They were standing to the left of the lines, completely still. They were younger than the people in the lines, 14 realized, and they were waiting.

Finally, the drum sounded and the lines halted.

There were several lines in front of 14 before the black mass began.

"Hello, my friends," a man said, smiling widely as he scanned over the lines with his eyes. "Your Makers are waiting for you inside the blackness. Is that not something to be thrilled about?"

An excited murmur echoed throughout the lines, but the man silenced them with a raised fist.

"You have lived properly, and fully, have you not?" he said, his smile unwavering. "You have been preserved, and therefore, lived."

Murmurs of agreement rippled through the lines.

"And now, I ask you, what is it that you are fortunate for?"

The lines recited their mantra, perfectly and angelically, as if they were one body.

"We are fortunate to be preserved," they said.

And then the drum sounded, and the lines began to step off the land and into the abyss.

"14, listen to me," Danny was saying, as they marched closer, grabbing her arm roughly. "We are marching toward our death. We need to break out of these lines. Now."

"But my Maker—"

"Isn't there," Danny interrupted. "They're lying. They are the Makers. The men are here. The women are back there. Giving birth."

They were nearing the drop-off. Five lines. Four lines.

"We are fortunate to be preserved," 14 said weakly, her heart beating at an unnatural rhythm that she had never felt before.

Suddenly, Danny stopped.

They were supposed to be marching, and Danny stopped.

He grabbed 14 by the shoulders and turned her toward him. They were old, and fragile, but Danny was stronger than 14.

The lines behind them wavered and then halted.

"We are all marching toward our deaths," Danny said again, more frantically, his arms on 14's shoulders. "14, we have marched our whole lives toward our deaths."

She saw the flat plain she had walked her whole life, and the lines of people. At the beginning were the babies, and then the children, then the adults. They were a constant forward moving mass, all marching toward the end, which 14 realized this was. The end.

The smiling man was still smiling, telling her to go forward. She would see her Maker in just a moment, he said, her Maker was waiting for her.

As 14's foot left the desert ground and she fell into the abyss, she heard the echoes of Danny's song:

"Many of those who sleep
in the dust of the earth shall awake.
Some shall live forever,
others shall be an everlasting horror
and disgrace.

But the wise shall shine brightly
Like the splendor of the firmament,
And those who lead the many to justice
Shall be like the stars forever."

Dear Mr. Wal-Mart

SOLA PARK, Grade 11, Age 16. Catholic Central High School, London, Ontario, Canada, Mila Lee, *Teacher*

Dear Mr. Michael Duke, President and CEO of Wal-Mart,
I write this letter with deep regret and repentance. I hope you take the time to read and consider the information and matters I have brought before you. I realize you are a very busy man, so I will attempt to make this letter as concise and cogent as possible. As the CEO of the world's largest retailer, you have fervently worked to reduce prices of goods for the public. Your company has accomplished myriads of achievements and ameliorated the lives of millions of Americans, and for that I truly admire the effort you've displayed.

However, I am highly concerned with the wrongdoings of your company in its product manufacturing practices. It has grasped my attention, and the attention of the international community, that child labor is an issue that perturbs each and every country. I was astonished to learn, after extensive research, that many of Wal-Mart's practices disregard the United Nations International Covenant on Economic, Social, and Cultural Rights, and the UN Convention on the Rights of the Child. Wal-Mart abuses international law and standards in numerous aspects through child labor and provision of unfair wages.

According to the 1998 United Nations Convention on the

Rights of the Child, Wal-Mart is currently in violation of Articles 2, 3, 6, 27, and 28. Millions of children work in deplorable conditions with wages so wretchedly low as 1.25 U.S. dollars a day. Many of these children work for your company as a way to climb out of poverty where they could live with an ounce of decency. As one explores the dark reality of child labor, it is difficult to comprehend how profitable companies, like Wal-Mart, can utilize innocent children as young as four years old. This is the sad truth that has been accepted as normal in our world today. It is in your hands to eradicate this horrible practice that hovers over this great company.

I am writing this letter to urge you and your company to put an end to this disgraceful treatment of human beings across the globe. The children Wal-Mart manipulates are stripped of education; children belong in school, not locked in sweatshops. Instead of receiving the education these children are well entitled to, they are exploited and coerced into manual labor for up to 15 hours a day. Their unacceptable lifestyles designed around providing goods for your company only condemn them to a life of misery and poverty.

By valuing economic revenue over the well-being of humans, Wal-Mart is only contradicting the latter half of its own slogan: Save Money, Live Better. Yes, consumers may be "saving money," but do you think they will truly "live better" when they realize your company has exploited naïve and innocent children to manipulate them for your own good? The sad reality of our world today is that Wal-Mart has become dependent on prioritizing economic gain over human life. However, I want to pose this question to you. Would you be willing to support child labor, as you acquiescently do now, if your own children were employed by force, coerced into manual labor with no freedom and voice?

As a citizen who wishes to see a halt to these horrible violations, I strongly urge you to eradicate these practices you allow in your corporation. You cannot run away from your responsibilities. I believe you, as a well-respected man and a high-ranking official, have the potential to do something about this atrocity. Use your ears to hear the faint cries of the children of this world and use your position to end this era of bondage. Your commitment to making the world a safer and happier place for all will be greatly respected.

In the Interest of All Humanity,
Student

Planned Parenthood: An Organization at the Mercy of Politics

NICHOLAS TEAGUE, Grade 10, Age 15. Brookstone School, Columbus, GA, Sherry Tomblin, *Teacher*

Since its inception, Planned Parenthood has been a controversial group. Recently, pro-life groups have pushed for the defunding of the organization, because it provides abortions. However, the denial of financial support to Planned Parenthood would deprive many women of reproductive health care and lead to an increased rate of sexually transmitted infections, death from breast and cervical cancers, unwanted pregnancies, and abortions.

Since 1916, Planned Parenthood has provided much-needed reproductive health services to both women and men. These services are particularly important to low-income women who could not otherwise afford health care. The goal of Planned Parenthood is to give people, regardless of race, gender, or sexual orientation, control over their family planning by providing information and services (www.plannedparenthood.org). At present, Planned Parenthood is the country's largest provider of sexual and reproductive health care. There are currently

800 Planned Parenthood clinics across the United States, with all fifty states having at least one clinic. Over 90% of the care they provide is preventative medicine, including education and counseling, family planning, contraception, breast and pelvic exams, breast and cervical cancer screening, and STI screening. In 2010 (the last date these records are available), Planned Parenthood provided medical services for more than 3 million people in the U.S. Contraception and STI screening each accounted for one third of their services, and cancer screening and prevention 20%. In addition to medical services, Planned Parenthood provided that year educational programs to more than 1.1 million people of all ages on such topics as contraception and family planning, safe sex, puberty education, STIs, sexual orientation, AIDS/HIV, teen pregnancy, and women's health (www.plannedparentood.org).

Despite the many beneficial services Planned Parenthood provides, in 2011 Republican congressmen made an effort to cut funding for Planned Parenthood, largely because conservatives in the House and Senate take issue with Planned Parenthood's offering abortion services. While a bill revoking funding to the organization was passed in the Republican House, it was later defeated in the Senate. In response to this, several states have attempted to withhold government money from the organization. These states, including Arizona, Florida, Kansas, Indiana, New Hampshire, New Jersey, North Carolina, Tennessee, Texas, and Wisconsin, have passed measures preventing the organization from receiving Medicaid funds, some Title X funds, and other government backing (www.sba-list.org). While many federal courts have subsequently ruled that a state cannot deny Medicaid to Planned Parenthood, the Fifth Circuit Court of Appeals of Texas allowed cutting abortion providers such as Planned Parenthood from the Women's Health

Program. Although the Obama administration has threatened to withhold federal resources for family planning services from any state that denies Planned Parenthood Medicaid funds, the state of Texas has responded by opting to forgo federal help for their Women's Health Program (Kliff). Furthermore, states such as North Carolina have tried to circumvent the court order there that says that states cannot single out a single health care provider like Planned Parenthood for defunding by preventing the state's Health and Human Services Department from contracting with any private provider, effectively barring Planned Parenthood (Bassett).

If Planned Parenthood ultimately loses government funding, the results would be disastrous. Planned Parenthood relies heavily on government assistance; the organization currently receives one third of its money from government grants and contracts (Rovner). Without this support, many of Planned Parenthood's programs would have to be cut, many low-income women would lose health care, and, in some cases, Planned Parenthood clinics would have to close. This has already happened in states such as Indiana, New Hampshire, Wisconsin, and Texas, where clinics have had to shut down and thousands of low-income women have been left without access not only to contraception but also to life-saving tests, such as breast and cervical cancer screening (Landrigan, Liebelson). Furthermore, for many of these women, Planned Parenthood is their only source of medical care. According to Cecile Richards, president of Planned Parenthood, "For more than half our patients, Planned Parenthood is the only nurse or doctor they will see all year" (Rovner). In addition, without access to Planned Parenthood clinics, many low-income women would not have effective means of preventing pregnancy, leading to a higher rate of abortions.

Planned Parenthood's providing of abortions is the point of contention for those who seek to defund the organization; however, their arguments lack validity. Opponents of Planned Parenthood claim that federal money should not be used for abortions, yet the Hyde Amendment already prevents Planned Parenthood from using federal funds for abortions. Opponents also claim that the majority of Planned Parenthood's services are abortions. However, only 3% of the medical services Planned Parenthood provided in 2010 were abortions. (www.plannedparenthood.org) Critics of the organization hope that revoking financial support to Planned Parenthood will reduce greatly the number of abortions in the U.S.; however, the vast majority of abortions in the U.S. are not even performed by Planned Parenthood, but by independent clinics throughout the country (Taft). Moreover, 34% of Planned Parenthood's service goes to providing contraception, which helps prevent unwanted pregnancies and, thereby, actually reduces the number of abortions. In 2010, services provided by Planned Parenthood prevented approximately 584,000 unwanted pregnancies. (www.plannedparenthood.org) Without publically funded contraception services like those Planned Parenthood provides, it is estimated that the overall abortion rate would increase by 34%, with the teenage abortion rate increasing by 65% (www.prochoiceameria.org).

Clearly, Planned Parenthood plays a vital role in women's health. Its defunding would only result in more sexually transmitted infections and more unplanned pregnancies. It would deprive many women of access to breast and cervical cancer screenings. Opponents of the organization focus only on the issue of performing abortions, while refusing to acknowledge that its services actually help prevent abortions. As Stephanie Kight, president and CEO of Planned Parenthood of Greater

Ohio eloquently states of Planned Parenthood's critics, "The overall attitude has been, 'How can we make abortion more dangerous and difficult to get?' rather than 'Let's reduce the number of abortions by improving access to education and health care'" (Sheppard). An organization that has and continues to provide much-needed health-care services, as Planned Parenthood does, should not fall victim to politics.

For sources cited: www.artandwriting.org/media/84030/

The Asian Misrepresentation: How the Portrayal of Asians in the Media Harms America

MIRANDA CASHMAN, Grade 12, Age 17. Home School, Concord, MA, Christina Cashman, *Teacher*

There are a whole host of bankable stars . . . Can you name one bankable Asian-American star? No. There isn't . . . One can't name a single Asian-American whose name you can take to the bank and get a project financed.—George Takei

This statement, spoken by George Takei about American film actors and actresses, brings to our attention the lack of Asians on film. George Takei, famous for his role as Hikaru Sulu on *Star Trek*, has long been an advocate for Asian-American social justice. In an interview about primarily white actors playing originally Asian characters, Takei stated clearly the problem in Hollywood with Asian-American actors—there aren't any "bankable" Asian stars. Asians are not accurately depicted in the media, and the lack of Asians in American media socially harms the country and negatively impacts how Americans relate to Asian-Americans.

Maybe it's because Asians have gotten the reputation for being successful in many fields, but the stereotypes made about

Asian people still prevail within American society, especially when it comes to the Asians portrayed in movies and on television. America is a television-driven society, with Americans individually watching on average about 34 hours a week in 2010 (Stelter), and therefore it is no surprise that we are all subtly influenced by what we see on the screen. Many racial minorities have broken through the confining bonds of stereotypes on screen, and we see a fair share of African-Americans and Latinos, but Asians still lag behind in American media. Essentially, this lack of Asians in the American media today keeps the stereotypes about Asians alive. These attitudes prevent the social integration of Asians into an unbiased country, and it limits the thinking of some non-Asians, resulting in socially stratifying the country.

Though famous Asian actors, directors, and screenwriters like Chow Yun Fat, Jackie Chan, or Ang Lee may be household names, movies with such rounded and intricate Asian characters who are successful in America are few and far between. Even though in 2010 Asians made up 5.6 percent of the United States population, roughly 17 million people (United States Census), the media does not reflect the strong Asian influences within the country. Instead, the majority of television shows and movies in the United States unconsciously influence us to hold on to the stereotypical and sometimes offensive views of Asians. For example, Margaret Cho, a well-known Korean stand-up comic, for one year starred in a sitcom called *American Girl*, which aired in 1994. The show centered on her struggles with her traditional Korean family and the desire to assimilate into American culture. *The New York Times* presented two different reactions to this show when it aired. Elizabeth Wong talked about phone calls from people who said, "Thank God, at last we're being seen." But others, like John H. Lee, a critic for *L.A. Weekly*, seethed about "'the butchered Korean language and pseudo-traditions' of the mostly non-Korean cast" (qtd. Southgate). This presents a question: Is it worse for Asians to be seen in the media, but with incorrect or offensive stereotypes, or not to be seen at all? "Both are unacceptable," should be the answer.

More questions arise: How does the lack of Asians in the media influence the views Americans hold about Asians? Or is the better question, how does American culture influence the media, resulting in the lack of Asians in the media? Both of these questions are absolutely valid, but my question is, which one came first? This leads us into a vicious cycle that somehow must be broken, because each influences the other, and both are hurting the perception of the Asian-American community.

The American public greatly influences what is portrayed on the screen. Hollywood, like all forms of media entertainment, is out to make money. When television shows do not receive high ratings or when movies are not box-office hits, studios are less likely to give funding to similar projects, even if a script featuring Asians is good for the world socially. When one of the first Asian-centered sitcoms, Margaret Cho's *American Girl*, failed to keep its ratings high on American TV, the studio canceled the show (qtd. Southgate). The character of Lane Kim from the seven-year run of *Gilmore Girls* was lucky to be on television for so long. Kim, the best friend to one of the main characters, is presented as a rebellious and free-thinking girl who lives with a very traditional and strict mother. This tense mother-daughter relationship was described on a blog as "grossly exaggerated . . . making the Korean mother seem almost like a totalitarian Nazi" (qtd. Dynamitekenji). The actress who played Kim, Keiko Agena, though, thinks that Lane was a complex part that broke all the traditional "good Korean girl" stereotypes. "Parts are very rare for Asian-Americans, and parts as good as this are even rarer" (qtd. Heldenfels). Lane is a character who breaks the Asian girl stereotype, but when will characters like Lane lead their own show? How long will Asians stay stuck as the "best friend" and not the hero?

Many adaptations of Japanese anime or manga done in the United States that present strong, usually Asian, heroes reset the traditional Japanese setting to an American one, and instead of casting Asian actors, studios cast big-name stars who are not Asian. In a CNN article, Stephanie Siek quotes, "Kent A. Ono, a professor of Asian-American studies at the University of Illinois at Urbana-Champaign, said the practice of casting white actors to play Asians and Asian-American characters has a long history in Hollywood. Until recent decades, this mostly took the form of white actors playing stereotypical representations of Asian characters" (Siek). The Academy Award–winning portrayal of O-Lan from *The Good Earth* was performed by Louise Rainer, a German actress (Higbie). The famous performance by Mickey Rooney in *Breakfast at Tiffany's* is currently thought of as racist, but at the time Rooney was applauded for his amazing performance in the Oscar-winning movie (Calder). If Asian actors cannot even get good parts that are specifically "Asian," how will they ever get parts that aren't written for Asians?

The lack of Asians on screen does do psychological and social damage to both Asian and non-Asian children. The lack of childhood role models for Asian-American children slows the social progression toward complete liberation. In 2009, Kevin Wu, a notable YouTube video blogger, mentioned his lack of Asian role models in his life as a kid. He talked about Goku, a popular anime character, as being his childhood hero. "There weren't any other Asian superheroes growing up, so Goku was like our only idol, our hero" (Wu). Asian children search for role models with whom to identify, and when they don't find them in Hollywood, some turn to the media coming out of Asia, like Japanese animation, for heroes. These stereotypes also change how non-Asian children socially relate to Asian children. For non-Asian children, images like these may lead to limited thinking: Asians are good at only certain things, or every Asian kid in their class will grow up the same way. Audrey Kwak supports this view in "Asian Americans in the Television Media: Creating Incentive for Change," writing, "For children, the visual absence of Asian-Americans on television establishes subconscious conclusions of what one can and cannot be—actors, anchormen and women—and perceptions of what one is—studious, exotic, nerdy" (Kwak, 409). The lack of confirmation that Asian-Americans can succeed in television can clearly affect how people think and what people think certain groups can do. Adin Kachisi, an African-American author of *Beyond the Talented Tenth,* spoke on Maurice Carver's show *Black Men Screaming,* and recognized "the invisibility . . . a veil is actually put on the Asian community when it comes to public media, nobody sees them. [The] public opinion that's created through the media is the quiet Asian that you never see" (qtd. Carver). We must improve and change the visuals to be able to change minds, but we must change minds before we can change visuals. Options must be opened and stereotypes must be overcome to socially liberate the world.

But what are these "Asian stereotypes" that are portrayed on-screen? In the first decades of television and movies, several Asian stereotypes became prevalent. One stereotype that Asian actors have encountered is the outdated idea that Asians can hold only certain clichéd jobs, like restaurant workers, businessmen, martial artists, and laundry workers. Audrey

Kwak, writing for the *Boston College Third World Law Journal*, describes the hardships of an Asian actor in the media. "One Asian actor's experience is particularly telling: in a 2003 survey of Asian-Americans in prime-time TV, he disclosed that he had played 'a dry cleaner and a Chinese takeout delivery man in 21 different prime-time shows' in the span of a few years" (Kwak, 407-408). Other stereotypes that affect Asian actresses include two-dimensional characters like the "dragon lady," an aggressive and usually sexualized woman, or the "China doll," a submissive, helpless, pure-hearted woman, which are offensive because they display an inaccurate view of Asian cultures. Jeffry Kimble, an African-American man, speaking on *Black Men Screaming*, also discusses certain stereotypes that Asians encounter on-screen. "If you look on television, you don't really see a lot of Asian-Americans portrayed in roles. There are a number of supporting roles. A lot of times they are the only single members of a cast, so if it's an Asian male, he doesn't get the luxury of an Asian wife" (qtd. Carver).

It is clear that the Asian misrepresentation in the media is damaging and pervasive. Though we must admit that we have become more supportive of "the exotic" in the media, we cannot say that the problem is fixed. Asian stereotypes are still very much with us. The media is expanding, allowing more opportunities to arise for Asian-American actors to seize their chances and change the media. Our country should applaud these endeavors, and show the mainstream media how important it is to represent all people in America today.

For sources cited: www.artandwriting.org/media/848791

KYUNGJOO HA, *Connection*, Grade 12, Age 18.
Interlochen Arts Academy, Interlochen, MI,
Melinda Zacher Ronayne, *Teacher*.

Save the Chicken Grease

ALEXIS PAYNE, Grade 10, Age 15. Pittsburgh Creative and Performing Arts Magnet, Pittsburgh, PA, Mara Cregan, *Teacher*

Be a democrat. Remove the "–ings" from the end of every one of your words. Cook everything you eat in chicken grease. Complain about your lack of money; blame your lack of money on the fact that you were denied 40 acres and a mule. Scream *nigga* in the street; make a scene when someone says *nigger*. Don't vote. Emphasize how useless voting is in conversations. Don't ask questions. Don't know who Medgar Evers is; don't care to find out. Laugh at racist jokes. Disassociate yourself from Africa. Kill your neighbor. Slaughter your brother. Jump into iron cells. Become products of a system. Conform to stereotypes. Own slaves. Break windows. Erase words. Discredit yourself. Blame slavery. Blame slavery again. Talk about Dr. King; talk only about Dr. King. Listen to music that objectifies. Listen to music that enslaves you. Listen to music that tells you to kill. Throw money into trash cans; buy cars. Maintain a cycle. Buy more cars; don't invest in anything. You only live once. Care about you. Wish you had better hair. Hate white people because they enslaved "you"; pretend like you don't hate white people. Eat watermelon. Work at McDonald's; be perfectly satisfied with working at McDonald's. Wear your pants below the waist; trip over them. Try to look cool while tripping over them. Add extra sugar to Kool-Aid; blame obesity on slavery. Take stuff. Convince yourself that you deserve what you take because of slavery. Vote for the black man because he's a black man. Listen to nothing he says. Care about nothing he says. He's black, after all. Blame stuff you can't control on slavery. Don't read. Please don't read. If you read, read books about—never mind, just don't read. Avoid the future. Avoid the past. Get angry; blame your anger on white people. Maintain a cycle. Get popped with hot chicken grease; save the hot chicken grease in a glass jar. Don't let it go. For the life of you, don't let that chicken grease go. Become products of this system. Don't have the time. No, really, don't have the time. Work and work and work and then come home and sleep and—maintain a cycle. Save that chicken grease. Be a democrat because your mama was a democrat, because her papa was a democrat. Vote for Barack Obama, because his daddy was black. Disassociate yourself with Africa. Forget that his daddy was African. Be offended. Be terribly offended. Cuss out a nigga 'cause you're so offended. Be offended. Keep telling me how you're so offended. Blame the fact that you're offended on slavery. Save that chicken grease. Prove me wrong.

Jump the Shark

MARLEY TOWNSEND, Grade 9, Age 14. Tamalpais High School, Mill Valley, CA, Jessica Variz, *Teacher*

On the day of your death, rain will fall in slanted, angry lines across your bedroom window. You will watch, from somewhere around the ceiling, as nobody cares to notice.

They will say you tripped. You tangled your cursed clumsy feet up and smashed into the posts of your cheap Ikea bed (förböveln!), leaving a murky pond of metallic blood on your landlord's new carpet. It will be your final mission. He will curse you and your leaky cerebral matter later with a finger raised to the sky, his glasses askew. But you did not trip.

It is exceedingly important you don't believe what they say.

At first, it's the lack of sound that will bother you. It's as if death has eaten all the noises, swallowed them whole. You can't hear the couple downstairs arguing. You can't hear your landlord as he mutters, disgusted at his dying mother. Because death, like theaters and libraries, is a silent beast, all teeth and nails.

But eventually you start to enjoy the newfound hush. You will start to subtitle things. Go ahead. Make children swear. Make a morose middle-aged banker tell his boss, quite solemnly, that he prefers bubble baths to the traditional scented candles. It will make you laugh silently, your translucent shoulders quaking with bored mirth. It will pass your time.

Do not attend your funeral. It will only make you angry. Your third-grade teacher, Mrs. Turnpike, will mouth embarrassing stories while the funeral home director eats all the free buffet food. You will notice he really likes champagne. Afterwards, you slash the tires of his new Hyundai. Whisper in his ear that he's a cheap bastard as he stares at it in sweaty anger, rubbing his too-big ears anxiously with pancake palms.

They bury an empty coffin. Your body disappeared while in the morgue. A potbellied reporter will sigh. Nudge a female cop named Elsie with an elbow. Take a sip of his decaf, and say, "Damn shame, that is. Damn shame. Can I have your number?"

Read the newspaper instead. You will find a neat, two-by-four article in the back, a picture of you, cropped accordingly, next to a column of nice things. You think it looks like ants. They call you a child prodigy, and a young, tragic victim. Again, they will say you tripped. "Such a sad thing, he jumped the shark at 21." It will not mention your drinking problem. Or the twenty thousand in cash you lost, red-faced, in Vegas last year. Breathe. You sound wonderful.

Another article will brief the city on the business, and then you will slip away from their minds like a failed reality TV show. You will notice it is smaller than your obituary, and it mentions the drinking. Don't cry about it. Mourn your wandering corpse, then haunt a Goodwill. Doze off in an alleyway, and wake to find a homeless man crying into his coat, yelling at someone named Rachel through snot and sour tears. Throw things, have silent tantrums, and run on water. Go to France. Break the law, then remember, somewhat loathingly, that you are invisible. You start to feel the silence; it weighs on you, twenty-odd pounds of bored frustration.

They will never find your killer. You know it was murder. Someone shadowy who climbed in through an unlocked window, and smashed your face with a signed Sammy Sosa bat. Wonder, dryly, if it was corked. You never liked baseball much.

Your tongue will start to feel dry. Your feet, eternally wrapped in old Christmas socks, will start to fade, and your arms will cave in on themselves. You know your time is ticking. It's been only a year since your death. You won't want to go. But you are tired. Every floating, faltering step feels like a marathon in molasses to you.

Return to your apartment, small, dark, and occupied by an up-and-coming British DJ named Paul. Wander the halls, before coming to a stop in your old room. There is nothing but a faded purple stain, a flimsy reminder of a kid who died a clumsy fool.

Lie down. Paul will be beat-boxing lonely in the corner. Be glad you can't hear him.

Give a last glance at the ceiling. It is speckled with age, a clump of fungus, and a tiny nest of spiders. You will feel suddenly warm.

Close your eyes.

It will be raining. Angry slants beat the window, and you can hear them, a final word in your aching ears. They are like delicate drums, simple, mindless rhymes to a strange poem. Probably spiritual. You don't care.

Let it put you to sleep.

You will never wake up again.

Reform

JACKSON TRICE, Grade 11, Age 16. South Carolina Governor's School for the Arts and Humanities, Greenville, SC, George Singleton, *Teacher*

My friend Jeb Lindy had been in trouble before. He made a point to tread the line between delinquent and mentally insane. He told teachers he liked the way human bodies tasted when they were cooked slowly over the stove for about forty-five minutes. The teacher had said, "Jeb," and she had said, "That is enough!" But everybody was laughing by then, and whatever they had been learning about was pushed far out of their minds. The teacher's cheeks had reddened, and her hands were balled into tiny fists. She had said through clenched teeth, "Mr. Lindy, you are disrupting the class," but he just went on about seasonings, the sauces that he used. He had shrugged and said, "Eh, I'm not a big fan of the Irish. Too starchy, you know what I'm saying? The darker the better!"

Jermaine Altois had agreed. He had said, "You know where it is, brother."

I sat next to Jeb in four classes. We passed notes, but they were odd, little conversations that say too much about us now. I ate lunch with him every day. He'd say, "Watch this," and blow milk out of his nose. It never got old. I wasn't allowed to have play dates with him because everyone knew the Lindy kid was, if anything, a bad influence and at the most, batshit insane.

But he was the class clown, the middle school's own super-star. We'd walk through the halls and hear only "Jeb Lindy, Jeb Lindy, Jeb Lindy." The teachers hated him, but he was smart. Or maybe he cheated. No one really knew.

The principal stared at him, asked him why he said those things about eating innocent people.

Jeb said, "I have divine powers from God."

The principal told him to shut his mouth. The principal said, "I will call your mother."

Jeb said, "You can't, because she's dead." Jeb's mother wasn't really dead. He just said that because it made people squirm.

The principal said, "Son, I am so sorry."

"You should be! She didn't even taste good!"

Jeb got expelled. Not because of what he said then per se, but for a culmination of things. There was the time he put gum in Eliza Bernelli's hair (accidentally, of course) or the time he skipped class for a month because he said he needed the "beau-ty rest." He always had something profane to say to our English teacher, Mrs. Harris, whose fat under her neck jiggled as she'd scream, "There is no sexual tension between Tom Sawyer and Huckleberry Finn, Mr. Lindy!" He came in late one day, said he just got back from Heaven. To be honest, the day Jeb got expelled was the day we all started actually learning things. School got worse from there.

There were rumors that he had been sent to a reform school. That he had shaved all his hair and changed his ways. He want-ed to be a Marine now, and fight for his dear country, and the freedoms he now acknowledged and enjoyed.

There were other rumors revolving around a speculation that he had killed his father and eaten him. I went to college and got a degree in business, ended up in accounting. I married a man of my race and of my faith, just like everybody had wanted me to. I even bought a house and kept a garden out in the back. I had done everything Jeb had fought hard never to have. I was reading the paper—mundane as the town I lived in, the life I led—when I read an article about a man my age who had escaped from a state penitentiary.

I said, "Well, I'll be damned."

In the picture, he had wrinkles, not of an old man, but of one who didn't have time to sleep, who didn't have time to stop. His hair was mostly matted to his head, but certain curls were still unruly, springing out in every direction. The deranged light in his eyes hadn't faded, neither had the mania in his smile.

My husband leaned over to read it, and he said, "Goddamn, is that . . . ?"

He didn't know that Jeb and I used to be close. I had met my husband in high school, when only the ghost of Jeb was there, in the form of rumors that swirled around. There were pictures, of course, "Remember that time Jeb said he ate his own shoe? I have proof!" and things of the like, but my husband didn't know that Jeb and I used to be friends. Maybe I wanted it to stay that way.

My husband read aloud the charges against him, put the paper down and said, "Goddamn," again.

I said, "That boy'll be fine."

He had been in trouble before.

Tattoo

CELESTE BARNABY, Grade 11, Age 17. Sage Ridge School, Reno, NV,
John Sloyan, *Teacher*

Jane stood before the smudge-laden bathroom mirror and un-
buttoned her shirt before lowering her arms and letting it gently sink to the floor, revealing her bare chest. The sun's tepid
afternoon rays shone through the frosted-glass window to her
left and illuminated her undressed body. She dampened a cotton pad in the sink and began scrubbing the afflicted area—a
small patch of skin just above her left breast. Slowly, the copi-
ous layers of concealer gave way and revealed the secret beneath. While it was perfectly normal for a twenty-something
such as herself to have one, the shame and tarnish that ac-
companied hers impelled its perpetual concealment. The image grew darker as she continued to scrub, transforming from
a cloudy, skeletal frame into a thick, dark-blue outline, con-
trasted sharply by her pale complexion. Upon completion, she
tossed the soiled cotton pad over her shoulder and into the
trash can, her eyes remaining fixed upon the engraving mere
inches away from her heart.

It was, by all objective accounts, a lovely tattoo. The letters swooped and curved gracefully, and were adorned by two
blooming roses. She could remember the ecstasy she had felt
upon seeing it finished for the first time—the sensuality and

confidence that it had endowed her with. However, those memories were all blurred and tainted now, and thinking of them filled her with a profound sadness, for she only now knew what was to follow. After staring at it for some time, she languidly licked her lips before letting the word fall out of her mouth: "Ian." It was a word she had said many times, a word she had thought and dreamed and tasted and cried. She remembered loving how easy it was to say, how little she had to move her lips and tongue. She used to whisper it over and over to herself at night, as if it were a lullaby. She had once looked it up and learned that it was a Hebrew name meaning "God is forgiving." She now hoped that wasn't true.

As she meditated upon the word, pictures of him began resurfacing. Little pictures at first: his large hands, his dirty-blond hair, his brown eyes that over time turned from sweet and gentle to angry and callous. Short featurettes soon began playing in her mind: his fingers combing through her thick, unkempt hair, his chapped lips upon her forehead, the sound of an open-handed slap on the cheek, a ceramic plate thrown against the wall. Connecting the word with its meaning, seeing this meaning—seeing him—permanently imprinted on her body made her nauseated, sick with grief and stupidity.

After showering herself with these memories, she retrieved the supplies from the drawer beneath her sink. They were collected in a small blue box with lavender trim. She placed the box on the counter and evaluated its contents. One bottle of peroxide, one bottle of dark-blue ink, one bowl, one washcloth, one sewing needle. Also in the box were a few pieces of paper and Styrofoam that she had practiced on, until the design was to her liking. She could afford to go to a tattoo parlor, yes. The product of a professional would surely be much more attractive. However, this was a deeply personal matter. The right to redeem her body was hers alone. Reaffirming this truth, she unscrewed the bottle of peroxide and poured a small amount into the bowl. She swirled it around for several moments and then added the entire bottle of ink. She picked up the needle and traced along her chest the outline that she planned to draw, lightly enough that it just tickled slightly. She then dipped the tip of the needle into the ink and, taking a deep breath, plunged the sharpened point into her skin, at the tip of the "n". She pulled it out and drove it back in, right next to the previous mark. She continued like this, making tiny blue spot after tiny blue spot, occasionally refreshing the needle with ink.

As she persisted, the pain grew noticeably distracting. This was a pain unlike most pains, one she had experienced only once before. It was a hot, stinging sensation, like scratching a sunburn, almost. She was flooded with memories of the last time she had felt such a discomfort. She had been lying down that time, her bare back pressed against a prickly cushion of Ian's craigslist couch. He had worked diligently and tenderly, and with much more dexterity than she now possessed. While his right hand maneuvered skillfully, his left hand had clasped hers comfortingly, with the same firm assuredness that he would later viciously clasp her throat. In an attempt to avoid an embarrassing cry of discomfort, she had focused her thoughts on the lovely lies that had led her to this moment: "I'm doing this for me," "I can't lose him," "I want him with me forever." Facing these memories of delusion and careless naïveté created far more anxiety than any discomfort from the needle.

The pain becoming too cumbersome, she stopped briefly, balancing the needle at the rim of the bowl so that only the tip was submerged. She drew the washcloth to her chest and gingerly dabbed away the excess ink. She took a moment to remember what she was working for, what she had worked for since she stepped out his front door for the last time. Since she had let the last bruise fade and the last scab peel off. The pain subsided, and she recovered the needle and continued in her endeavor. It was an arduous labor, and took far longer than she had originally expected. The sun eventually dipped so low in the sky that its light alone was no longer substantial enough for her to see clearly, and she was forced to momentarily stop and flip the switch by the door. Instantly, her cramped bathroom was filled with intense brightness from the fluorescent lights in the ceiling, giving it the same sense of sterility and artificiality as a hospital room. She looked up at the lights, recalling the feeling of lying on an examination table, the thin paper crinkling beneath her as she cradled her swollen wrist, waiting for the doctor to return. It had been then, at that moment, that she had decided to make a change, to forever stop grimacing as she dabbed concealer over tender, darkened patches of skin, to stop apologizing as tears welled in her eyes, to be unfettered and, maybe, after a while, even happy. Reendowed with motivation, she went back to work.

After two painstaking hours, she was finally done. It was by no means perfect; some might have even called it unsightly. But in her eyes, it was gorgeous. It was liberating. It was no longer a reminder of inadequacy and despair, but instead one of survival, of renewal, of hope. Sure, there were some obvious errors. The spot where the "n" had been altered to an "m" was clumsy and uneven, and the "I" was far too close to the "a" to be a distinctly separate word. These details were irrelevant to her, as she dabbed away the extra ink one final time and, with a slight smile, gently whispered the words that her body now held.

"I am free"

Skipping Rocks

SERINA CHANG, Grade 10, Age 15. Hunter College High School, New York, NY, Caitlin Donovan, *Teacher*

"I went to church yesterday."

Ronnie leans over and flicks the metal tab of my soda can. I wait for a response. He flicks the can again then looks up at me. "Yeah?"

"It was alright," I begin. It's a sore topic, I know, and I have to tread carefully. "At least nobody tried to stone me or anything."

Ronnie scoffs. "They don't know."

"I know they don't."

"You were lying to them," he adds.

"It wasn't lying; it's just not full disclosure. Everyone hides things."

"Whatever." Ronnie leans back and stretches, his right arm landing behind me on our park bench. I watch him warily, wondering what his next move will be. He smirks. "Hey, check out that chick. Nice."

Girls. Of course. "C'mon, Ronnie."

His dark eyes meet mine. "Come on, what?"

"You know . . . " I can't say it either. "Anyway, church was weird."

"I thought you said it was alright."

"It was. It was actually kinda nice, but that's what's weird—that it didn't suck. I mean, not bad weird. Just weird, you know?"

He shrugs. "I hate going to church."

"I know."

"It's stupid. I don't get why you still go."

"I told you. It's not that bad. It's not even that religious."

"What the hell does that mean? Church is religion."

"Not really. I mean, the preacher reads from the Bible and all, but he doesn't mention God much. It's more about us."

He chuckles meanly. "Us? Like you and me? Sure, I bet God just loves us."

"God loves everyone, Ronnie," I say quietly.

This time he actually laughs out loud. "Are you kidding me? You of all people should know that's not true. The only reason you're even allowed in that church is because you're a goddamn liar. You think they would let you in if they knew?" Ronnie takes a deep breath. "God doesn't love either of us, Matt. You gotta know that."

There's no point in responding so we sit in silence. I drum my fingers and Ronnie half-heartedly watches the girl from earlier. Eventually he sighs and rubs his forehead. "She's cute, isn't she?"

"How would I know?" Wrong answer.

His eyes widen then quickly narrow. "You're a guy, that's why you should know."

I open my mouth, not sure whether to defend myself or apologize, when he suddenly grabs my shoulders and shakes me. "You're a fucking guy, okay?" Ronnie sighs and releases me.

The wind picks up and the dead leaves stir on the ground. I hear Ronnie unzip his jacket, and I don't need to look over to know that he's taking out a pack of cigarettes. He takes his time, waiting for me to say something. But I don't want to fight with him again.

I leave him and walk over to the lake. The sun is setting and the lake is a collage of murky water, painted sky, and me. The colors remind me of stained-glass windows. I crumple my soda can and toss it into the water. The windows shatter.

"You shouldn't litter." Ronnie's gravelly voice interrupts my thoughts, and I turn to see that he has followed me. He stands a few feet back though, hands stuffed in his pockets and cigarette nowhere in sight. The setting sun makes his brown hair red and he looks younger, like from when we were little kids and played cowboys and Indians together on my bedroom floor. We were best friends then.

I shake my head. "It doesn't matter. There's crap in the lake already." As if it proves my point, I toss in a dirty pebble.

"What are you doing, anyway?" he says.

"I don't know."

I throw two more pebbles, one for the lake and one to him. He catches it with ease.

"I bet I can skip this farther than you," he says, smirking again. It's a sweet smirk though.

"Oh yeah?" I say.

"Yeah." He's grinning now, eyes shining and eyebrows lifted teasingly.

His comical face confuses me, so I bend down to look at the ground instead. I try to find an appropriate skipping stone, although I have no idea what I'm looking for. Ronnie squats down as well and hands me a flat, circular one. "Thanks. Alright, man, let's see what you got."

Ronnie makes a big show of winding his arm, baseball-pitcher-style, and sends the small rock flying. It dances across the lake, endless circles exploding from where the earth comes into contact with water. And then, three bounces later, the pebble is gone, sunk far beyond where the human eye will ever see.

"Easy. I'll make it past that floating log, watch me," I boast. It's a bluff and Ronnie knows it. I can't skip pebbles. No one ever taught me.

I throw Ronnie's pebble like a Frisbee and we wait. To our surprise, the rock skips once, no, twice, no, three times . . . before, strangely enough, landing right on the log. And there it rests, atop the gnarly wooden trunk.

"Dude, how'd you do that?" Ronnie asks.

"I don't know. I didn't mean to. I've never skipped anything like that before. They always sink right away."

"Huh. Well, that one's not sinking anytime soon." A strong breeze now pushes the pebble and log farther and farther away from us and into the sunset. "Well, I guess you won."

I grin at him. "Thanks to you. It was your pebble."

He laughs a little. "Okay then. Tie?"

Ronnie's hand sticks out of his frayed sleeve, hesitantly extended toward me. I watch it waver a little but nevertheless stay there, and I can't help but to remember something I had heard in the pews yesterday. Love bears all things, the preacher said, believes all things, hopes all things, endures all things. I thought of Ronnie immediately when he said that but knew I could never tell him. Yet now, seeing this uncertain hand reaching for mine, I'm not so sure that I can't. The wind ruffles my hair comfortably, pulling me out of my reverie, and I shake his hand.

"Tied," I agree.

Voices in the Sand

BENJAMIN HAIDT, Grade 7, Age 13. Bexley Middle School, Bexley, OH,
Linda Kelley, *Teacher*

A gust of desert wind prickles my olive skin. It's a feeling I've
been experiencing for days now, the wind whispering to me in
its scratchy voice: *Go back, Nahla. Return to your clan.*

I don't listen to the desert anymore. My mother died three
days ago, and the caravan abandoned me to the shifting sands.
They sent me away because I saw things not for what they are,
but for what they could be. At least, that's how I understand it.
My clan thought differently; they saw me as a threat to tradition. For instance, I saw no reason to serve the person at my
right hand first, or to fear the number seven, or to accept the
Sheikh's decisions without question. And because I refused to
heed such customs, I was treated like a noxious stench, though
my mother pleaded with the elders for patience, promising that
I would learn to respect their ways, just as she had. But they
knew what I knew: that I never would.

It has been three days without food now. As I trudge through
the sand, the folds of my russet tunic flap around my blistering
legs. The wind moans: *Go home, Nahla, go home to your tent.*
Your mother misses you so. I turn my head away from the sound,
but the desert's voice seems to whisper the old *ghinnawa* that

my mother taught me long ago: "I've lost their tracks, the loved ones./Perhaps my singing will bring them."

My mother. I halt my dreary slog up and down the dunes, and fall on my knees. The memory comes rushing with the force of a sandstorm: I was standing in our tent, the lamp dimly flickering. A looming essence of sorrow hovered in the air. The bleached body of a woman—Mother—lay sprawling on the rug bed before me. The thought of losing the only person who ever loved me made me burst into tears. I sank to the carpet next to my mother and lay there sobbing by her side. Then in a weak voice, my mother began to sing a *ghinnawa*: "Despair of them, dear one, made you a stray/Who wanders between watering places." Our hearts intertwined, sharing our sorrow. We sang the old song as the wind howled into the night.

But I knew I wasn't supposed to be in that tent. In our clan, it is taboo to be with the dying. I did not care. In singing, I was sharing my mother's grief. A booming voice from outside the tent intruded roughly, shouting "Who dares to be with the dying?" The Sheikh pulled aside the curtains of the tent. "Show yourself!" I left my mother's side and stepped out onto the sand. His voice snarled, "You're breaking tradition yet again. When will you see that tradition is tradition and cannot be broken?!" Frustration swelled inside me, and I felt that I was glass breaking into a million shards as my words erupted in response: "What if the tradition is unjust? Shouldn't someone dying be able to share their spirit as it says goodbye?!" The Sheikh frowned deeply. His eyes were like hot black coals. "Nahla, in our caravan you have been the weak link for too long. And I am sure that our fragile hold on these sands will slip because of you. Our council of elders decrees that it is time to expel you. Now starts your blind journey. May you never return. Leave us!"

I shake this bitter memory from my head, stagger to my feet, and keep walking. For I cannot bear to wonder what mother must have been thinking as she heard the Sheikh bellowing and me shouting. To remember how I went back into the tent and found my mother's spirit gone. How I walked over to my mother's body and took her hand in mine one last time.

And yet I cannot stop remembering. I sink on my knees to the sand and recall leaning over and kissing my mother's pale forehead. And I remember the rage that blew inside me, white hot against my heart. I burned with fury at these elders who were commanding me to leave behind my home, our tent, this space where my mother loved me even when nobody else did. I felt an impulse to shriek with anger. I could have hurt anyone or anything in sight. Yet at that moment I heard the wind seem to cry out: *Nahla, stop! Clear your head. You must calmly ask them to take you in as one of them.* I took a deep breath, unclenched my fists, and walked toward the Sheikh's tent. But a half hour later, I was looking back over my shoulder at the caravan's dim lights, tears slipping down my cheeks.

That was three days ago. I am fatigued from thirst. Beads of sweat drip from my eyebrows like tears and trickle down my sand-peppered nose and cheeks. The sand scrapes my blistering legs like hot needles. I know my goatskin bag is almost depleted of water. As I stare out into the endless sand and wind, I miss my mother. I miss our tent.

I'm shaken with surging frustration and anger, knowing that this aimless journey will never lead me home. I will never find food or water alone in this harsh desert. Alone. I am overtaken by a frenzy of fear and hopelessness, and reflexively clutch the amulet around my neck, ripping it from my skin as though I were pulling away my pain and anguish. I feel between my fingers that the sealed silver *hirz* has cracked open and I unclench my rigid palm to find not verses from the Quran, but what seems to be a note.

Immediately I recognize the handwriting. "Mother," I hoarsely whisper to myself. I read her words: "Dear Nahla, I write this note to give you light in a time of darkness, and have placed it in your *hirz* so that I might always be with you." I feel my eyes opening wider, and I feel saliva—water—return to my tongue and throat.

"And Nahla, a desert may be dry and desolate, but there is still water beneath it if one has the faith to find it. You may be tired, grieving, angry, and confused, but if you hold strong to your faith in what you believe, and in what your spirit tells you, then you may find water to help you quench your thirst and keep on going in life."

As I look up from the note and out at the desert, the sun no longer harshly beats down on my skin, but now gently warms it. The dunes seem like rolling waves. As I look around me, the sand twinkles like stars in a cool night sky. The wind has stopped howling and has slowed to a gentle breeze. My life is blooming with colors, fantastic shapes, and spirit. Gently, I roll my mother's note and place it back into the *hirz*. I raise the amulet necklace high, and then lower it over my head as though laying a baby into a cradle. I am no longer aware of the nagging thirst. I know, even though I can't see it, that there's water somewhere.

I set out to find it.

Gulf of Mexico

JACQUELINE KNIGHT, Grade 12, Age 17. Lafayette High School, Lexington, KY, Liz Prather, *Teacher*

Rosa dated the moon once. He took her to a movie and they discussed that if there were magic in the world, it must be contained in water. He, a quick-thinking boy with pocked gray skin, did not believe in magic, and she told him about her grandfather, who could turn lead to gold.

He had been twelve when he discovered the trick. Twelve and made of sun-warmed beach sand. A traveling girl in colorful skirts had tried to take the secret from him with a temptress hand tapping his upper leg. The girl made the wealthy boy's bones rattle like ice in a full glass. Her grandfather, whose riches had turned him into a baby shelled sea turtle, fell for her, and they found a home on the coast.

The woman went out on a boat the day they were to be married, her neck heavy with African diamonds and rubies plucked from a princess's garden in the east. The bride ran her fingers through the water, and when a swell hit the side of her boat, toppled over like a small stone. The waves swallowed the girl, twisting her body in seaweed and tearing at her delicate body. When she washed ashore, her lips were the color of the sky, and the jewels she had worn were long lost.

Rosa's grandfather wept over her battered body and his arms became as the wandering seagull. He cried out and begged for the girl who was his to come back. He swore his fortune, his land, and his life, and the gods dried his tears. The girl's heart glowed crystal clear, and life flowed through her once again. The ocean that had taken her, however, demanded she remain his own, so her body turned the color of pearls, her eyes into the flesh of an oyster. The girl fell back into the salty breath, never to walk dry land again.

The man, having given his vast riches to the gods, married a girl from his village. She was kind and nurturing, with a face like his mother's. Every night he would walk the lonely shore and watch his mistress shepherd the tides. His children with the lost bride never grew from bubble-eyed preteens with legs like streams of warm water. His children with the soft-hearted wife from the village were forged of sun-warmed beach sand with skin of turtle shells.

Rosa and the moon's fling was short-lived, but no more than a day after they took separate paths, the moon appeared in Rosa's window. His hair was frazzled, so stars were falling out as he trembled by her bed. He confessed he could go no longer without the hollow sound of her voice and the feel of her palm against his fingernails. Rosa batted her oyster flesh eyes and twirled her colorful skirt. "I know," she said. "We are shepherds of the tides."

Who You Are

INDIA NABARRO, Grade 12, Age 18. Chamblee Charter High School, Chamblee, GA, Adrienne Keathley, *Teacher*

Twenty-three weeks and five days ago, your body was covered in a fine layer of soft fur called lanugo. The next day, you began sucking your thumb. You began to kick your legs and then— soft and malleable—your eyes opened. They are unseeing, but it matters not, because nothing rocks you like the ever-present rhythm of your mother's heart.

You will be born in one week and three days. The lanugo will shed, and you will enter this life completely naked. The physical tie to your mother will be severed and, though many will flock to you, you will be incomparably alone for the first time.

As of yesterday, you have spent a total of nine months and four days in the womb. In ten days—247 hours and 53 minutes —you will be expelled from this place, this unbelievably protected, flawless, and comforting place.

You will spend the next eighty-four years, eleven months, and two days searching fruitlessly for this original and wholly unattainable, entirely and all-consuming overwhelming peace. Of these years, you will be blessed with 333 months and 24 days of sleep, one-thirty-fifth of which will be spent on the most vivid and terrifying nightmares imaginable.

These terrors will plague you. When you wake, your eyes

will be swollen and crusted shut from the incessant tears and mucus secretion. These nightmares will be caused not by the guilt stemming from your mother's suicide, a theory you will have convinced yourself of by age seventeen, but rather by your collective unconscious speaking to you whilst you are in the deepest and most vulnerable trance.

This voice is your voice; the voice of your soul. It futilely tries to bring your past memories and knowledge to light for you. It is trying to tell your body—a strangely scientific and mechanical edifice—about your true history.

Sometimes, you remember.

During the Ming Dynasty, you met with Death, leaving that four-year-old female form that trapped and caged you in the streets for other peasants to pillage. You died of starvation, but your mother was relieved, for daughters were a burden in that society, but you were taught the value of perseverance and dignity. These lessons are what will eventually give you the assiduity to become a craftsman of fine furniture in the Golden Age under Queen Elizabeth's rule in England.

You subconsciously recall killing 162 Jewish women and children in the fall of 1941. This event, however, eludes identification by your more reasonable and logical self. In truth, to have the ability to isolate and trace the source of the effects of these past choices is impossible, but the crippling guilt is evident and takes a notable toll on your elderly being.

In the winter of 1982, your older brother's car slid off a bridge in northeastern Michigan, ultimately trapping you under the ice. This is the sole explanation for your seemingly inexplicable disdain for all large bodies of water.

In these times you have loved and you have gravely sinned: these elements lift your soul and blacken it. You eternally strive for the equilibrium between good and bad. On your shoulders lay the consequences of your actions from long ago. They suffocate and mold you. They are there to guide you, but you must comprehend that you are not the same individual that you were centuries ago.

You are not the same person you were twenty-six seconds ago.

You are a polymorphous energy that controls a tangible being to visibly express itself.

Energy is never created or destroyed—you were neither created, nor will you ever be destroyed. This intangible force that is you will never die. You are a collection of emotions, thoughts, ideas, opinions, and possibilities. You will live on forever, a parasite among trillions, and, however unfathomable, you will find those you lost again.

As flawed as modern science may be, Aristophanes was correct in one regard: The soul is always engaged in the insatiable game, the never-ending quest to find that absent fraction of itself—yourself—that is vital to the illusion of being complete. This deception aids you in accepting and comprehending your own importance.

In 247 hours and 16 minutes, you should be blinded by the most sterile of white lights, but that thin membrane of new skin will become translucent, and all you will see will be red. Your eyes, bulbous and unseeing, will remain shut until six days after your expulsion from your mother.

Your sleep will be fitful for two months and thirteen days, because you will crave to return to that soft, dark place that suspended you in a warm, viscous liquid for approximately nine months. You will begin to suck your thumb and cry for that haven inside of your mother.

You will not be awarded the pleasure of this return until your 84 years have lapsed.

In an effort to commit all your failures, your losses, and your precious learned lessons to memory, you play them in a reel in your head in the hours before your birth. They hit you like the ocean's relentless tides, and you pray that some sense of these past lives will accompany you into your next life.

Remembering these traumas is painful, and soon you begin to physically ache.

You are crowning.

The light is unfathomably bright and makes a bloody filter of the skin protecting your eyelids, through which you are able to see every vein and capillary coating the concavity.

You take your first breath, and you remember how wonderful it feels to breathe.

That is all you remember.

What She Learned

MELANIE ABRAMS, Grade 12, Age 17. Commonwealth School, Boston, MA, Melissa Haber, *Teacher*

Beginning . . .

The ceiling rock cracked open and yellow light streaked Strat Marmel. Benzy screamed, because Benzy had never seen anything so bright, had never wondered if there was anything above the twisting stalactites of the Strat Marmel ceiling. It was as if the floor under your feet had opened up, reader. It was as if someone had slashed open the fabric of the universe. Benzy had been born in Strat Marmel, had grown up in Strat Marmel, and up until this moment, Benzy had never questioned that she would live the rest of her life in Strat Marmel and die in Strat Marmel.

Benzy lost a lifetime of the faith in a single moment. Benzy had believed, as everyone who had lived in Strat Marmel had believed since the Creation, that her existence would be a journey from darkness into light and back again. The matter from her mother's womb had grown into the matter of a child, a child as unlit as the fry of the pskol. Benzy knew that the unlit child had grown brighter each time it nursed, as all children had since the Creation. Benzy knew that the child had been taught as it grew, as all children had been taught by their mothers, the story of the Creation and everything else that one must know to live in Strat Marmel. Benzy knew that the child had grown brighter with each meal of pskol and each passing day, till it caught its first meal and became a girl named Benzy, till it set out on its journey through life, alone, as all who live in Strat Marmel had done since the Creation. Benzy had believed, as everyone who had lived in Strat Marmel had believed since the Creation, that she would brighten still more with each passing day and with each meal of pskol, until light would finally leave her and her body would feed the pskol fry with a lifetime of light and matter. Benzy had believed that matter was as infinite as Strat Marmel, whereas light was finite and therefore sacred. Here, through a crack the size of her thumbnail, was a lifetime allotment of light, sudden and unearned. Here was a crack the size of Benzy's thumbnail in the constant matter of Strat Marmel. Reader, you cannot begin to imagine what this would feel like.

Benzy found a lifetime of color in a single moment. Benzy had been born and had grown up in a world of thin blue light and deep purple shadows, of the dim glow of pskol swimming through the dark trickle of the Strat. Benzy had been born and had grown up in a world of deep musky smells and low rippling noises as dark as Strat Marmel. In a single moment, the warm yellow light flew in shocks over the sparkling Strat and outlined the pale pskol fry in a ripple of color, sent reds and greens dancing over the skews of stalagmites, and flared over the gauzy webs of Benzy's outstretched fingers. I am sorry to inform you, reader, but you cannot begin to imagine what this would feel like either.

. . . *Middle* . . .

Outside of Strat Marmel, they have little dots for eyes, noses no bigger than a fry, such dark skin. Benzy still marveled, months after she had seen the sun and far curved horizon. Outside of

Strat Marmel, their fingers are nearly webless and they have flat dull teeth. In the dark, they are dark, and they can hardly smell or hear.

Months after she had heard the crash of thunder and tasted chocolate, Benzy still saw a hazy square of flash when she closed her eyes. Dr. Wilson had thought to bring a photographer with the digging team. As Benzy soon learned, Dr. Wilson thought of just about everything. But even Dr. Wilson hadn't imagined the thrall of that picture; there were simply not enough magazine covers in the world. None of the magazines or newspapers that ran the picture mentioned that Benzy had been rushed to the hospital right after it had been taken, knocked senseless from the hot white camera flash, that Benzy had suffered more pain in that instant than she had in her lifetime. Reader, if you have ever had your eyes dilated for a vision test, then you still have no idea what this was like.

Dr. Wilson, in her defense, had taken every precaution to smooth out Benzy's journey onto the surface of the earth. When Benzy had come to, she had found herself wearing dark circles of glass over her eyes, in a dark room with a low ceiling, next to a woman with dim blue lights strapped to her fingertips and forehead. The woman had introduced herself professionally—reader, even I don't know Dr. Wilson's first name—and had sat for hours trying to teach Benzy in a few hours what people outside of Strat Marmel are taught over a lifetime.

Benzy learned that people on the surface eat tall green creatures that grow in rows on land and orange squares that come in red boxes. Benzy learned that some people on the surface of the earth kill each other to find food. Benzy was taken into a forest and scuba diving through the coral reefs. Benzy learned what electricity and alphabets are, what art is, what war is, how bottled vanilla smells. Benzy began to dream in color, to listen to recorded music, and Benzy began to wear clothing, which itched terribly at her sunburned body.

Benzy remembers everything she sees and hears and touches, and Benzy gave Dr. Wilson hundreds of vibrant details at the end of each and every day she spent outside of Strat Marmel. At the end of each and every day she spent outside of Strat Marmel, Benzy wept and wept, overcome with beauty and strangeness, color and pain. Reader, try to spend one day seeing every single thing around you for the first time.

. . . *End*

Outside of Strat Marmel, they have melanin in their skin to bear the rays of the sun, as everyone who has lived in Strat Marmel has had the blue light to bear the darkness since the genes of our ancestors adapted to living in cave systems. Benzy wept and wept when Dr. Wilson informed her that she had not developed sufficient melanin and could not stay upon the surface of the earth. Outside of Strat Marmel, they know you are sick before you do, and so the sick do not always die. In a single moment, Benzy learned that her life was a journey from darkness into light and back again.

Benzy did not take anything with her when she returned to Strat Marmel, except for a laminated copy of her first photograph. By the time she left the surface, Benzy knew that batteries would die in time, that apple seeds would not sprout in Strat Marmel. Benzy left Dr. Wilson, and museums of ancient skeletons, and the brilliant light of the sun as it sets like marmalade. Reader, if you have ever mourned your own life, then you know what Benzy felt in that moment.

When Benzy returned to Strat Marmel, she could not see her photograph by her own blue light. She could not see the pskol that swam in the Strat around her or hear the soft ripples of their fins.

Cowboys vs. Bear

ELIZABETH MILLER, Grade 7, Age 12. Camp Hill Middle School, Camp Hill, PA, Katherine Niederoest, *Teacher*

The day was overcast, with low-lying clouds. When a pair of cowboys, Larry and Jack, rounded the corner of the barn, they saw a gruesome sight. The cowboys were brothers and were aged six years apart. What they saw was a humongous bear snacking on one of their prized bulls. Jack, the elder brother, pulled out his shotgun and fired at the bear. He unfortunately missed, and the fact that he had shot at the bear made the bear very angry. Next, Larry pulled out his pistol and aimed at the bear and shot. Larry missed as well. You would think that with such a big target, since the bear was so big, that they couldn't miss, but the fact is they were both lousy shots and probably would have missed the bear if he was right on top of them. Fortunately for them, the bear had been taking anger-management classes recently and counted to ten, shook the two brothers' hands, said he was sorry, and trotted away dragging the bull corpse with him for lunch.

The two cowboys were flabbergasted and rode home on their horses with their mouths wide open. The cowboys, on their way to their ranch, decided that it was all a dream and that they had had too much to drink last night and went on with their chores.

A few hours later, in the early afternoon, they came across a female bear looking around the barn. Remembering what had happened earlier, they turned and walked away, but before they could get any farther than a few steps, the female bear called out, much to the two brothers' horror, and said, "I am terribly sorry for what my husband did to your bull. He was hungry, and he would always take meat from the ranch that we used to live by. We will not trouble you anymore if you do not hunt us or trouble us any longer."

The two cowboys looked at each other and Jack replied, "Okay, we will not bother you if you do not bother us." The bear shook hands with Jack and then Larry, and trotted off to her cave. Wondering what the heck was wrong with themselves and if the well was poisoned, the brothers walked home to take a nap to see if that would cure their "hallucinations."

Meanwhile, at the bears' cave, the two bears were finishing up the leftovers of the bull for a snack. Their two cubs were playing kick the spleen with the bull's spleen. All was happy in the cave, and they had excellent neighbors that would leave them alone. It was an excellent environment to raise two cubs. The male bear, Bob, got up from his wicker chair, which was imported from Japan, and stretched. He then said, "It is very annoying that to stay alive and out of a cage, we must keep our hair short and walk on all fours. Every day when I come home, my back is sore and the hollowed-out bear's head stinks when it gets hot. We Sasquatches should be proud of who we are and should share the world with humans as equals. We are just as intelligent as humans; we just don't use the technology. Sasquatches are more civil than humans, and we never have wars."

His wife, Jennifer, then replied, "I know that we don't live the best of lives, but the cubs are happy and we have a roof over our heads and food in our stomachs. What more could you ask for?" She got up and said more defiantly. "We should be grateful that we are alive. It was a sad situation with the farmer over in Kentucky, but at least he tasted good. We are grizzly bears and nothing more to the locals and that is how it will stay. Like I said earlier, we should be grateful for everything that we have."

Back at the ranch, the two brothers were talking about what had happened and decided to tell their friend Joe what happened. They called Joe and asked him if they could meet up for some coffee and to talk. The three of them went to a café nearby called The Clean Kitchen Food Place, which was called that because of some salmonella cases a few years back. They started talking. "It was the strangest thing," Larry exclaimed. "The bear talked and shook my hand."

"Yeah, and the other bear did too. The other bear made a deal with us," proclaimed Jack.

"Well, you have a problem, and I think you might want to see a psychiatrist or at least a therapist," replied Joe.

"We are not crazy!" Larry screamed. All of the people in the café stared at him. Joe, while Jack and Larry weren't looking, switched on his phone and Googled insane asylums in Montana.

"Everyone, calm down," said the head chef, coming out of the kitchen, "Everything is under control." The chef was just trying to help, but it only made it worse, because to be honest, he wasn't very pretty and the sight of him made a baby start crying.

With everyone occupied with the baby, which is all of seven customers, Larry and Jack were sneaking out the door because they really did not want to go to an insane asylum. Joe was occupied, because as he was looking up insane asylums he came across an ad for the new Iron Gym and was ordering one off of Amazon. Joe was a little skimpy on the muscles.

Jack and Larry ran back home since they didn't live that far away. When they got home, they locked all the doors to make sure no one could come and take them away. By this point they were a little paranoid, because no one else but Joe knew where they were, and Joe was a little busy at the moment doing pull-ups since he had the Iron Gym delivered with express delivery. After a while of hiding in the basement with a shotgun, Jack came upstairs to make himself something to eat. He went upstairs to see where Larry had gone. Jack went into Larry's bedroom, and he saw Larry on the floor. Thinking Larry was dead, Jack screamed and ran out of the room. In a few seconds Jack came back and checked his brother's pulse. He wasn't dead. Larry had fallen and wacked his head and was now unconscious. Jack saw a puddle of water near the bed and suspected that Larry had slipped on the puddle and wacked his head on the edge of his desk, since it was wet with blood.

All of a sudden, there was a knock at the front door. It was Bob, the "bear." "Sorry about the water balloon. My kids were playing with two that we made out of your bull's lungs. It went in through one of your open windows upstairs. I hope that it didn't break anything," apologized Bob. "That's okay," replied Jack. Then without warning, Bob lunged and ripped out Jack's jugular vein. "Sorry, I had to do it. You might have told someone."

Meanwhile, upstairs, Larry was recovering from unconsciousness when he heard footsteps on the stairs, loud and heavy. Something big was coming up the hallway now. The large something continued into his room and loomed over Larry. It spoke and said, "Ready to join your brother?" Then all the lights went out.

Holy Cow! A Profile of Dairy Farmer and Cow Caretaker Edgar Pless

JAKE KUHN, Grade 12, Age 18. Buckingham Browne & Nichols School, Cambridge, MA, Eric Hudson, *Teacher*

Edgar stops by a light-brown Guernsey standing at the opposite fence. "She's going to give birth soon," he says, gesturing at the cow's rear, where a long, dirty strand of goo dangles eighteen inches. Cows emit mucus as the birth date nears. With his bare hand, Edgar plucks the mucus from her and drops it on the ground. He feels her udder with two fingers, pressing the pink flesh. "Not for a few days," he concludes; when she's ready to give birth, her udder will be swollen and tight with her first milk. Her vagina will stick out the back, distended and jiggling "like jelly." During calving season, Edgar checks the herd for these signs every few hours, looking especially for cows by themselves. The day before they are due, he moves them to a special birthing pasture in the back, a lawn with white-picket fencing and shady oaks where they can deliver in peace.

"We have to separate the mother from her calf after she licks her clean," Edgar says, rubbing his knuckles as he closes the pasture gate. The two hours with her calf gets the cow's hormones and milk production running, but any longer makes the necessary separation even harder. In Edgar's ideal world, the mother raises and feeds her own calf, but dairy cows must give their milk to humans. "It would be wonderful to have an animal farm, keep the moms and their babies together," Edgar murmurs as if daydreaming. "That's the most beautiful thing."

To Edgar, his job is nothing but beauty. Seven days a week, he begins work before dawn, when the air is still and stars fleck the sky. "Nobody is around. It's just outstanding," Edgar sighs, his words dripping from his lips like sweet cream. "There are certain fields I work in, chopping fresh grass, where there's nothing in sight, and you could be in Montana. There's really natural quiet." After dusk, just he and his cows remain. Some nights he even sleeps in the barn with them. "It's just unbelievable. The noises and smells, very . . . nurturing. I guess it must be nice in the womb," Edgar laughs, opening the door of his large, blue pickup truck. "Sometimes I'll be driving around, and I just look up at the sky, and—" he opens his arms and tilts his head backward, wrinkled eyes closed in reverie. "Smelling the roses."

He climbs into the truck's high cab, settling into his seat with a small grunt. The truck grumbles to life, making the clutter of farming magazines and the empty Fanta bottles and the trunk-sized lunch cooler vibrate on the floor. Maisie, Edgar's aging Australian cattle dog, jumps up from her back-seat slumber to lick his face. A collie-dingo cross, she is semi-wild—that's what Edgar likes about her. Her flares of feral instinct are responsible for the chewed headrests. "Somebody once told me, 'Your dog owns you,'" Edgar says as he pulls out of the driveway, "but nobody owns nobody here. It's not about owning."

It's four-thirty, and the herd over at Eastleigh is ready for the afternoon milking. At a fork in the road, Edgar chooses the narrow lane that disappears around a sharp bend. Just a mile from the Home Farm, Eastleigh sits at the foot of Framingham State Forest in a valley with sparse neighbors and few visitors. Edgar motions at the dense trees flanking the truck's right, explaining that on the other side of those woods is the Sudbury Valley School, where students set their own agendas and "do whatever they want." He and his wife Juliette moved to Framingham so that one of his kids and two of hers could attend the school. "Kids—let 'em loose," he says. "Be there, as a friend, consultant, advisor, whatever, but let them do what they want to do, and they'll be just fine."

He turns into the driveway marked by a yellow sign advertising Fresh Milk! Four ivy-covered silos rise like steeples over the picturesque farm. Forest-green roofs shelter beige barns, lush pastures roll on gentle hills, pieces of rusting machinery lie strewn about the lawn. Edgar's destination is the milking barn, a long hall lit by sun seeping through cloudy windows. The aroma of milk and manure pervades the air. A row of stalls on each side faces a central passageway where Pedro, at twenty the youngest worker on the farm, parks a battered wheelbarrow containing the cows' afternoon snack.

Pedro beams when he sees Edgar. They embrace, Edgar's heft burying Pedro's compact build. When Pedro started working at Eastleigh a year ago, he was skeptical of Edgar's seeming "passive" manner and "scrubby" look. But Edgar soon proved Pedro's impression wrong. When teaching him farm jobs, Edgar would not simply tell him what to do, but why. Their greetings went from hellos to hugs. "Even if it's just for three seconds, you distinguish the difference between hugging someone else, like your mom or your girlfriend," he says. "That becomes a routine, but every time he hugs you, every time he looks at your eyes, there's a connection."

After a long moment, they release each other. Grabbing a pitchfork from its hook on the wall, Edgar preps the cows' snack by tossing a pile of brown, mulch-like material in front of each stall. This is chopped corn silage, undried grasses collected in summer and stored in the airtight silo for winter, fermenting to take on a flavor that the cows love. Edgar nods to Pedro, and Pedro slides open the door at the end of the barn.

Seven cows jostle through the doorway—the early crowd. They trot to their stalls and munch on their snack, snorting in delight while the rest of the herd trickles in. Using one hand, Edgar chains their collars to the stalls, and they are ready to give milk. Hygiene is the first and last step of the milking process. Edgar sanitizes with a teat dip, a plastic blue cup that fills with a disinfecting iodine solution and molds to fit the teats. From behind, Edgar reaches under the first cow's udder, lifting the cup to engulf each of her four teats. The motion is as quick and noiseless as dipping fingers in water. He finishes the row of twenty cows in two minutes, returning to the first cow with a steaming rag. He wraps her teats with the rag, wiping away all traces of the disinfectant. Sterilize the teat, wash away the sterilizer. Edgar scrubs around the teats on the udder, scraping away dirt to reveal the soft pink skin beneath.

"Pedro, can you get the cart and start the pump?" Edgar asks. Quick to oblige, Pedro disappears into a side room.

"He's not a boss," Pedro says. "Even though he is, he doesn't talk to you or approach you like that. He's more of a friend." Pedro scratches his stubbly cheek as he flips open a mechanical box. "Having someone you work with that doesn't act like a boss, and they're not full of themselves, they're a humble person, it makes everything beautiful," he grins, flicking a switch before wheeling the cart into the milking room.

A rhythmic beating emanates from the black vacuum pipe suspended from the ceiling above the stalls. This is the main line, bringing milk from teat to tank. Pedro's cart looks foreign in the rustic barn—a chrome rack on wheels carrying a tangle of tubes. Edgar takes one of the pulsators, a spider-like contraption with four thin, black-and-chrome suction cups sprouting from a central chamber. A clear blue tube runs from the chamber to the main line. Edgar attaches the suction cups to the teats one at a time, slurping them up. The cow's bloated udder deflates as the milk surges into the tube. The fresh milk is a steaming 110 degrees, making the room warm and humid as it travels through the tubes. The cow flicks her tail once, and Edgar pats her haunch before pulling the pulsator from her teats. He dips each teat into another cup, this time coating on an orange sealant that prevents bacteria from entering the teat and infecting it. Safe cow, safe milk. Done in ten minutes. He moves on to the next cow.

"The care that Edgar has for these guys, the love—wow," Pedro says, refilling the cows' silage. "That amazes me." He pauses to watch Edgar humming to cow number 577, who gave birth this morning. Her first milk will feed her calf back at the Home Farm, so the pulsator sucks the milk into a huge silver pot rather than the main line. When the pot is full, it cools for an hour and a half while Edgar finishes milking the herd. He then separates the milk into two white buckets and drives them to the Home Farm.

Lifting the buckets from the bed of his truck, Edgar's hands quiver under the weight. He brings them into the front room of the barn, a cozy space lit by a bare light bulb encased in a jar. Clutter swallows most of the room: baskets of wool socks, piles of folded shirts, cases of power tools, containers of dog biscuits and cat food. Edgar's children and grandchildren smile from photographs crowding every ledge. As Edgar plops the buckets onto the swept concrete floor, Juliette turns from her place at a sink built into a spotless white countertop. Exchanging a silent greeting, she and Edgar gaze at each other and smile.

"That's the colostrum?" Juliette asks, brushing her long gray hair from her face. Colostrum is the cow's first milk, full of antibodies that the calf needs to build its immune system.

"Yeah, she can have this tonight," Edgar responds. Even if they have to tube feed it, they need to give the calf colostrum. Without it, her chances of survival plummet. Edgar pries the lid from the bucket. The life-force liquid, bright yellow and thick with globs of congealed minerals, reaches the brim. "It's like snot," Edgar laughs, lifting it to the counter. Juliette rinses clean another bucket, placing two sieves over it. After stirring the colostrum with an oversized wooden spoon, Edgar pours it through the sieves. Since the colostrum goes straight from the cow to the pot, sawdust can get in—Edgar isn't taking any chances. Juliette stands beside Edgar with four-pint bottles waiting to be filled. They work as one, moving around each other in wordless harmony. He pours the strained colostrum into the bottles, she caps them with red rubber nipples fresh from the dishwasher. She soaps up the buckets, he stores the extra colostrum in the fridge.

Edgar and Juliette met when they both brought their first families to Sirius Community in Shutesbury, Massachusetts, where people lived together under a consensus government. "I had built all these walls around myself to protect myself, protect my reality," Edgar explains. He decided that he needed to put himself in a situation where he was forced to talk to strangers and be more open. There, he realized that there were other people who shared his ideas about life. The community believed in the sacredness and intelligent nature of all life, including plants. They worked "consciously" with "nature spirits" to grow forty-pound cabbages and two-pound tomatoes.

He was harvesting vegetables in the garden when Juliette first visited the community. "As soon as we met, we knew," Edgar whistles. "Damn."

"It was like he was somebody I'd known forever," Juliette says as she caps the last bottle. "I felt like I had met a kindred spirit." She and Edgar each take a bottle of colostrum and head for the back of the barn, where the newborns spend their first weeks. Edgar and Juliette never had a baby together, but together they raised three children from their first marriages. "I was always atypical around how to be with kids, and it wasn't until I met Edgar that I met anybody who was similar," Juliette remembers. Both were against using threats, intimidation or fear with their children, instead seeking a respectful relationship built on clear communication. "I had to learn to do that. I wasn't sure how you commanded respect if a kid was blatantly doing something you didn't want him to. Edgar was like that naturally."

Edgar's oldest daughter, Anisa, who left for college before her father married Juliette, remembers him as gleeful and open-minded. When she was ten, she wanted to have two friends sleep over but wasn't sure if it was okay. Edgar not only agreed but invited every kid in the neighborhood. She says that he was the perfect mixture of playmate and parent. "I don't remember him ever yelling," she says as if realizing the novelty. "He would just sit down and talk to us, and we responded to that. He understood kids and treated them like people."

Edgar and Juliette are more than just parents—they're mentors. None can attest to this better than Pedro. He recently moved away from home and is trying to become a better man, to "do things right." He says that Edgar and Juliette listen to him, look past his wrongs and see him for who he is. They enable him to open his heart. "They're like people who lived on this earth and then came back again," Pedro says. "Nothing but knowledge, nothing but heart, nothing but love to offer. I feel like they're angels."

Angels they may be, but Edgar and Juliette are convinced that the true divine being rests with the animals. In the back of this barn alone, both of them have experienced an extraordinary connection between themselves, the cows, and what Edgar calls "the other side." Juliette recalls nurturing to health Mason, a calf born with a heart defect. He was more than thirty feet away in the barn when she murmured, "Mason, I love you," and he looked up, trotted over to her and pushed his head against her. "It's like the animals know what I'm thinking," she says, fingering a small braid above her ear. "It amazed me at first, but now it's just part of the fabric woven into our everyday life."

In its hay-lined hutch, the unnamed calf lows when she sees Edgar and Juliette coming. She wobbles to them on unsteady legs. Juliette kneels beside her and Edgar rubs her cheek, letting her nibble his fingers. He straddles the fledgling calf and semi-locks her head between his knees to keep her focused on finding the bottle. Nudging his free hand with her rosy nose, she licks his skin, jacket, pants. "Hey, girl," he coos. She locates the bottle and almost yanks it from his hand, inhaling her milk. "She's not shy; she takes what she wants," Edgar chuckles, stroking her velvet fur. "I can tell she has attitude." The calf hiccups and moos. He offers her a second bottle, and she takes it, her ears wiggling with pleasure. Edgar feeds his calf and hums a low tune, filling the farm with the sound of his spirit.

The Mammoth, No Longer a Thing of the Past

BAILEY HWA, Grade 8, Age 13. J. Lupton Simpson Middle School, Leesburg, VA, Debra Sheridan, *Teacher*

Falling back into time, to the ancient, long-lost age of dinosaurs, colossal giants towered over the blood-stained land, mercilessly eviscerating their prey with teeth as sharp as knives. Lush vegetation painted the world in a multitude of bright colors, as if it were a masterpiece collage. One fateful day that would change the course of history, they met their end as countless, burning meteors rained down from the sky, tearing the earth apart, leaving only death and mass destruction. For many years, these beasts have been ghosts of our long-lost past, with their faint essence imprinted in rock. However, it will be a matter of time before scientists resurrect these massive creatures via genetic engineering. In Japan, scientists have set their eyes not on the dinosaurs, but the woolly mammoth, an ancient, extinct cousin to the modern elephant. However the result turns out, this project will make a crucial impact on our nearing future.

The project, led by Akira Iritani and a collaboration of the world's brightest geneticists, hopes to bring back this gargantuan by the year 2017 for a multitude of reasons. In particular,

Mr. Iritani is primarily interested and engrossed in finding the underlying, shrouded truth about the mammoth's unknown lifestyle. He says, "After the mammoth is born, we'll examine its ecology and genes to study why the species became extinct and other factors." In addition to the mammoth, other extinct species, such as the dinosaurs, could be brought back to life, allowing scientists to examine the creatures to the upmost capacity. From cloning a beloved, deceased pet to growing replacements for people in need, this project can open many doors for new methods and improvement. To an extreme, this technology can be taken to the next level, when applied to humans.

The roots of this magnate project lead back to 2008, when Teruhiko Wakayama, a brilliant, eminent geneticist, successfully produced a clone from a dead mouse. Frozen in a laboratory for sixteen years, the mouse and its minuscule cells were dead, but mostly intact. With the utmost caution, his team of scientists removed the dead mouse's nucleus, thousands of times smaller than the sharp, piercing tip of a needle, fusing it into an egg cell. As a result, thirteen thriving identical clones were produced. This breakthrough conveyed a clear, yet significant message; cloning a mammoth was no longer a mere idea but a reality. All that was needed was the genetic material of a woolly mammoth.

Fortunately, in 2010, the remains of a mammoth were discovered in isolated, frozen Siberia. The mammoth, though dead, remained preserved and frozen in the motionless ice, almost intact as if time itself had never passed. Frozen deep in the ice for 10,000 years, the mammoth, presumed to be three years old at the time of its death, was given the name Yuka. Unlike other mammoth remains, Yuka's matted brown fur, which protected her from the biting winds and extreme temperatures, still remains on isolated patches on her massive body. A closer look at Yuka's body reveals bloody gashes lining her flesh, showing its end by the bloody, sharp fangs and claws of saber-toothed cats. Taking a closer look inside, one can see that the mammoth was severely injured by predators, with broken, fractured bones and missing organs, in addition to its pink flesh torn to shreds. The most unique aspect of the mammoth is that it was preserved well, despite being in permafrost, a rock-hard, deep layer of ice, which is known to devour organic matter, leaving nothing behind. Because of Yuka's cell preservation, its cells would be used a year later, at the start of the mammoth project.

After many tiresome years of research, on January 2011, Akira Iritani and his team began the project, hoping for the best in the next six years of perspiration. Using the valuable research from Teruhiko Wakayama, he created an accurate, theoretical process of his own. By extracting the nucleus from one of Yuka's minuscule, preserved cells, which were frozen in a laboratory, he can then implant it into an African elephant's egg cell, which will then be put back into a female elephant. From there on, the mammoth will begin its lengthy birth process. However, before beginning the process, the team is still debating on the ethical concerns if a mammoth is successfully cloned. Some members fear the public's negative reaction of a cloned mammoth. Biologists are concerned with the ecological damage it could cause. Others are terrified of the mammoth's unparalleled power, as it could toss aside a car with a mere flick of its head. To the greatest extent, the return of extinct species, portrayed as a fantasy in *Jurassic Park*, is now one of the ominous possibilities of this controversial experiment.

Despite what the public's conflicted opinions are, the project will continue to move forward, shrouded in secrecy.

Binary Switch

HANA LEE, Grade 12, Age 16. Oregon Episcopal School, Portland, OR,
Art Ward, *Teacher*

CHARACTERS

STEPHEN–male human, about twenty-five, zoo specimen,
also known as X13 or Mimicry Platform Mendacity

TOUR GUIDE–android, gender irrelevant, dresses fashionably

WOMAN–female android, zoo visitor, dresses fashionably

MAN–male android, zoo visitor, dresses fashionably

SETTING
The setting is a small, bare room with gray walls. In the
center of the room is a zoo cage with iron bars, about six by
six by eight feet, roped off for viewing. No other furniture is
necessary. The scene is meant to look stark and artificial.

TIME
Either late fall or early spring. The time period is vaguely
futuristic.

SCENE ONE
(First setting—the room with the cage. Sitting inside the
cage, playing idly with a broken yo-yo, is STEPHEN. He

looks about twenty-five and is wearing a gray business suit faded and torn by long years of use. From his posture and expression, it's obvious that he's been locked in the cage for an interminable amount of time—perhaps a dozen years or more. Trickling in and out of the room at random are the zoo visitors. From appearances alone, they seem to be ordinary people, but their movements are sometimes strangely inorganic. Their outfits are impeccably fashionable, as if picked straight from the pages of designer magazines. They speak in hushed voices as they gaze upon STEPHEN but do not interact with him. At length, a woman enters the room, followed by a group of people.)

TOUR GUIDE
And here is our number one exhibit, the one you've all been waiting for, the pièce de résistance: Homo sapiens. Or "people," as some of you prefer to call them.

(The group of visitors crowds around STEPHEN's cage, but in an orderly fashion, so everyone gets a good look. STEPHEN does not react to their presence. He continues to play with the broken yo-yo, his eyes dull and his movements mechanical.)

WOMAN
I have a query.

TOUR GUIDE
Go right ahead.

WOMAN
Does this specimen suffer from Mendelian Syndrome?

TOUR GUIDE
Great question. X13, as we like to call him, is one of only a few captive specimens on the planet. Like the rest of his kind,

the virus of the syndrome is present in his cells, but as far as we can tell, he is healthier than ninety-nine percent of the specimens we've studied.

MAN
What is he wearing?

TOUR GUIDE
That is his tribal costume.

MAN
It looks a little like . . . clothing.

TOUR GUIDE
Yes, we have determined through analysis that it is composed of the same material and through the same procedures as our own clothing. His species is difficult to observe in the wild, but it is possible that they acquired the technique for manufacturing clothing from our own service sector.

MAN
I see. Thank you for the addition to my data banks.

TOUR GUIDE
No problem. That is my purpose.

(One of the visitors approaches the rope surrounding the exhibit and gazes intently at STEPHEN. As he does so, STEPHEN fumbles and drops the yo-yo.)

WOMAN
What organic behavior! How fascinating.

TOUR GUIDE
Try commanding him to pick up the toy. Sometimes he responds to verbal stimulus.

WOMAN
A command? I don't have the proper superiority protocol to do that.

TOUR GUIDE
No problem. X13 is an organic. He doesn't require superiority protocol. Go ahead and give him a simple command.

WOMAN
X13, Command. Pick up the toy.

(STEPHEN rolls his head slowly to the side to look at the visitors for the first time. The entire group is silent, waiting for him to act. After a few moments, he looks away and buries his head in his hands. His shoulders tremble noiselessly.)

MAN
I've heard that Homo sapiens are prone to self-deletion in captivity. Has he made any attempts?

TOUR GUIDE
X13's brain patterns have been regular for the past eleven years. We have not detected the chemical imbalance that usually precedes an attempt at self-deletion. No, I don't think we have to worry about losing our star exhibit for some time yet.

MAN
It's a shame their lifespans are so short.

TOUR GUIDE
Yes, it is. We have run some genetic reprogramming simulations, but nothing is foolproof yet. We hope to discover a solution to his species' high mortality and low fertility rates, as well as a way to counteract Mendelian Syndrome.

MAN
Why haven't more data resources been devoted to the task?

TOUR GUIDE
Well, we are also working on recovery programs for several species of Bovinae and Sciuridae. The dung beetle also has a fascinating life cycle that we would like to devote some of our resources to studying. Our aim is to preserve these species physically as well as electronically, to allow a more holistic integration into our visitors' data banks.

MAN
I understand.

TOUR GUIDE
Good. On our way out, I invite you to peruse our data wall. There are some entries there on Homo sapiens recovery efforts that you may find educational.

(The visit to this exhibit is over. The tour guide leaves the room, followed by the rest of the group except for HEGEMO-NY. She is dressed in a brown vest, knee-high brown leather boots, and a burnt-orange scarf straight from the pages of an autumn-issue fashion magazine. She moves closer to the cage, remaining beyond the rope line, and studies STEPHEN in silence for a few moments.)

STEPHEN
I can feel you looking at me. Why are you still here?

HEGEMONY
You're speaking to me.

STEPHEN
Haven't you seen enough?

HEGEMONY
I've never communicated with an organic before.

(STEPHEN lifts his head from his hands.)

STEPHEN
You don't communicate. You exchange data. I don't have anything to offer you. Go away.

HEGEMONY
On the contrary, you have much to offer me.

STEPHEN
Nothing you can't find on the data wall.

HEGEMONY
I have already exhausted the data wall.

STEPHEN
You mean . . . you read the whole thing?

HEGEMONY
Yes.

STEPHEN
But you can't possibly have stored everything. That's . . . I don't even know how much that is.

HEGEMONY
Slightly over two exabytes of data.

STEPHEN
Exabytes? That's 2 million terabytes. You've got to be kidding me. Where are you keeping it?

HEGEMONY
(places a hand on her sternum) Here.

STEPHEN
So you're a walking Library of Congress.

HEGEMONY
Approximately three hundred Libraries of Congress.

STEPHEN
But why? Why would you need that much data?

HEGEMONY
I value data equally. I am a singular platform with no purpose
other than to assemble random data.

STEPHEN
But that data has already been assembled. That's what the
wall is for. You wouldn't make a hard copy of the Internet.
It isn't logical. You things are all about logic. (He comes to a
realization.) You're broken. Aren't you?

HEGEMONY
(quietly) There is a flaw in my programming.

STEPHEN
So that makes you . . . what? A datamaniac?

HEGEMONY
I do not know that word.

STEPHEN
That's because I made it up.

HEGEMONY
Oh. Invention.

STEPHEN
Yeah. It's something we humans do. You know, when we
aren't locked up in cages.

HEGEMONY
Cage? This is a container for your own protection.

STEPHEN
Doesn't matter what it's for. It's still a cage. And caged birds
don't sing. We have to fly free for that. You . . . do you get
metaphors, or am I just wasting my time?

HEGEMONY
I have recorded data on metaphorical language.

STEPHEN
Of course you have. Hey, listen. You're broken, right? You're
not like the rest of them. The machines, I mean.

HEGEMONY
I am unique.

STEPHEN
Good. That's great. We have something in common. Could you
do me a favor? Could you bypass that lock right there? It only
responds to electronic pulses, so I can't do it, but you could
open it. There isn't even a code.

HEGEMONY
You wish to be released.

STEPHEN
Yeah. You wouldn't mind that, right?

HEGEMONY
It is against zoo policy to release a specimen without
authorization.

STEPHEN
But you don't follow their rules, dammit. You said you were broken.

HEGEMONY
Flawed. Not broken.

STEPHEN
I should have known. But I had to try, didn't I? You could have been the one in a million. My ticket out of here. A free ride home.

(STEPHEN picks up the yo-yo from the floor of the cage and turns it over in his hands, staring at it. Suddenly, he smashes it on the floor, shattering the toy beyond repair. His mood appears to swing rapidly from casual to enraged.)

Just get out of here! Useless hunk of blasted metal. I should have known.

(STEPHEN turns his back on HEGEMONY, curling into a ball on the floor of his cage. His frame quivers, but it isn't clear whether he's sobbing or laughing silently. HEGEMONY observes him coolly for a few more moments, then leaves. End scene.)

YIHAN CHOU, *Manticores, Set #1 (Shame, or Just Separation Anxiety?),*
Drawing. Grade 11, Age 17, Sharron Art Center, East Brunswick, NJ.
Sharron Liu, *Teacher.*

Bronx Rooftop Song

GABRIELLA GONZALES, Grade 11, Age 16. Bard High School Early College, New York, NY, Elizabeth Poreba, *Teacher*

On the mansard roof, girls stick like flies
to the sloping shingles. Little buggers
with Lucy's kaleidoscope eyes,
omniscient in the pinkening sky.

One-two: the neighbors shut their windows tight
to steep in inner dimming light. The dishes
stack up sweetly on the countertop.
Behind their curtains, couples fight

while girls sing love songs to the sky.
Their skirts flutter about their unlotioned thighs.
Their breath catches in their wreathing hair;
their ankles flex in the gutter where

their toes strain against dead leaves & silt
with a Balanchine air. One-two:
they let their stockings slip and fall
like burnt and blackened embers to the ground.

The boys below file by like sheep.
The girls' throats test a reveille.
One-two: the neighbors shut their eyes;
they might have heard a lullaby.

Expanding

HALEY LEE, Grade 11, Age 15. Basis Scottsdale, Scottsdale, AZ,
Hadley Ruggles, *Teacher*

Wings dipped in the iron of the sun slice like butter knives.
Clipped, combed.
You are a cosmonaut, a moon dancer.
Your pastpresentfuture is ripe and blushing,
sweeter than the time the night fluttered on our lips, unfurled
on our hips.
Locked, looped.
I am sorry
for the broken glass
and the way we were constantly expanding,
but for every breath we spend, the universe takes one more
step toward chaos.
Fall into me; teach me how to sew the layers of us into
something new.
Bloom, burst.
Your eyes remind me of velvet mornings when the gray-
tinged-pink-sprayed-orange
spilled onto our thighs like a prayer.
We are heavenly bodies pickpocketing the cosmos.
Warm-blooded, bold.
I know the way spring skies will pulse.

daughter one

ALINE DOLINH, Grade 9, Age 14. Oakton High School, Vienna, VA,
Katherine Hovanec, *Teacher*

My mother was the one who taught me
how to turn my heart to stone. Make your eyes dark like
bullet holes, she whispers softly
while braiding my hair. Set your mouth like a razor blade. The
war is not yet over.
Of all the children, I was old enough to remember
the acrid tang of napalm, blooms of crimson on the humid air,
the swelling flares of gunfire. I tell myself
to get used to the weight of that stone hanging heavy in my
chest.
They'd said I'd never be pretty here, so I want to become
beautiful instead—
but the terrible sort of beauty, the kind that makes men die,
the kind that launches a thousand ships. I want a revolution
that brings up the blood.
A long time ago, I tore out the threads
fastened to my heart. There's electricity in my veins
that could burn cities to the ground.

pulp

STEFANIA GOMEZ, Grade 12, Age 17. University of Chicago Lab School, Chicago, IL, Stephen Granzyk, *Teacher*

years sit on her
vertebrae like young
nectarines. She curls,
dripping
condensed tongues
on paper
like mercury,
licking them and
sticking them
down with her
thumb, gripping
canvas dish so they don't
blow away, rounding
corners with her fingers
like bits of inky earth.
She has stopped flinching
when her nails fill
with purple viscera
like ripe plum circles
or black eyes.
She rakes
them deeper into
porcelain, mixes her mud
with sewer grates,
bark, warm
teeth, Chicago
accents, flecked cement

Haiku for an Extravagant & Wheeling Stranger

LUCY WAINGER, Grade 10, Age 15. Stuyvesant High School, New York, NY, Eric Grossman, *Teacher*

Oppressed, repressed, compressed, depressed, hard-pressed, expressed, impressed; hollowed out, inside-out, I'm moving out, my insides are out. My insides are brick red. My insect insides are iridescent. My insides are sprawled all over the sidewalk in a Fibonacci sequence spiraling toward the edges, the edges of the city, the spherical planet of surgery, the edges of the discriminant which equals negative twelve which equals "nothing is real" plastered on the faces of every boy who dared to look down. Every boy who showed me his hand streaked with semen & seaweed-green tattoos, a jack of clubs, the queen of hearts, the queen of the heartland, my insides embedded in the mountainside. The jack of clubs is a soldier & he looks down, dares to look down the cliff like a woman's shirtfront, where crushed cars lay rusted to the grass, moving out, men, we're moving out. Fracture, fixture, mixture, picturesque postcard pasture infested & festering with love, filtered through love, supersaturated with love! I am depressed but I am also impressed. I am radioactive. I am gripping this basement couch like it's my ticket to nirvana & I am kissing him everywhere in the dark, his chin, his throat, the walls, the floor, his scientist's hands (in the city of depressed & also impressed) that are obsessive & compulsive & impulsive & convulsing across my hollow chest, but are also careful, his hands which are also careful.

Halidom

MCKAYLA CONAHAN, Grade 11, Age 16. South Carolina Governor's
School for the Arts and Humanities, Greenville, SC,
Mamie Morgan, *Teacher*

spring pee·per
(ˈspring ˈpē-pər) *n.*
small, chorus frog,
esp. one that makes
a peeping sound: as
in, a peeper found
my toes; the peepers
under the eaves
predicted the
oncoming rain with
their faint, alien
singing; peepers
flung themselves
into swimming pool
filters; my brother
buried dozens of
dead peepers.

ver·te·brae
(ˈvər·tə·-brā) *n.*
the bones of
the spinal column;
the hinge of the
body: as in, frogs
have nine vertebrae;

I have twenty-four
vertebrae corrupting
the direction of my
toes; that frog's nine
vertebrae hinged
the wrong way,
turned that body
vacant on the
swimming pool side
concrete.

tac·it
('ta-sət) *adj.*
understood without
having to be said: as
in, the pool party
was; my little
brother's pitter-
patter run from
there to the pond;
his carrying two
frogs at a time; the
children sitting feet
drawn up from the
water; Mia, the only
little girl I ever
babysat, girl pope,
her fingers over
broken frog limbs,
and all that
chlorinated holy
water, she was, she
was.

In the Summer

KIRA PELOWITZ, Grade 12, Age 17. A.I.M.S. at the University of
New Mexico, Albuquerque, NM, Ben Mitchell, *Teacher*

in the Summer, I write ripe poems;
I write honey and sun poems;
I write fermenting poems, I write mushroom poems;
I write sweet-scent dirt poems.

nothing is ripe here during the Summer,
but I don't write char poems;
I don't write dust poems;
I don't write poems slick with sweat.

I write wind and sandstone poems instead;
I write poems where the wind makes the mountains a flute;
I write ribcage and hipbone poems;
I write poems that crumple below the weight of swollen
stone-fruits.

I don't write poems that wake up damp;
I don't write parched poems, or
poems that shrivel around the edges;
I don't write sunburnt poems.

I write heartbeat and blood poems that disguise as love poems
instead;
I write rain poems disguised as love poems, and
love poems that pool on the collarbones of rain poems, and
I write lying poems instead.

I don't write moist-palmed nervous poems, or
poems that have to catch their breath,
but I do write moon poems, and
oyster poems instead.

I write sulfur-geyser poems.
I write deep-sea, translucent poems.
I write night-time poems, and I
write moon poems instead.

because I cannot reach the moon:
I write lying poems filled with rain;
I write poems full of the sumptuous night
and poems that ripple when touched.

I write moon poems that hide in oyster poems,
and palm poems full of oysters;
I write poems where I drink the moon
slick, and soft, and cool.

The Coming of the End

CALEB RAK, Grade 8, Age 13. Integrated Day Charter School, Norwich, CT, Melissa Dearborn, *Teacher*

The coming of the end
Gather round from all the Villages
Breathe dissent on the treaties
Forget the heirlooms
Leave without copper pots in the bag
Escape the fallen suns
Unleash the corks
Free the wines roaming essence
Keep the Jovial till safety

Timelord's Burden

RACHEL HARGRAVE, Grade 10, Age 15. Charlotte Latin School, Charlotte, NC, Richard Harris, *Teacher*

Running through the trees
From red-faced devils
Murderous angels
Creeping along rotting tunnels
Sneaking through the hulls of abandoned alien ships
The curve of your smile as you laughed
This is why I don't walk by angel statues anymore
Fighting dragons on horseback
Watching stars begin and die
Fading, exploding into dust
In the same day
Your eyes as blue as a midsummer's day
So full of wonder
At every new thing we found
You, golden glowing,
Energy coursing through you
Laughter bursting out in the darkest of nights
You, staring at the stars
Their ethereal light shining in your curious eyes
The whole universe in your imagination
Stars that burn cold as the souls of the monsters we slayed
And planets made of diamonds, glittering crystal
Midnight suns and twin galaxies
Swirling, twirling, never ending
Before you left
Before you were taken
Stuck on opposite sides

Of a permanent wall
Between realities
And all I have
Is a lingering scent of roses
A pair of reading glasses
And a jacket you forgot
Like you forgot me
Your Raggedy Man
Martian Boy
Your Doctor

Wolf in the Desert

ROBERT BEDELL, Grade 12, Age 17. Pine View School, Osprey, FL,
Paul Dean, *Teacher*

I long to be a wolf in the desert,
assassin of the sands,
conspirator with the moon.
    Two hunters,
    the wind and I,
    sink teeth like scimitars
    into dying apathy,
    savor each leap and lunge,
    each succulent taste of meat;
        Raging
        for a world of fertile danger,
        life or death
        by the strength of my will.

—to be an explorer on the shore,
star-crossed lover of the endless sea,
in a world neither scouted nor surveyed,
its secrets kept safe from the ink of a map.
    By night, to sleep,
    and in sleep, to dream,
    of the waking dawn and a new unknown;
        To corner the horizon,
        tear off all its mystery,
        and make passionate acquaintance
        to its naked curves:
        To taste the sun
        like honey on my tongue.

—to be a poet in the wilderness,
carving sagas into the green earth,
digging for verses in writhing dirt,
to bleed crimson emotion
into the virgin soil;
    Then, panting,
    to bathe in a crystal stream,
    drawing zealous artistic fantasy
    with the palette of the wild.
        Embracing base desire,
        to ride creation's beasts.

I long to be a vision,
with a fire in my heart
and a lover by my side,
guiding me onward through
the luscious insanity
of nature at its richest.

—to live,
and then to die,
to fall into the arms of one last sleep,
and to sleep
knowing that I have lived these dreams.

steeplechase rd.

ALISON LIU, Grade 11, Age 16. Edmond-North High School, Edmond, OK, Bjorn Bauer, *Teacher*

it was the fall of dead crickets.
we swept them out of the garage with
the brooms that came in our halloween costumes
and sat on the curb to hear the crackle
of tired rubber grinding new asphalt.
sometimes we walked to the gas station,
bought orange soda to drink through sour-patch straws
and with the change, we laid
rusted pennies to sleep on the train tracks
and carried thin copper luckthings on thread.
we dug up summer's last dandelions
and raised them in Mama's glass bowls
until she made us replace the holes in the yard.
well that was okay, we just ran to the creek
and folded our once-upon-a-times
into paper boats.
witches trickled tears shed from
God's cruel lashes
onto children who climbed electrical towers
to hold the nervous currents at their toes
and we raised our faces like november turkeys to taste
october rain.

Survival Is a Roast You Have to Keep on Carving

MEGGIE ROYER, Grade 12, Age 18. Ames High School, Ames, LA, Joe Brekke, *Teacher*

Because no matter how hard you try, your grandfather will always
keep coming back into your sister's room.
In grade school you learned how to carve a steak with both hands
and a knife, the fork weeping in between your fingers.
They put the shank on a platter with the blood pooled like wine
around the ribs, and all you can do
is stare at it until the meat vanishes from the bone
and everything is beautiful again.
Because your sister's door will always be locked, the key tossed over
his shoulder like salt at a wedding
to keep the evil spirits away.
You are proud of your wounds
and display them on your sleeves where your heart should be.
Inside the cupboards at age four you found
a box of matches and twenty-five candles,
laid out polished and clean like quiet slivers of the moon.
You wondered what the strip of rough red on the side of the box will do,
and struck a match against it just to find out.
The room ignited; for years after you will dream of your mother's hair
orange and golden gossamer around the cool white circle of her scalp.

Because even your father stops trying
to shine a light under the door, and you can hear the bed
rattling even with the pillow pulled taut over your head.
Once you caught a moth in a mason jar and left it on your neighbor's
doorstep, where she picked it up the next day
and set it free,
its tiny body shivering feebly through the trees.
Because when you visit your sister at college
she still has the old family photo album
tucked away in her desk drawer
with dirty singed Polaroids of your grandfather and her
laughing during summer,
his arm settled firm around her shoulders
as if trying to keep her from getting away.

Destination

PARKER ELKINS, Grade 7, Age 12. Center for Teaching & Learning,
Edgecomb, ME, Nancie Atwell, *Teacher*

The car stops, and you leap out
without waiting for me,
too eager to begin our lifelong tradition
of running down the driveway,
tree branches snatching at our faces,
soft moss on bare feet.
And I run, gasping, sprinting,
stumbling after you, until, at last
I reach the cabin, far behind you,
and, at last, we sprint down the rough-hewn
wooden stairs and onto the beach
of hard stones and sharp, dry seaweed—
a counterpoint to fine moss—
and we sift through pebbles
worn smooth by pounding surf
and twelve-foot seas in the winter,
and we search for elusive seaglass,
brother and sister left with memories
of days spent lounging in the sun, sitting on the rocks,
beachcombing on the way to Parker's Point,
and I will treasure them all.

The Heroic Actions of a Girl Stuck in the Middle

MARY ROSE WEBER, Grade 7, Age 13. Saint Joseph Grade School, South Bend, IN, Melissa Green, *Teacher*

It happened so fast
One moment Kennedy was pulling up in his limo
He was right next to us
He waved right at me
I swear he did
Then I heard a shot
And he was slumped over in his seat
Blood was covering Mrs. Kennedy
Mass panic swept through the area within two seconds
Charlotte's parents tried to push us aside to get us away
When
There was another shot
And I saw pieces of my hero's skull fly through the sir
In that I swear very moment the world stopped
I stood stock-still
And all of a sudden I figured it out
I knew who killed Kennedy
I knew what my parents had been talking about that night
I knew I could have prevented this before it had happened
But I hadn't
I hadn't told anyone
I let my father continue to do those awful things
And it had come to this
I knew what Da had told me about his time in the Marines
Where you could make that shot

I looked up and saw the Texas School Book Depository
Where Da worked
And I knew he would come up guilty
I knew the evidence would point to him
They would find his gun
He wouldn't hide it very well
But the question burning inside me right now
Mixed with the sudden grief was
When Da came up guilty in court
Would I stand by him?
Or even could I?

A Crane-ian Homage

KATHERINE FANG, Grade 12, Age 17. Bellaire High School, Bellaire, TX, Carole Bagley, *Teacher*

I.
On the corner of Wisteria and Oak
I saw a woman, half-clothed, hair flying,
Who, lips pulled down at the corners,
Tugged along her heart in a cart behind her.
I inquired, "Is it heavy, poor one?"
"It is weighty," she answered.
"But I don't know how else to transport it."

II.
At the park
I saw an old man, weary, allergic,
Who, leash in hand,
Chased behind his heart as it led him among the trees.
I observed, "That is a good pet, sir."
"But it wants much airing out," he countered.
"In winter, it shivers,
And I have to swaddle it in laundry."

III.
In the forest
I saw a creature, clear-eyed, rebellious,
Who, kneeling upon the ground,
Held his heart in his hands and prayed to it.
I investigated.
"I wearied of listening to it," he answered before I spoke.
"But I wondered, if I whispered to it,
Whether it would respond."

IV.

On the gravel driveway

I saw a young man, absorbed, muttering,

Who, magnifier in hand,

Focused sunbeams on the asphalt and on his heart.

Shocked [he was so young], I asked, "What is it you intend, lad?"

"What I intend," he frowned,

Batting distractedly at the air near where I spoke,

"Is of course for it to shrivel.

But it has yet to look like a raisin.

Perhaps it is not the right time of year."

V.

In a garden

I saw a sprite, eyes twinkling, wearing leaf-garlands,

Who, squatting upon the ground,

Planted her heart in the earth and beseeched it to multiply.

I asked, "Will that work, elf?"

"Of course," it answered.

"All seeds populate.

I breathe over it and wait until its progeny rings open."

Judgment Day

FRANCESCA SEDLACEK, Grade 7, Age 12. P.S. duPont Middle School,
Wilmington, DE, Tracy Selekman, *Teacher*

The fawn-like children scream shrilly,
As they venture through the lush green jungle,
Aware of silent black hunters eyeing them like vultures.
The drip drop of the after rain leaves
Are the only sounds they hear
Before the sickening smell of death is upon them
Judgment Day has begun in the quiet velvet night.

Ate My House for Dinner

ASHLEY CRUTCHER, Grade 8, Age 13. Cornerstone Homeschoolers, Salunga, PA, Elizabeth Jones, *Teacher*

I ate my house for dinner,
It tasted very good.
It took about three days
Because of all the wood.
First I ate the windows,
And all the shutters too,
Though there were lots of nails
That I wish would have been glue.

Then I ate the siding
Leaving nothing but bare wood,
It tasted much like plastic wrap,
Which isn't very good.
I ate the doors and doorknobs,
Which got stuck down in my gut.
I wish they had been open
Instead of being shut.

After the doors and doorknobs
I ate right through the walls,
Which wasn't very easy,
So I began to bawl.
Last I ate the furnishings,
The chairs and tables too,
The whole meal was very tasty—
Don't you wish that I was you?

The Cleaner

BRIANNA BREAUX, Grade 11, Age 17. New Orleans Center for Creative Arts, New Orleans, LA, Lara Naughton, *Teacher*

Your keys are rubbing my thighs
like come on
in. I know you
will be out all day

anyway
so I do. I ghost
backroom to parlor, opening
blinds to let in light
as soft as clean
sheets on Sunday morning, tender, pure,
if unclean; I could be

in Church.
Your house
is quiet as dust. Alone, I kneel
in the mouth
of the drains, and open each

jewelry box, hungry,
but I know you
trust me.

Origin

OLIVIA LINN, Grade 11, Age 16. Wyoming High School, Wyoming, OH,
Keith Lehman, *Teacher*

I saw a goddess yesterday. She was dressed in all pearls and sil-
vers; the long, light, gauzy fabric that just brushed the tops of
her feet was quietly shocking in February in line at the Seven
Hills DMV. Her skin was like spring mulch. It glistened and I
thought it might have smelled like earth. The creases in her
wrists were folds of night against the lace of her shawl like
snow. Her

lips were roses and words fell from them like poems. I
thought it must have been the language of her ancestors—of
her people of the earth, people who might have been trees so
many years ago—her hands still resembled the toughness of
oak and work.

Her language was full of vibrant undertones, clicks and
throaty syllables, pockets of color like music, so that it cannot
be spoken. What I imagined is her

singing her origins softly, but resolutely, to her sixteen-year-
old daughter, who has forgone her mother's angel-garb for dark
wash jeans and a teal Aeropostale T-shirt. The harshness of
this color clashes with the music in the woman's voice as the
daughter responds sharply in English.

Unyieldingly, the goddess of language and color and roots
pushes forth with ever-more-urgent clicks of her tongue in a
language the teenager can't help but understand. She switches
to English: Evidently, she was reminding her daughter to go to
the grocery store. "Eggs, milk, bread," she said. "Please do not
forget."

The Human Condition

JOHN LHOTA, Grade 9, Age 15. Hunter College High School, New York, NY, Rebecca Wallace-Segall, Molly Haas-Hooven, *Teachers*

Corroded. Dull. Broken.

I remember the day I first saw this watch. The glass was so clean I could see my reflection in it. The metal was the kind of shade that shouldn't even exist, but does. Too beautiful to be real. So reflective, you can barely even see what color it really is.

It doesn't even work anymore. They've put it in a museum now. "Artifacts of the pre-intellectual capitalist period."

It smelled like metal, the kind of bittersweet smell that burns your nostrils as you smell it, but makes you long for it right afterward.

Now that it's locked behind glass, I wonder what it smells like. I can barely even see it through my own reflection, so I switch to looking at that.

I don't recognize my face. Is this what I looked like when she gave it to me?

Is this what I looked like on the day they all died?

I wander around the museum for the rest of the day. Part of me wants to go back and look at the watch, and the other half of me wants to get as far away from this place as I can. I hurry past the whining children, the sacred headdresses, the works of art, the bored security guards. The tourists with sunglasses. The school-groups of unruly children, and the underpaid teachers. None of them could understand. I wonder if this is really how they think of their past.

And suddenly I realize I am all alone. I've found my way into a dark hallway in the back of the museum. I look around. I don't see any exhibits. I keep looking, but don't remember how I got here. In this room, there are no exhibits. No artifacts. Nothing from the past. And suddenly, it's starting.

I hurry out of the room. I can't take this anymore. A man in a dark suit and sunglasses gives me a strange look, but I don't care. I need some air. I see a glass door, opening onto a balcony. It has a beautiful view. I can see out over the whole city. Toward the horizon, the sun sets over a dark-green forest. It is a mellow tangerine.

I blink slowly. Muffled laughter rings through my ears. I wince. It feels as if someone has been banging my head with an iron sledgehammer for the past hour. I try to open my eyes, then quickly close them again. I take a deep breath, and slowly squint them open. I'm in a dark hallway. I limp toward a door, and peer outward at the sight of several politicians cheerily eating shrimp.

* * *

And now I am standing in the hot sun, holding a muddy brick. I look around; I am one of many placing mud bricks on top of each other, to dry in the hot sun. A little over, there is a house already dried. It doesn't have a door, but a ladder leads up to the roof. I suppose there might be a door up there.

* * *

I'm driving a car down a 1950s street. I look to the left, and see a store selling books.

* * *

I wake up and look around. I'm on a bus. A school bus. I look down. I'm wearing a blue shirt and jeans. I look at my hands. They're small. I'm probably in second or third grade. I'm sitting in the window seat. Another child is seated next to me. He has sandy hair and looks energetic.

Now all the children are getting up and walking out of the bus. I follow them.

It appears that we're in Washington, D.C. The teachers are leading us toward a big building, probably a museum. Upon closer inspection, it looks like the Smithsonian, the Air and Space one.

Once we enter the museum, the teachers let us walk around. Something about one of the rooms draws me in. The ceiling is tall, and suspended from the roof are three large planes. From left to right, I see the Wright Brothers' flimsy-looking mess of paper, wood, and dreams; a robust metal contraption that they say Amelia Earhart flew in; and a military jet painted with an angry-looking, out-of-place tiger.

For some reason, I'm entranced by this display. I don't quite know why, but there's something beautiful, something horrifying about this. I look at the tiger. On closer inspection, perhaps he's not angry. He really just looks confused.

A sharp voice breaks the solitude. "Jason! Hurry up!" It's one of the teachers. They're herding the children out of the building, trying to get them back to the bus. Based on what I'm hearing, we're visiting the White House. One of the teachers is explaining the elegance of our democracy.

And before you know it, we're back on the bus. Someone from across the aisle is whispering into the ear of the child next to me. It sounds like he said something about bananas. Then the child whispers the same thing into my ear. "The bananas fly planes!" he says enthusiastically. A girl from two rows forward shouts at us,

"Hey, what is it now?"

"No, we've gotta wait 'til it gets to the back of the bus," whines the sandy-haired boy.

"Just tell me!"

The boy sighs dejectedly. "Fine, it's 'The bananas fly planes,'" he says, matter-of-factly.

The girl giggles. "Ours was 'Cupcakes are yummy.'"

Chapter 0

Back before this all started, I belonged somewhere. It was before the leviathan of civilization ever reared its ugly head.

We were not so different from everyone else. We were cavemen, like them, banging rocks together.

They were bad at surviving, so I am the only one left.

* * *

I'm back in the dark hallway. I think I'm the same person. I now realize that the politicians must be at some sort of party. I notice that I am wearing a suit. I must be one of the politicians as well. Not knowing what else to do, I walk out and greet the others.

"Ron!" exclaims a man with gray hair in a black suit. "Good to see you."

I grin awkwardly, not quite sure what to say. "It's, uh, nice to see you too . . . "

"The shrimp here is great," comments a sleepy-eyed man. "By the way, what have you been thinking about that new thing . . . uh, HB1776 or whichever one it is."

* * *

I wake up on a sandy street. Bright midday sun is shining down on my face. I sit up and yawn. My face feels tight and dry.

There's not much activity on the street in front of me. I realize I must be some sort of homeless person. I look around. Up on a hill a mile or two away is a huge marble building. Considering the architecture, I figure I must be in Ancient Greece. Suddenly, I see some angry men running toward me and shouting. What would this man want me to do? Would he run?

Well, they're already here, and there's no point wondering anymore.

The men drag me down the street. And then I am gone.

* * *

I am an old man in a boat, with a damp, salty beard. The water is clear blue, and I can see all the way to the bottom of the ocean. I am holding a rope that leads to the water, so I pull, and up comes a cage full of lobsters. The lobsters look at me and blink.

* * *

I am wearing a suit and drinking champagne. A man sits next to me, talking about a book he is writing. A woman sits next to him and nods. A tear drips into my drink, and plunges through the pale liquid; why, I know not.

Chapter 1

My people were smarter, more creative. If souls exist, theirs were more beautiful than the most vibrantly pale flower ever written about in a rough draft of a movie script that was turned in as a college project and accidentally thrown out by the writer's professor. They cared about each other, and they just simply did whatever they knew was to be done. They knew that if everyone did that, they all would be fine, and they trusted that their friends would do the same good as them.

They were bad at surviving, and their time soon came. This is how I escaped. This is why I am the only one left.

* * *

And now, I am back with the politicians.

"—that people need to have guns that bad. I mean, when you look at the number of violent crimes that take place every year in America, you realize that you've gotta tighten the restrictions."

"Well, I'm just saying, people need the right to defend themselves from—"

* * *

An angry dog says woof to me. I pet it and say hello. It frowns and walks away.

Fur the color of chocolate.

* * *

And there I am, an Ancient Roman soldier, dragging a shouting Jewish man down the street. Should I let him go? What would happen to the soldier? He's hardly the helpless one, but—

* * *

Paris, sipping a wine that tastes so peculiar, it has to cost at least a few thousand dollars per bottle. I think back to a few seconds ago. It seems so surreal, and yet I can't deny that it happened. I keep staring at the red liquid for a few minutes, and wonder why it's so expensive. I pick up the glass, and slowly swish it around.

* * *

They holler, running down the street with their inverted metal crosses. The rush of sunburnt energy fuels their shouts as the last of the troops enter the Holy City. The crosses whip around through the air like leaves in a hurricane, the soldiers using all the solid adrenaline for the impossible task of barely hanging on. Even as the men around me pierce their armored hearts and blood pumps to the flat and dusty earth, I hear shouts of death to Muslims, and cheers for the disciples who will at long last worship on this land again. I'm horrified, and I don't know where to go.

But as I whirl around in this scarlet kaleidoscope, part of me wonders if it would really be so bad to just let go, give up, release all the love and fury and pent-up exhaustion that's been building and building for as long as I could think and breathe and feel, to lift the sword and look into his eyes and let it fall. And suddenly the sword feels heavy, heavier than anything I've ever had to lift, and I can't hold it up anymore.

* * *

As I fall into the waves of the dark black sea, hitting their surface and feeling the sudden cold, I realize that I do not want to die, and with the single fact, a frenzy of emotion washes over my body just like the cold, briny splashes that slowly spread goosebumps across every inch of my skin. I realize this means I'm going to have to swim, so I lift my arm forward—

* * *

And the blade penetrates his chest. I barely register that I'm back on the batteground from before, and as I look around, I still feel faint prickles of the icy abyss, just beyond the feel of my skin and the reach of my mind and the armor I wear. And yet it somehow feels warm, and stuffy, and I need to do something, to fight, and though I don't know what will happen if I die here, I can't find out, and as the next soldiers advance up the line to the fight, and they roar at the top of their lungs, I find myself caught up in the sheer volume, the sound waves lifting up my arm, and I join in the cry, rushing forward with the gargantuan mass of human flesh, ready to die for their cause, and

* * *

I'm still shouting, still rushing forward, barely taking an instant to see that I am now on the other side, rushing toward the others

* * *

And I'm still shouting, and I lift my sword

* * *

higher and higher with every scream that joins in the incomprehensible blurring of sound and passion and energy

* * *

And I don't even know whose side I'm on anymore, but I just keep shouting, back

* * *

and forth

* * *

and back

* * *

and forth, and the two sides blur, it's all one continuous scream, and as our lines meet, and our swords finally fall, it doesn't matter. I don't need to know where I am, there is no order or formation or confounded clever strategy; now the only thing left that can matter in this world is how I thrust my sword forward with every last piece of ragged put-together strength in this feebly muscular body—

* * *

and kill

* * *

and kill

* * *

and kill.

Chapter 2

There is no past, and there is no future.

There is only an infinite amount of isolated, unrelated moments.

None of them contain any context. They all must stand for themselves.

An End

I walk into a shop and see an old man sitting behind the counter. I awkwardly walk out of the shop before he looks up, not knowing what else to do. Out of sheer curiosity—what other reason do I ever seem to have?—I look up at the sign above the door.

"Clockmaker."

Simple as that. No name, no brand, no copyright and trademark.

And I don't even have to wonder. I know it's the same one.

I hurry back into the shop. "Excuse me, do you know what year it is?"

The old man looks up. "Why, yes, it's 1999. Can I help you?"

"Um—yes, yes, I think you can." I say it quietly, almost afraid.

We exchange a few words.

And then, like a whisper, I am gone.

Dreaming of Stars

HELEN COPP, Grade 8, Age 14. Oyster River Middle School, Durham, NH, Susan Renner, *Teacher*

It was well into the second week of the flood when I awoke freezing from the clearest dream in months. It was lucid, more like a vision than a dream, and it left me in a cold sheen of sweat between the rough blankets and the thin mattress in the captain's quarters. After shaking the sleep off my back, I threw myself topside, my feet, rough with calluses, smacking the smooth ladder as I ran. Shielding my eyes from the afternoon sun, I leaned out over the rail, trying to find some trace of life on the vast expanse of blue. No luck today. I flicked my chestnut mop out of my eyes and tried again. The water was bare and flat, as it had been every day since the floodwater had settled. My gaze trailed downward to the infinite depths of the water. On some days, when the angle was good, and the water was illuminated with the slanting shafts of sunlight, I could see right down into the dark. Once, I saw an old church steeple, complete with a cross wavering a few yards below the surface. That was the luckiest find, however. Smaller buildings never came close to the surface.

Without any landmarks or land of any kind, navigation proved to be quite difficult. Standing at the helm, I tried to direct the craft in a straight line across the open water. A voice, warm and casual, sounded behind me, lazy as the afternoon sun. I didn't turn.

"Got us on a steady course, Caleb?"

"As always, Mom."

"You're a good girl, aren't you, *September*?" I heard her murmuring to the boat, pretending not to hear. It was kind of a private thing Mom did. She'd always loved the *September Song* as if she was another member of our little lost family. Now, I suppose, she was. "Yes you are, you'll keep us safe, won't you?" Keeping my gaze forward, I felt a smile crawl across my lips. The *September Song* was our literal lifeboat. She was all we had, a young craft, but an experienced sailor. The honeyed wood was worn from padding feet, the rails beaten by spray, but the ropes were strong and the slice of sail stronger. She was no more worn down than any other well-loved vessel.

Finally glancing around from my post at the wheel, I observed two catastrophes burst from belowdecks within a minute of each other. One was my sister Gracie, nine years old, basically the human embodiment of fireworks. The other was my father, who immediately went to work checking the tightness of ropes and lines, as if I couldn't do it just as well myself.

"Caleb, can we go swimming? Can we can we can we please?" Gracie tossed her yellow hair and drew out her please into a whine that rattled in my ears until finally, I had to crack.

"Alright, you can take a dip," I chuckled. "But just for a short while. I'm not stopping this boat forever." My sister's energized yelps popped and cartwheeled across the deck after her as she dashed to the break in the rails, and propelled herself into the shining water.

"She didn't even wait for you to drop anchor," Mom laughed as I belatedly heaved the small deadweight anchor overboard. "Adult supervision is always needed with that one." Striding to the gap in the rail, she swung her legs over the edge and disappeared soundlessly into the water.

I watched her go with the ghost of a smile. These days, happiness came and went in waves, not unlike the gentle lapping sounds the endless water made against the edges of the *September Song*. It seemed to me the world was suspended, like it had been silenced by the crashing flumes. Unable to be seen, it didn't have to be thought about anymore. Everything was buried and quiet. With everyone together, on our literal lifeboat, we lived a life on pause.

The last inhabitant of our vessel emerged only when the wheel had spun and the gold of the sun had shrunk to the silver of the stars.

"Glad to see you up before midnight, San," I shouted to the figure across the deck. He made his way from the raised cabin roof toward the helm, resting against a mast as he glanced spiritedly toward me.

"I like the cool air," he protested, with a trace of a smile.

"No, you don't, you just like to sleep," I shot back, receiving a playful punch on the shoulder as payment for my honesty.

"I've been awake since midday. That sister of yours ever had a lid on it?" Smiling, I shook my head wearily. Gracie hadn't shut up since she'd been born. "Did you find any—" I cut San off before he could continue with a sharp shake of my head. The topic of possible survivors made everyone tense. A shiver trickled down my spine. We hadn't seen so much as a flicker of another living person, and I couldn't decide if this was entirely bad news. Sighing, I turned, and made my way to the bowsprit, clambering out to the far point, where I could watch where the sun had drowned in the eternity of water. San followed.

"When we were kids . . . It's just funny, thinking about this. I mean, down there," I gestured to the endless blue on either side, "there used to be people. They walked the streets down there. Now fish do, if anything." I turned my head as if to get away from the bitterness in my voice. It was a long way to the bottom.

"I think one day, maybe kids will swim down there. Explore. Maybe they'll dig it out again, what we used to be," San pondered. We sat and watched the stars, tiny pinpricks of hope in a midnight closer than it looked. When they were the only source of light, it was apparent just how much the world was not the world it had been. The churning water had devoured the streetlights, the skyscrapers, all the lights humanity had relied on. Without the electric pulse cities once provided, there was no familiar orange glow to the night. It would be scenic if it wasn't tragic. The stars were small and far away, but they made a difference in the seemingly unconquerable chasm. With a mirror of darkness on either side, both above and below, life unpaused. Pensive thoughts slipped into dreams. My dreams didn't look so different from the strange sea of stars that took the place of all the trivial things the world once had. Gracie and Mom must have clambered back aboard and gone to sleep themselves while us boys were lost in thought, because I only fell asleep when I knew within me that every member of our lonely family was safe.

I dreamed of noise. A clammer and a buzzing that grew in volume until my ears felt like they were going to burst outward. Wrenching my eyelids open, the world flashed in sepia as I adjusted to the approaching sun. The boat was often still and empty in the morning, so I ignored it now. Stepping atop the raised cabin roof in the middle of the deck, I scanned the edges of the sea out of habit. Everything was mundane except the tiny black triangle that wavered in front of the sun. Then the noise returned. Every shadow leaped at me, stretching and running from every crevice. Everything flashed. Disoriented, a sharp pain in my back chased away the lights. I'd fallen off the cabin roof. Pushing myself back up, I glanced around frantically, my sight clear of feverish visions. It had to be a boat. There couldn't be anything else out in the endless expanse of motionless sea. It was the impossible. One would think I'd grown accustomed to the impossible, but the truth is, the universe keeps surprising me. Deftly hanging halfway over the rail to get a closer look, I noticed with a jolt that the vessel appeared to be heading toward us, the shadowy triangle growing larger even as I watched it. For weeks I'd searched for life, and now I wondered if that had been a good course. The blood beat behind my eyes and ears, taking place of the absent waves. Everything was silent, and too loud.

I was frozen in my hope. It was most definitely a boat, and as it grew nearer, I began to make out figures. Actual people, moving about the top deck. Faint whispers of shouts flew past my ears, and as I watched, paralyzed, to my horror I recognized one of the people. San. San was across from me, on the other impossible craft, waving.

The world rushed by and pain shot through my lower back. I'd fallen over again. From my vantage point on the floor, I felt a scraping shudder go through my beloved boat. A shadow shivered across my face, and I kept my eyes shut, not wanting to see what might be there. But sooner or later, we all have to open our eyes. Squinting through reluctant eyelids, I stared at the hand hovering in front of me. A solid hand, real and welcoming. When I grasped it, it yanked me into a hug that was unbearably familiar. I could feel San's body shaking as it pressed against mine, but whether it was from tears or laughter, I couldn't tell.

"I'm so glad we found you." His voice was trembling as much as his body. My throat worked against me and even if I could find something to say, my voice would have cracked and squeaked until it didn't come out at all. We slid down to sit on the hard planks together, still shivering, although not from cold. "How did you do it? On this boat? Alone?"

"What?" As predicted, my words came out mutilated and dry. A great hand was squeezing me, and all the floodwater on earth couldn't have moistened my voice.

"How did you survive, alone on this boat? She's a good craft and all, but it's been weeks, Caleb, weeks . . ." San trailed off, staring at me. I could feel his gaze, though I didn't meet it. Now I could see just how much the flood had changed us. He was talking nonsense, because I hadn't been alone, I'd had Mom and Gracie and Dad, sometimes, and San.

"But . . . you were there. With us," I protested wearily. "You were with me. You don't remember?" I had to push to make a sound, as if I hadn't spoken in weeks.

"No, Caleb. I was here, on the boat we scrapped. With the others. We haven't been able to find anyone else. You're the first one we found alive." I could hear it in his voice, that heavy tone, the vocal shadow people get when they talk about bad things. I knew.

"Alone."

"Yeah, Caleb. You were alone."

"Nobody else?"

"No. Nobody." His voice cracked on the "no" of nobody. "But I'm here." For some unidentifiable reason, the world was un-paused and now on mute and fast forward at the same time.

"Are you, though?" I trace a stain in the wood over and over again, gentle little swirls. Simple things.

"Yes. So now you'll never have to be alone again," he pleaded.

"It's okay now. The flood can't have reached everywhere, we'll find some sliver of land and—"

"And what?" My anger rises, yet I feel strangely detached from it. "What will we do? Live again? Everyone is missing, the earth essentially gone to ashes! What can we do?"

San placed one hand on my shoulder, cooling the fire. "We can start over." Then for the first time, I looked at him. He was older than my dream, than my hallucination. His face was etched with sorrow, but in his dark eyes there was something that reminded me of the stars. We strode to the edge of the *September Song*, the gap in the rail loomed, but I was not afraid. He kicked the boarding plank; it lost its balance and splashed into the chasm. There was a moment, one taut, detached moment, where we did not jump. We turned around, and I went to the helm, and he followed. We charted a course west, toward the hopeful mountains. We followed the stars. The dome stayed constant. Our lifeboat sailed above the trees, under the stars, and I didn't dream. I didn't need to anymore.

The Shortest Short Story in the History of Short Stories of All Time Ever

ADAM SCHORIN, Grade 12, Age 17. Stuyvesant High School, New York, NY, Kerry Garfinkle, *Teacher*

I. *The Rise*

Long is my favorite of the bunch.

At each visit, he's in his black-and-gray fireproof pants, black army boots, black fireproof gloves that he slips on and off, FDNY crew sweatshirt—which, as I've told him, I also own—and Engine 47 button-down work shirt. He always greets me the same way, with a suave fist bump and a nod in the opposite direction. (He thinks he's cool or something.) Then we sit down at one of the open, supervised tables and he asks me if I've ever seen *Rescue Me*.

That's what started the fireman thing for him. I don't think he understands the show but he thinks Denis Leary looks cool in a firesuit so he wants to be one too. I always answer no, which is something he can't believe. Long shakes his head and raises his arms in disgust to the guys at the neighboring tables. Like antagonized clockwork. When he calms down, we talk about the show, which I've never seen, so he talks while I nod and listen and shake my head and check my watch to see if I've maxed out on my hours for the day.

Throughout our conversations, Long jumps into a set of ten pushups, ten sit-ups, and fifteen jumping jacks. He's training for his career as a firefighter, he tells me—he even refers to firefighters as "we"—but I don't think he knows that the FDNY doesn't accept applicants from the New York City Division for Special Education.

The others in the group sometimes sit at our table or sometimes at the other tables and often get up and switch during the visit. Angela is colossal. She has huge flabby hands that swing from her stumpy arms like she's a T. rex, these massive sagging breasts that look like U-boat torpedoes, and a loud voice that is too clumsy to form the words she wants to say. She can't pronounce a hard C, for example, so she says my name "AAAriiii" instead of "Eric." Every time she sees me, she gives me a big, shaking hug even though I can barely stand to look at her. Pamela is almost the same. She's always smiling and trying to say something, but her tongue is too thick to get the words out. So she nods yes to everything. When I catch her cheating at Connect 4, she breaks into a shrieking cinematic laugh that is more proud than evil. Carl sits in the corner, with big white tracks on his tongue and mouth always hanging open kind of dead, rubbing his arms against his crotch, like he's masturbating with his elbows. When he gets upset, which is often, he slams his palms against his forehead and yells until he runs out of air. Almost anything can set him off: wind whooshing against the window grates; a pebble hitting the floor. And Alfie I don't know too well, but he says he likes war, and he's constantly hunched over an imaginary assault rifle, going *pew, pew, pew, pew* at an imaginary villain.

For some reason, these four—and Angela's monster hugs in

particular—scare me more than Kareem, the violent hood re-tard and unknowing drug-runner in his brother's gang. Their complacency unnerves me.

There are, of course, others at the Julius Project, but they don't really talk much (or try to). They stay in their corner and I stay in mine.

This happens:

On Tuesday, Long rushes up to me in the lunch line and hits me with a fist bump of such force that it knocks me back a foot. "Hey, bro. Eric. Man." He can't speak in full sentences and the pauses become fault lines between the fragments of his speech. He thinks he's cool. "Have. You seen. *Rescue Me*?"

"No, Long. Not yet, man." I'm cooler than he is.

Scoff.

We cut to the front of the line and the hairnetted lunch lady offers, "What'll it be, honey?"

"What day. Is it. You know?" Long asks.

"Uh, Tuesday," says the lunch lady.

"Steak and eggs," Long says, because he always has steak and eggs on Tuesday. I get ditto and we shuffle through the double doors at the end of the line. Long's face, like his speech, is more composed than that of the others. Just the part from below his nose down to his chin has been crushed by a giant cartoon anvil.

We sit down at one of the oval tables facing the Hudson that smells like it's been quadruple-washed with high-strength ammonia. Long sniffs the steak and eggs. In the same way that idiot savants have a genius for math, Long has a superhuman sense of smell, a trait that he often reminds himself of. He sniffs the steak to inhale the little particles of blood and ash and the eggs to see if they are powdered or not. (They are.) I start the timer on my watch and lean in for the latest installment of *Rescue Me* reruns. The first few minutes of the conversation are always the hardest. Okay, Long. Let's hear it.

"How're you doing, Long?"

". . ."

"Didn't catch that. What's up, man?"

". . ."

"One more time?"

"Eric!"

"Long?"

"I'm in love!" Pause. "You know?"

"Really?" I'm only a little skeptical. "Terrific, buddy. Who's the lucky lady?"

Long giggles. "Yeah." Hehehe. "Ms. Chester."

Before becoming a "guiding motivator" at the Julius Project, Ms. Lillian Chester taught math at my preteen alma mater, Edward R. Fleisch Middle School for Boys, where she was known almost exclusively as Ms. Chesty, and, as implied by her moniker, is a very ample object of Long's affections. She's at least ten years Long's senior, but through some strange regimen of fitness, diet, and wrinkle-clearing medical scrubs, maintains the same countenance and figure she proudly wore in her math teacher days.

"How do you know you love her?"

"Errrrriiiiiiiic . . . Eric! I know! I really. Really know!"

I nod with my post-adolescent understanding. This, I understand. I fall in love so often—quickly, randomly, and obscurely—with girls I do and do not know, that I was already in love with Karen, my current girlfriend, a good two weeks before I knew her name and some four months before I even saw her naked.

II. The Stretch

Over the next three weeks and five visits, Long changed. He began to draw very abstract portraits of Ms. Chester embedded in wobbly red hearts or plastered against fire-truck color-ins from the Web. He tried to write to her or about her, saying things like: She. Is. Beautiful. He stopped eating on his schedule, and increased his workout regimen, and wore ties and plaid shirts on top of his FDNY crew, and poured cologne through his crew cut, and bowed low and painfully when she entered or exited the room, and stuffed uncomfortable cardboard squares into his shoes so that his spastic limp (the "swagger," I used to call it) became even more exaggerated, all with the desperate hope that he would be tall and beautiful and loved! I could tell you about all of these changes in painstaking detail and repetition, but would they even make sense to you? Would you regard the irrational actions of this irrational kid with any amount of gravitas or understanding? Would you understand him like I sometimes do?

What I mean is: Are you Harris or are you me? I can't tell.

I'll tell you instead the biggest details, the obvious occurrences that beg to be read:

1. Long got a Facebook account. I think his cousin or brother set it up for him, and he checks it pretty regularly. Now consider the Facebook Ratio Principle of Happiness, one of the guiding rules of social interactions in the iEra. The FRPH states that "the ratio of one's own wall posts to one's posts on others' walls is directly proportional to one's happiness," a sentiment similar to that of Charlesberg's Theory of Sent vs. Received Text Messages, the runner-up for the 2009 Bell Science Award. His only wall post is an emoticon from me: :-). Meanwhile, he posts daily on my page or Harris's page or the FDNY's fanpage.

With a ratio of 1:17, he is decidedly unhappy, well below the standard range and only slightly above the Joan Cusack Line of Misery.

2. Long made a list of his favorite things to smell. (Superman kept records of his escapades in the Fortress of Solitude; Batman charted his intellect and strength on the Batcomputer; Long—the Super Sniffer, the Great Olfactor—writes down these scents as a record of his one superior ability.) After he dies, I find part of the List in the pile of his stuff we dissect at the Project. Here it is:

Apple Sause with ginger And cherry. It is sharp aNd sweet in My nose.

Paper on Fire. I feeL STrong. I smell it MiLes away.

Steak and EGGS. Tuesday.

Perfoom. Ms. Chesters perfooM. ByootiFuL.

Me. I smell ME. Do yOu smell mE?

3. I also published something else. A list of my own that I sent to an editor friend at *The Punch*, an underfunded lit magazine in the Village. She liked it and stuck it in the latest bare-boned issue. It's a list of things I hate—my superpower, I guess. An excerpt:

1. The following phrases—straight up, no doubt, dead-ass, nigger please, that's dirty (meaning good, and not covered in filth), that's dope, word (or werd), filthy (meaning good, and not covered in dirt), etc.—are pathetic attempts at conversation and are inexcusable offenses against the English language.

2. The following words that are used to mean other words—smacked, plastered, sick, Gucci, gay, gone, random, sweet, solid, tight, beef, baked, bag, stoned (and filthy and dirty), etc.—are disgusting idiosyncrasies of our generation and are inexcusable

offenses against the English language. (But I have no problem with using nouns as verbs—river out, let's basketball, beer me, coffee me, ice him, are you uptowning, etc.—because they are creative and new and fresh.)

3. The following abbreviations—fml, omg, brb, nfw, omfg, l8r, pce, ttyl, ttfn, g2g, etc.—are, except when used in necessarily rushed text messages, inexcusable offenses against the English language.

4. I hate white people who say "Fo sho" ironically.

5. I hate white people who say "Fo sho" for real.

6. I hate women who get offended when I tell them they're pretty.

7. I hate complainers. (Especially those of the female variety.)

8. I hate people who say "I'm sooooooo drunk." Or "I'm sooooo highhhhh, maaannn."

9. I hate people who say "like" too much without being ironic.

10. I hate people who post pictures on Facebook while they are out so they can prove to the Internet-browsing world that they do, indeed, have a social life.

11. I hate. . . .

4. Karen broke up with me. It was clean, really. She was tired of me, and she said I was a freak and emotionally retarded and that it wasn't worth it for her. "Freak" because I didn't like her friends or going to loud places or doing things that involved dancing or not having sex. I told her she didn't know what retarded was and that I loved her, but she didn't hear me, and she knocked over my trash can on her way down the stairs.

I took a few days off from school for the Breakup Film Festival—my standard post-relationship cycle of nineties rom-coms, *La Dolce Vita* and *Wild Strawberries* and *Citizen Kane* hold-

ing up my high-art backbone, and bizzaro horror flicks rang-
ing from *Nosferatu* to *The Incredibly Strange Creatures Who
Stopped Living and Became Mixed-Up Zombies.* Usually there
is also a series of obscure Japanese mob thrillers, black-and-
white detective stories, and stoner favorites from the last few
decades, but I always end with *Top Gun,* the greatest and most
enduring bro-pic of the flaming eighties. I'm okay now, really.
I'm not a sentimentalist.

This happens:
It is Creativity Time at the Julius Project and Long and I work
at one of our favorite ammonia-steeped tables by the window. White cardboard paper, masking tape, and crayons are
sprawled out on the table in front of us. I doodle sharks and
harpoons and weird figments of my imagination while Long
works intently on something underneath the crook of his arm.

The silence has been getting to me recently, so to break it I
go, "What're you working on, Long?"

"Just. Writing. Eric. Man."

"Oh yeah? What're you writing about, man?"

"Just . . . Writing." His cheeks are tense here, and with his
weird chin he looks kind of like a frustrated blowfish.

"Oh, okay. That's cool." I keep on drawing. A shark is about
to be speared by one of the harpoons. I look for a red crayon to
draw the blood. Long is using it though, sketching ivied strands
down the sides of his cardboard. "Hey, can I see that?" I say.

He hands me the cardboard. Written in his lopsided font is:
MiSs ChesTer. I LovE yOu.
LovE, LoNG.

"Wow, this is a very sweet letter," I say. "Are you gonna give it—"

"Not. A letter."

"What's that?"

"It's not. A letter."

"Oh, okay. That's cool. Are you gonna give—"

"It's a. Story." He says this without looking up.

"Oh? It's pretty short," I say.

"It's the. Shortest. The shortest. Short story. Ever."

"Oh."

"Do you. Like it?"

"Yeah, sure." I'm not just saying it. "I love it." He blushes and claws at his arm. He hasn't looked up yet. "But it's not very short." This makes him look up and stare me in the face.

He chokes. "Not. Short?"

"Yeah, I mean seven words is good and everything, but I bet you I can write a lot shorter. I can write a shorter short story. The shortest of all time."

Now he laughs. "But this. This is the shortest!" Hehehe. "Ever. You can't. Beat this!"

Ms. Chester is rolling an archaic dodgeball to a spread-legged Angela on the floor. Harris is playing hand games with Pamela at the next table. The sun hits ours in a way that makes the ammonia burn stronger. It's caustic in my nose. "Oh yeah?" I say. "You don't think I can? Watch me. This is the shortest short story in the history of short stories."

I turn over the cardboard and write something in purple crayon. I hand it back to him and he reads it over. His eyes widen and he turns red and he shakes his head side to side and then, first as groan or a rumble, and then louder and chaotic, he begins to laugh. Hahaha. Louder and louder, slapping his hand against his thigh, he cranes back his blockish head and bellows. HAHA. Hehehe. HA!

And I start to laugh too, and we're both laughing now, falling over our arms against the side of the table, brutally tickled by thousands of electric fingers. Heehee. Hoooo. HAHA. Laughter pulsing down the sides of my arms, pulling out my vocal chords, choking on hilarity!

And as we go off, he lets the cardboard drop to the floor, and it bounces on its side before falling with the love letter faced down. If you were to look at the paper now, you would see, written in my steady, grade-school block print, in thick purple letters that fill the center of the page, in plain and non-elegant prose, imposing with capital-letter/period and sharp measured lines, a single four-letter word, my short story to end all short stories:

Fuck.

III. The Punchline (i.e., The Fall)

Two days later, we are sitting in the same place. I'm the only volunteer in the room. Mr. Peterson shows up on Wednesdays and Fridays and today is Thursday so he isn't here either. Ms. Chester and Harris are nowhere to be seen. Instead of acting as a general overseer for all the "population" in the room, I sit with Long as he colors in fire-truck printouts.

We're not talking. I continue to work on my shark-attack doodles. The others just sit there. Complacent.

About twenty minutes in, Ms. Chester rushes through the double doors and sits down with Angela and Pamela. Long eyes her in his peripheral but keeps on coloring. I don't think he's given her his love story. A few minutes later, Harris walks in slowly and sits down at our table. "What's up, kiddos," he says. "How's the bro sesh going? No more breakdowns?" Haha.

"I can see that. How're you doing today, Longy-boy?"

"Okay. Very okay."

He keeps his face down. "Swell, swell, swell, man. That's real swell." He looks like he's searching for a cigarette. When we don't say anything, he leans in. "I'm just swell too. Real swell."

Long's nose is in the air and he's sniffing now. He pulls hard on his nostrils and the sound is sharp. "Oh, look at him go!" says Harris. "What a nose! What are you smelling now, Longy-boy? The eggs in the kitchen? Is there bird shit on the side-walk?"

"No. No eggs. No birds."

"Just leave him, okay?" I say to Harris.

"Leave him? Long doesn't want me to leave him, right Longy-boy? We're just being sociable." He winks at me. "Isn't that right, Longy? Sociable enough for you?"

"I smell. Something."

"Oh, I'm sure. What is it then?"

"Ms. Chester. I smell. Ms. Chester."

Harris laughs hard, and I feel something in my throat, like it's stuffed with a rag. Hahaha. "Ms. Chester's right over there, Longy," Harris says. "Normally you can smell much farther than that, am I right?"

"No. Not over there."

"But that's where she is, Longy-boy! She's—"

"Over here. I smell her. Here. I smell. Her perfume. Here."

The laugh is frozen on Harris's face. I stare at my sharks and spears and won't let myself look at him. "Well," he says. "That's odd, I guess." And he turns to me. "I was right though. Some real Meg Ryan shit. Infuckingcredible. "

I dig my nails into the crayon.

"But, anyway," Harris goes on, "fine spring day and we're stuck inside coloring. What's the deal with that, Long?"

"No."

"What's that?"

"No." He doesn't meet Harris's eyes.

"There's no deal with that?"

"No. She smells. Here. No."

"I know man. It was awesome. But I'm asking you about outside, Long. What do you think about outside?"

"No. No. No."

"You don't think about outside?" Harris laughs.

"No. No. No. No. No."

"Okay, dude," he frowns. "Be cool. Be cool, dude."

"No. No. No. No. No. No." Harris looks at me but I am drilling my eyes into the shark. I change crayons to draw its teeth. My hand is stained with its blood. "Relax, man. Come on, Long, it's okay," Harris says.

"No. No. No. No. No. No. No. No. No." Long's face is twisted again, the vein in his neck is expanding. He breathes fast and stares at the table. He digs his hand into his leg. "No. No. No. No. No."

Harris stands up, and Ms. Chester looks over. The other patients stare. Angela is clapping slowly, not looking at anything. "No. No. No. No. No. No. No. No. N—"

"Hey! Just be cool, okay?" Harris reaches out and grabs Longs hand, but the kid pulls away.

"No. No. No. No. No! No! No!"

Ms. Chester perks up from her table and asks, "Long . . . ?"

"NO!"

This is what gets Carl going. Aaaargh! He screams. ARGH! He pounds his fleshy nose and forehead with the sides of arms. ARGH! Pamela covers her ears with her palms. ARGH! Angela claps faster. NO! AAARGH! Pamela starts to cry. The whole sound is painful, cutting, terrible. Lactic acid against my eardrums. Clap! The ammonia mixes with the air. Harris starts shouting at Long. "Be cool! Okay?! Be cool! Just shut the fuck up and be cool!" Ms. Chester doesn't move. ARGH! I stare into the shark's eyes.

Pew! Alfie joins in now, firing his rifle at Harris. *Pew*! *Pew*! *Pew*! He doesn't even know what a rifle sounds like. ARGH! The cork in my throat expands and my guts start to twist, contorting my intestines into a ball. NO! *Pew*! *Pew*! Angela bounces up and down, swinging her dinosaur arms together faster and louder, the two torpedoes on her chest flailing about. Shut up! ARGH!

"NO! NO! NO! NO!"

Chris bangs his fists against the table now. Slam! ARGH! NO! Shut the fuck up! CLAP! *Pew*! NO! Long hits the table, his face is falling apart. NO! The screaming is animal now, chaotic, a living thing of its own. NO! The shark is bleeding fast all over the page. NO! Pamela squeezes her ears and moans. *Pew*! My stomach is killing me. *Pew*! My throat is crushed. ARGH! It thickens. NO! I don't look at Long. NO! I feel something run down my arms and prick through my skin and sting at my veins. NO!

I look around at them and feel empty. NO! I feel sick. NO! I feel the bile in my throat. NO! I feel my brain NO! shaking in my skull. NO! My groin is crushed NO! my arms electric NO! and all the population is screaming. NO! And before I can help myself NO! before I think about what I'm doing NO! I get up NO! throw back my head NO! and now I am screaming too.

I Am All That Is

GARRISON ASMA, Grade 11, Age 17. Central High School, Salem, WI,
Vincent Kuepper, *Teacher*

Day broke in the forest just as it did every day.

The morning light danced in amber columns while the dawn rain fell, gently agitating every needle, leaf, and branch. The trees grew tall and quiet, living out their lives as the mute guards of this green nation. The quiet chirp of distant birds and the slow rush of the wind through the undergrowth were the only sounds for miles.

Apart from the steady march of the Nomad.

With each step came a subtle squeak from his disintegrating rubber boots. They carried a thin layer of earth and grunge accumulated from years of trekking. Despite the ruggedness, their pristine matte black tone still laid boldly underneath.

The Nomad also sported a severely tattered fume hood. At one point in time, it must have been a brilliantly sterile stark white, but this was not that time. The heavy-duty latex of the hood had clearly seen its time in action. It had reverted to a drab yellow from its exposure to innumerable days and nights of hard rain. The spots of mildew gave it a distinctive bitter smell that stung the tip of the tongue.

The Nomad wore nothing, save for his boots and hood. The rest of his body was subjected to the wrath of the forest. Exposure to the elements had left his bare skin a browned, weathered suit of armor; adaptable to whatever trials the environment could force on him.

The Nomad pushed on just as he always did.

As the cloud cover receded, almost seemingly in his presence, he could clearly see the pale blue sky.

He had never paid as much attention to the sky as the other parts of his kingdom. It was so beautifully desolate, reminding him of something he could not completely recall.

Was it the memory of a familiar place?

A different time?

Someone from his past?

No, a memory of someone else would be just plain silly. The Nomad knew that he and Steven were the only two individuals left in existence.

The Nomad pulled Steven out of his boot and chuckled, "How absurd!"

To which Steven replied nothing.

Steven was an incredibly old and incredibly rusted .38 caliber revolver. He had been with the Nomad since the start of the world. Steven was so ancient that the thought of him being made of any sort of sleek and clean seemed as preposterous as the idea of him being able to successfully fire. The only part of Steven that was even remotely intact was his finished wooden grip. The dented cherry maple handle was the only thing that seemed at home in the forest. Just like the Nomad's minimal clothing, Steven's rusted metal frame seemed like an unwelcome relic of a different life here.

"We are all that is," the Nomad proclaimed confidently for the empty space to hear.

And with that, they trudged on.

They walked through the forest without a sense of urgency, knowing the edge of the world would never come. Walking was, however, their only purpose.

They marched through the valleys and glens where the sun sliced through the treetops, illuminating every minuscule detail of the woods in a strikingly sepia tone.

They decided to rest on a bluff not unlike any of the other bluffs.

It stood tall, confidently overlooking a vast, clear patch of his kingdom.

But something was different here.

There were noises coming from the forests at the edge of the clearing.

Different noises.

These weren't the usual noises of the Nomad's subjects.

This something was moving with determination.

And from the woods burst a creature that made the Nomad recoil from atop his perch.

It caught sight of the Nomad.

It ran on two legs, it's other set of legs flailing wildly in the air.

He hadn't seen one of these in longer than he could possibly recall.

"Hey!" it shouted.

"Down here!" it continued on.

"Hey! Hey! HELP!"

The Nomad made no effort to acknowledge the creature with anything more than a probing stare.

The Thing came nearer and nearer to the Nomad and his bluff.

"HEY!" it persistently shouted to no success. The Nomad was unfazed.

The Thing was but 15 feet away recklessly running toward him.

It happened quickly and without hesitation.

Like a basic instinct.

The Nomad leveled Steven at this . . . this Thing. It tried to stop its approach, raising its savage arms.

But the Nomad couldn't let his kingdom become impure.

And then Steven shouted.

There was a great flash, and Steven's voice echoed throughout the forest, becoming the only noise in the world.

Bits of Steven and the Thing lay on the ground, serenely motionless. The Nomad stared down at the two of them, feeling nothing.

He and Steven had been through some hard times together, but Steven was no more.

"I am all that is," the Nomad said quietly.

Scanning the surroundings, the Nomad spotted a dejected-looking tree. Its bark had begun to gnarl, twisting its body in a downward fashion. A sliver of a branch, having been viciously ripped apart by perhaps lightning extended from the trunk.

"Is that . . . Is that Henry? I've missed you old boy!" he hollered and cheerfully ran toward the weak tree.

With a deep, hollow crack, the branch was freed of the grasps of the graying tree.

"Yes, we've got so much catching up to do, Henry."

The Nomad kept a firm hold on the branch. The side that was torn from the trunk had a malevolently sharp point.

The Nomad liked Henry very much.

But before they had time to discuss any personal matters, more rustling came from the clearing's tree line.

This time it was not just one Thing. These were the sounds of a whole pack of them, shouting the same nonsense the one that now lay gently still had cried.

The Nomad held Henry tight.

He knew what had to be done.

"I am all that is, and all that will be."

The 2-Hour Clock

NIKLAS THEORIN, Grade 9, Age 15. University Scholars Program, West Chester, PA, Sue Giordani, *Teacher*

Finally the news reaches Seattle; the end is in 2 hours.

1 Hour, 59 Minutes

Neighbors say 120 minutes, anchors say 7,200 seconds, but it is all the same spectrum of time, no need to dramatize it. The end is the end, and 2 hours is 2 hours.

The end is near, that's for sure. Anyone who says otherwise is desperate or drunk. Most are both. But who am I to judge what they say in their last moments? I am no better than the fools who say such things, in fact I'm worse. I could be at a bar now, drinking my thoughts away, or out on the streets, hardening them to clay, but instead I sit here drinking tea and gazing at a buzzing screen of black and white thinking, "To hell with it all. I'm going to watch *CSI*."

1 Hour, 45 Minutes

"To hell with it all." Story of my life. You graduate, expatriate, compensate, for what? Do you know what you're doing? No. Everyone around you knows what you're doing, and they can say yes or no, but in the end you don't care, because you've been spinning your whole life and when the world clicks in place, the room's still moving counterclockwise, and no one can see it but you . . .

. . . no one wants to.

Until . . . "Bob" from the news says that some foreign bomb is going to turn you into a mushroom cloud in two hours, and there's no escape. You panic, you forget, you remember, you turn the TV off and only really think of one word: "Hell."

At last, you wake up . . .

1 Hour, 10 Minutes

There's an old man singing outside my apartment. He's singing something sad . . . but too sad to hear what the gurgled words mean. He plays his guitar in a terribly melancholy fashion: He barely plucks the strings. The whole thing is sickening. It builds to an icy crescendo, and as I wait for the last note, it doesn't come. The man has broken his guitar.

50 Minutes

Some lunatic is waving a gun outside the window a few stories below me. I hear him say "my family!" and other blurbs. I have no idea if his problem is real, but his gun certainly is. It went off in his hand . . . by accident I think. A woman of about my age is on the street, bleeding. Saving her . . . is useless. We're all going up in the cloud anyways, bleeding on the street or not; gun in hand or not; blood on hands or not . . .

40 Minutes

Bob on the TV is beginning to lose his cool. You can hear it in his voice. His hands are twitching, and his eyes take on a persona of hunger. He's forgetting his cues and neglecting his fellow anchors. He's looking to the cameramen for help. You can almost imagine them holding up the script, or even maybe acting the thing out. Bob is stumbling through the words like a chain being pulled up a stairwell. From the way he moves his rigid hands, you could almost think this sort of raving he's doing is completely impromptu . . .

30 Minutes

It's totally impromptu. He's not even using real words anymore, and he doesn't know what he's saying most of the time. What's come upon this man? Bob: the man who commentated on the fall of empires; the man who watched starving children skittering on the floor, while telling the story of some kind of dictator. Bob: a genuine let-them-eat-cake kind of guy . . . now as crazy as the rest of us. Actually crazier . . . if you don't count the guy with the gun . . .

Actually, count the guy with the gun . . .

25 Minutes

Bob just swore on live TV. The whole show is cut. Right there. Should it be canceled for that? I don't even know why the cameras were still running after Bob told us about the nuke soaring above our heads. I don't think anyone was watching in the first place after that. Who would even care?

20 Minutes

The old man with the guitar is back! It's a stellar, crimson-red beauty! A flimsy tag is still ringed around it: It's stolen. But who cares? It hums as he plays it. The melody becomes sweeter with every note. Sweeter, and softer, and . . . sadder. I sit here wishing the man knew some happier songs . . . when it hits me that he probably does.

A small crowd is forming around him now. The huddled mass is full of faces sticky with tears and alcohol, but I can make out a few oblivious children, whose mothers have taken the initiative of not telling them about the end, or the ticking 2-hour clock that's almost up. They've got to be catching on though . . . drunks tend to shout what they're thinking . . . and what else are they thinking now?

13 Minutes

I am walking away from the window when the man plays a new song: one more upbeat. It sounds familiar, but I've been tuned out for so long I can't put my finger on it. Another voice besides the man's chimes in. It's a little girl's voice, which is strikingly different from the man's. It is a mystical contrast, and a phenomenon that the song doesn't sound abnormal. Slowly, more voices join in. They all know the tune . . . and the words . . . all of them but me. Who am I to not know this song? What is it? They start to sway, and I am trying to get this song in my head! The words, the words! With each one I feel a nerve in my mind ringing, crying out, as if it missed another chance. How many will I get? Does the song repeat? Oh, I wish I knew what it was! It is killing me . . .

It's the national anthem.

The whole thing would be beautifully cinematic . . . if the woman of my age wasn't bleeding out into the streets, right next to the singers . . .

8 Minutes

I'm standing at the door to the outdoors. I can feel the wind seeping through the cracks in the door, running up my skin. It's summer, but it's the coldest day I've ever known. I think I'm going to go to her . . . the bleeding woman. I don't know why. I don't care why. I just can't ignore her. Is she alive? Yes. She tosses and turns as if in an endless nightmare . . .

Oh, I don't know what I'm doing! I'm in my pajamas for god's sake! I think I have between five and ten minutes 'till the mushroom cloud. Five to ten. The bar's about a six-minute walk away. There's money in my pocket. I could go there, forget it all. But I'm standing here about to walk out the door to a woman I don't know who's going to be as dead as I am in about 7 minutes. Why? Some would say compassion. Some would say pity. Some would say love. Some would say, "To hell with it all."

"To hell with it all." Story of my life. But where's that all going? Up in smoke, right? This isn't how it was supposed to end. But had I really a plan? A goal? Anything? I had no idea what I was going to do. I was still spinning! People see that woman bleeding on the road and say, "To hell . . . " And why not? Isn't that where we're all going? But we're going together, right? Doesn't that count for something? But I don't see the woman on the road singing a song with the others. Isn't she going with no one? Some could say, "No time," but sometimes you've just got to hold your breath and check the ticking 2-hour clock and say:

"Don't I have 7 minutes?"

Luke and the Moon

AARON COOPER-LOB, Grade 12, Age 17. New Orleans Center for Creative Arts, New Orleans, LA, Lara Naughton, *Teacher*

Luke Loomis was not a particularly remarkable man before his tenure as the Moon. He was a regional cargo pilot, flying a small propeller plane along the same scheduled route every night. He would, each workday, get up at 6:00 p.m., leaving enough time for a bleary-eyed shower, a small black cup of coffee and an egg before trudging downstairs to the garage where he kept his beaten old sedan. He would pull the car out onto the street as his fellow tenants started to trickle back from work. He would make the half-hour commute out of his city, through the sparsely foliaged forest, and past the bay to his airport of operations, and by the time he got there the Sun would have gone down. Luke hated the cutting florescent glare of the airport lights, so Luke's friend the Moon would do his best to light the airport himself on the nights when he was working; he could never really do a great job of it, but Luke appreciated it nevertheless.

Luke spent many of his waking hours musing on the endless plain of his life, a place not grounded in the realm of melancholy but rather skirting its borders. He often found himself staring listlessly at nothing, exhausted from his life in repetition but unsure if there was anything to be done. Many of his conversations with the Moon, who too worked almost every day out of the month, ended up being about their frustrations with work. "I've been flying the same route for two years," Luke complained one night, "and I still only get one day off a week. Hell, I still make less than a preschool teacher. I thought being a pilot was supposed to be glamorous. My life is like some endless circle."

"You're complaining?" the Moon would snicker. "I've been doing this job longer than I can remember, and I don't get a single day off. It is hard work, and I'm lucky to have lasted as long as I have."

"Wow, that is harsh. How do you stay, y'know, sane?"

"Ah, that's a trick of the trade, my friend! Here's the secret: I take a nap during my new moon. Nobody's looking at me anyway cause my face is in shadow, so they're not gonna notice if I'm slacking a little bit." Luke couldn't help but laugh. The Moon was a clever one indeed.

Another popular topic of conversation was the Moon's love life; more specifically, his crush on his colleague the Sun. The two didn't work intimately, but, during the two weeks that Luke didn't see him, the Moon would be close enough to the Sun that they would be able to converse. Therefore, he would often greet Luke after their hiatus with news of his time with the Sun. Luke had listened to the starry-eyed Moon's daily updates for months, and knew the game well at this point. The Sun was a flirtatious woman, always laughing brightly at the Moon's hackneyed jokes, or throwing him a wink that could burn a hole in his composure, but the Moon was too unsure of himself to interpret these signals as anything more than vaguely promising.

"I don't know, Luke. She's just so great. Why would someone

so . . . so fiery even bother talking to an icy old boulder like me?" the Moon would gush.

"My friend, don't sell yourself short!" Luke chuckled. The Moon broke into his deeply dimpled white grin.

"I mean, she's so amazing at what she does. I wouldn't even be able to do my job if she didn't leave a bit of light for me to shine. She's brilliant, Luke!" He turned his head forward, to the east, a contented shine on his face.

This was a regular exchange between the two. Luke had a hard time imagining the Moon being so confident as to actually approach the Sun, but, timid though he was, the Moon seemed to be getting more and more bold as far as Luke could tell. He was still taken by surprise when the Moon broached the subject of the Sun from a totally new angle.

"I have a plan!" the Moon exclaimed, his excitement palpable.

"Huh, what was that?" Luke said, somewhat surprised.

"A plan. For me and the Sun." His eyes were determined. Luke had never seen him so sure of anything in his life.

"Really? Care to explain?"

"Luke, it's so simple that I can't believe it didn't hit me sooner. Do you know what's happening in a week?" Luke shook his head. Nocturnal as he was, he never really kept himself fully apprised of current goings-on. "It's an eclipse, my friend. A total solar eclipse." Luke's eyes widened.

"Oh! Ohhh." The Moon grinned at him.

"You see? We'll be really close during an eclipse, and, for once, we'll be totally aligned, looking each other right in the eyes. It's the perfect opportunity for us to finally connect." The Moon began to babble enthusiastically about all of the things they would finally be able to do together.

"But what happens after the eclipse?" Luke tried to ask, a slight disconcertedness punctuating the question, but the

Moon's earnest chatter drowned him out.

The Moon disappeared the next night, as usual, and a week later he eclipsed the Sun. The eclipse was, as always, a huge deal for one hemisphere of the world; Luke slept through it. After another week, Luke broke through the clouds to find the Moon waiting, grinning his wide crater of a grin. Luke was unable to open his mouth before the Moon burst with his news. "She wants to see me again! Oh, man, this is so great!"

"Wow, congrats! So you're gonna get together at the next eclipse, huh?" The Moon shook his head emphatically.

"Are you kidding? It'll be decades before we get that close again. No, I think I'm going to go see her," the Moon stated matter-of-factly. Luke's jaw fell an inch.

"What? How could that even be possible?"

"I'm not sure. It's driving me crazy though." The sky filled with silent tension as Luke tried to figure out what to say.

"Well," muttered Luke, "don't do anything brash, at least." The Moon nodded absently. "You are pretty important, you know," but the Moon had already stopped listening, staring off at the distant east horizon.

The next two weeks were of little interest. Luke felt that the Moon was somewhat more distracted than usual, but Luke was not bothered; after all, he'd spoken no more of going off to see the Sun. Luke therefore had no reason to suspect that he would sneak off to see her during his new moon.

The first few days were a typical Moon-less week. Luke would sit quietly in his plane, listening placidly to the muffled chatter of faraway stars. Nothing of any real concern happened until the week ended. Luke left his apartment, and though at first nothing appeared to be the matter on the sluggish two-lane highway, as he drove on he found the forest in disarray. Birds were shrieking nervously and flapping about in confused circles; a deer leapt out into the road and stared at Luke as he swerved by, looking more puzzled than afraid. Luke continued on past the bay; waves were crashing haphazardly into each other in total disregard of any tidal organization. Luke was somewhat perplexed, but not being a particularly curious person he just kept on to the airport. Upon taking off and arriving above the clouds, Luke felt unsettled.

The Moon was absent, as expected, so Luke was hearing only the voices of the stars. Tonight, though, they seemed to be whispering toward the Earth. Luke felt uneasy; normally, the stars buzzed joyfully, albeit in a subdued manner, but tonight they seemed almost concerned. Luke tried to put it out of his mind and continue his flight.

The next night, all initially seemed to be well. The animals were calm; the tides were neat; the stars had resumed their peaceful discourse. Upon arriving at his destination, Luke unloaded his cargo and went into the lounge for a quick cup of coffee. The lounge was empty at such a late hour, but the owners left the dim lights on specifically for Luke. There was a fake marble countertop along the wall, equipped with a pot of lukewarm coffee and some snack for the pilots: tonight, a tray of stale biscuits. Of particular interest, however, was a rifled-through newspaper from that morning lying on the table. Luke's eyes were drawn to the headline: "MOON DISAPPEARS OVERNIGHT; ASTRONOMERS PERPLEXED." Luke put his cup down and picked up the paper, skimming the article.

People the world over are mourning the sudden absence of the Moon. The Moon, known best as Earth's sole natural satellite, was officially declared missing last night... Luke skipped ahead. *... the tides were the first to report the incident; when contacted for comment, they stated, "We suddenly felt really listless, and we had no idea why. At first we didn't even consider checking* *the sky—it's not like the Moon had ever gone anywhere before!—but sure enough when we did, we couldn't see him anywhere!" The tides appealed personally to the Moon: "We need you, Moon! Come back!" Social correspondent Sandra Stonington took to the streets to find out who else was affected. "We'll be out of a job!" complained the astronauts. "We can't eat dinners by candlelight alone!" cried the romantic couples. "What are we supposed to howl at now?" lamented the wolves . . .* He skipped past a long scientific discussion of potential causes. . . . *clearly the Moon's disappearance is affecting humanity deeply. The question is, will he come back?*

Enraged, Luke took the paper with him and left at once. Everything had seemed alright in nature today, so he presumed the Moon had returned; nevertheless, he was furious. He spent the next few days seething until finally the Moon was waiting for him above the clouds, smiling a deep crescent smile. Before he could say a word, Luke slammed the front of the paper against the windshield of his plane for the Moon to see. "Explain this to me." The Moon chuckled.

"Oh, man, I didn't think everyone would notice so quickly! You can't deny it was clever, though! Sneaking off to see her like that." He was still laughing when Luke began to yell.

"How could you be so irresponsible?!" he shouted. The Moon stopped laughing.

"Wait, what?"

"You can't just take off for a day like that. You're the Moon, for god's sake. We need you!"

"Well what about me? Am I just supposed to ignore my desires forever? You know I like this job, and I've been doing it longer than anyone else ever has, but that doesn't mean I don't need a bit of time to myself sometimes too. That's only fair," protested the Moon.

"Look, I'm sorry, but you can't take time off. It's not about fair here," said Luke with an air of finality.

"Luke, why are you being so hard about this?" The Moon's eye shone with a sudden betrayal. "I mean, I'm in love. Isn't that supposed to be cause for celebration?"

"Grow the hell up. Love is bullshit; you know you belong here with me."

The Moon stared at Luke in consternated disbelief. As a few silvery tears began to leak from his eyes, he turned eastward and did not say a word.

The next night, the Moon was absent from the sky.

Luke flew through the great empty vault, pissed both at the Moon for just walking off and at himself for pushing him away. The stars were once again chattering toward the Earth, only this time they seemed to be directing their discussion toward Luke himself. Luke began to tremble under the pressure of the distant stellar susurration; after an hour of it, he could take no more, and shouted "What are you talking about?!" He heard a faint static from above, not unlike cackling. Then, they spoke to him.

"Your Moon has gone, no?" Luke was taken aback. The stars had never actually spoken directly to him before; they sounded like angels buried in gravel.

"Uh, yes. It's sort of an issue." The stars cackled again.

"You need the Moon?" they questioned.

"Yes, desperately. Do you know where we can find one?" More cracked laughing from above.

"Oh, yes, yes. You, Luke!"

"Uh. What?"

"You take the Moon's place!" they snickered.

"Are you serious?" Luke demanded, but the voices had already retreated.

Luke pondered the suggestion for three days, during which time he awaited the Moon's return with the rest of the world. He had come back the day after the last disappearance, they figured, so he'd probably be back soon this time as well. No such luck. Luke thought at first that the idea was deranged, Sure, he could probably do the Moon's job—lord knows he'd watched him do it enough times—but he couldn't imagine himself, Luke Loomis, ever being the Moon.

However, by the end of the three days, Luke was having second thoughts. He was flying his route, mulling over the situation. It was the fourth consecutive moonless night, and the world was tripping all over itself trying to figure out what to do. Luke had realized that nobody was stepping up to take the Moon's place. An image flashed in his head: billions of people cheering up into the sky, all praising Luke Loomis, the Moon. He exhaled slowly, and considered what he had to lose. Then, hesitantly, he turned the plane eastward, toward the horizon.

Luke wasn't quite sure how long it had taken to reach the edge of the world, but he got there with barely any fuel to spare. He climbed out of the plane and looked upward; the trek up the horizon would be arduous. He realized he was wearing no kind of Moonly attire, so he went back to his plane to look for something to put on. A white tarp-like sheet was tied over the boxes; he took it out, tore a hole in the middle for his head, and put it on. That will do nicely, he thought. Sheet donned, Luke began to ascend the sky.

After endless hours of hand over hand over hand, Luke finally reached his perch atop the heavens. The view from up high wasn't as startlingly different as Luke had expected it to be, though he could definitely see a lot more. He did not feel very planetary, to his surprise, though he expected that would change with time; no moon could be expected to get it right on the first day. He began his long trawl across the sky's edge, taking small steps at first, sheet billowing behind him as he slowly gained speed. The Sun was hurling her light at him with the rapidity of a true professional, and Luke did his best to toss some down to the Earth. He gained some confidence as he went; surely he wasn't yet as luminous as the Moon had been, but he felt like he was learning the ropes pretty quickly. Nevertheless, the job was far more challenging than the Moon had made it appear, and Luke worked hard to prevent feeling overwhelmed.

Luke felt as if he perceived everything differently as the Moon. His hunger had vanished, and his desire to sleep had diminished severely. Moreover, though his life had already been somewhat of a hurried blur, time lost most semblance of meaning as he circled the Earth. Luke regarded these developments with passive intrigue; after all, he had more important matters to focus on.

After a few days, as he was approaching his new moon, he got his first good look at the Sun. She really was stunning, and Luke could see now why the Moon had been so obsessed. The Moon was a mere speck next to her, but Luke could see the Sun clearly laughing joyfully with someone; perhaps they really were meant to be with each other. Luke called out to them, trying his best to be chipper, but he was ignored by both. Upset, Luke concentrated harder on his work.

After a few more days, a couple of astronauts arrived in Luke's vicinity. They told him he was doing well enough; the tides were still grumbling dissatisfactions with his leadership abilities, but he was better than no Moon at all. The astronauts told him to keep up the good work and started off on their return trip. Luke plaintively watched them disappear back into the Earth. He received the occasional visitors from below, but never for more than a few days; for the most part he revolved alone in his silent vacuum. As time wore on, he took the Moon's advice and began to nap in his new moon. His face in shadow, he would close his eyes, restless images of circles spinning through his mind. He would drift to sleep, the Sun's jagged rays pricking at his back.

Windigo

URSULA GRUNWALD, Grade 12, Age 18. Peak to Peak Charter School, Lafayette, CO, Kristie Letter, *Teacher*

Hunger.
Hunger hunger hunger.
Empty woods. No people. Only squirrels and raccoons. Not good eating.
Hungry. Hunger. Hunger hunger hunger.
Winter? No. No snow, no cold.
Summer. Yes. Warm. Lots of raccoons and squirrels for when the eating is bad.
People?
Soon.

Cracking of sticks underfoot, gleam of moon on bloody, sticky, silvery fur. Not his blood, no no no, not his. Too fast, too clever. Smart him, too fast and too good for the humans who come with their shiny sticks that reek of fire and spit sparks. Stupid slow humans—smarter than squirrels and raccoons, but not as clever and fast as him. Humans better eating, more fun to hunt than squirrels and raccoons.

Eyes glow gold in the flickering of dying stars overhead. Needs meat. Needs human meat. Once human, he was. Once upon a time. Once upon a time, no fur and no golden eyes and no endless hunger. Once upon a time, slow and stupid and easy hunting. Once upon a time, tangled black hair and bright brown eyes. Used a bow and slept on mats and cooked his meat before he ate it. Raccoons and squirrels were once upon a time good eating.

Hunger hunger hunger.

Long winters. Too much snow. His brothers died. Youngest one first—black skin on toes and purple on lips, glazed brown eyes and ice-caked hair. Made a good stew, sprinkled with pine needles. No other choice. No other food. Long winter. Bad harvest. Not enough grain, nor prey. Needed food. Younger brother was food, saved him and his brothers until oldest brother died, and then he saved them too.

No end to winter. Spring was late. Spring didn't have enough squirrels and raccoons. No good eating. Third brother died. Then fourth, then alone. All alone, and no one to share the good eating with. Girl he loved—girl with long braids and warm, warm brown eyes and big, friendly smile—she died. Good eating. Stew flavored with the bitterness of tears.

Teeth. Getting longer. Animals coming back. Plants and squirrels and raccoons. Don't want them, can't have them, they are not enough. Human meat. Human blood, sweet as honey and bitter as iron and as salty as tears. Hunger. Hunger for the honey-iron-tears.

Teeth get longer. Cut chin if mouth shuts fully. Hair on back, on stomach. Legs skinny, arms skinny. So tall. Runs faster than the eagles and hawks can fly.

Hunger hunger hunger.

Eats a hawk. Not good eating.

Finds a girl. Eats her heart. Slowly. She's screaming. Bright, sweet brown eyes and lips that could smile warmly. Love the taste of her blood on the tongue.

Good eating.

No remorse.

Nothing left. No one left. Only *hunger hunger hunger* and honey-iron-tears.

Hide in caves until hunger too much. Claws long. Feet long. Can run like the wind and climb like a cat. Hunt. Herd. Trick. Laugh as hearts slide down throat. Lick claws. Lick blood off fur. Fur stained pink. Don't care. Sleep.

Wait for the smell of honey-iron and add tears.

Miss brothers and girl once loved. Give in to the hunger. Hunt, herd, trick, laugh. Hide in cave. Repeat. Endlessly.

Forget about once upon a times and black hair and brown eyes. Forget when squirrels and raccoons were good eating. Forget everything but laughter and honey-iron-tears and running faster than the hawks fly.

Forget, and hunt.

The Doormen

NATHAN MEYER, Grade 11, Age 16. Dixie Heights High School,
Fort Mitchell, KY, Kris Gillis, *Teacher*

The first thing I noticed about the door was its ordinariness.
It wasn't large. There were no locks. In fact, it reminded me
of a closet door. It didn't seem like something that men would
devote themselves to. It didn't seem like something that would
inspire hundreds of mottos and sayings. It didn't seem like
something you would even look at twice. It was just a plain
white and wooden door. And, yet, men had spent their entire
lives gazing at its white paint and protecting its lockless knob.

The door had been closed for as long as I could remember.
I thought it would remain closed long after I was gone. The
first man who watched the door has been dead for over 150,000
years. Or maybe 200,000. We doormen, we have a saying. It
goes: Time makes it's own pace at the door.

I'm certainly not the first doorman. There's my predecessor. And his. And his. And so on. When my predecessor was
showing me my post, he told me that he'd watched the door for
what seemed like centuries and that his predecessor had said
the same thing. And so on, so forth. I once asked my predecessor why the door was always shut. Wasn't anyone curious what
was on the other side? He responded simply by saying that it'd
always been like that. I guess, after a century or so, curiosity
just dies.

I miss my predecessor. He wasn't much to talk to, nor did we have much to talk about, but I miss seeing him. Truthfully, I'm not sure how long it's been since I have seen him. The doormen left a ficus, a chair, and a fish tank. They forgot a calendar. As time passes, you realize there's only so much to see. I've got my ficus. I've got my fish tank. I've got my chair. And I've got the door. The ficus tree doesn't do much. The fish tank is empty. And, after a century or so, watching a door just becomes boring.

My predecessor was a young man, like me, when he started his shift. He didn't know why he did. What exactly made him decide to watch the door. All he knew was that, one day, he simply did. He asked me why I'd decided to watch the door. I didn't know either, truthfully. I simply did. Eventually, we all find ourselves watching the door. There's not much to do besides watch, is there?

My predecessor warned against the door. Said it robbed him of his youth. Robbed him of his life. But, then, he said he didn't know what he'd do without the door. Gotta watch something, I guess. After a century or so, the door becomes that something.

My predecessor died almost immediately after his shift ended. Don't ask me how I know that. I just do. They all do, pretty soon after the shift changes. We doormen, we have a saying. It goes: A doorman without a shift is like a flower without a pot. Or a ficus tree, I guess. After a century or so, you forget how to make jokes.

I've got no complaints about my chair, I guess. I mean, at least they give me one. Standing for a century, or even sitting on the floor, would be tiresome. After a century or so, sitting becomes tiresome too. Anyway, I was just sitting when I noticed IT. The Crack. Creeping right up the middle of the door. After a century or so, you forget most of the words that you used to say. I thought of the perfect words for right now, though. The Crack meant I was in deep shit.

My predecessor didn't leave me with much advice on how to watch the door. We doormen, we have a saying. It goes: The door is just a door. So, of course, I knew how to watch a door. However, my predecessor did say that he heard, once, about a doorman who let the door break. I figured that it was just a fable. A boogeyman bedtime story. Anyway, this doorman that let the door break . . . bad things happened to him. That's why I thought it was just a fable. Every time I'd heard it, something different had happened to the incompetent doorman. Besides that, why would the door be in perfect shape if it had broken? Doors can't rebuild themselves. But, either way, it's our duty to watch it. Even though I didn't believe in my predecessor's fable, I still feared the door. What would happen if it did break? The fable was almost a comfort. If it did break, obviously, it wasn't the end of the world. But the door clearly hadn't broken. The world could still end. After a century or so, you don't forget fear. You never forget fear.

And so I began to search for something to fix The Crack. Of course, there was nothing but the fish tank and the ficus. We doormen, we have a saying. It goes: Simplicity in duty goes hand in hand with efficiency. Of course, that saying is over a couple of centuries or so old. I know the doorman who came up with it never broke the door. After a century or so, it's okay to disagree with a few of the sayings.

As I scrambled, The Crack grew up the middle of the door. As I scrambled, my life flashed before my eyes. Of course, career is probably more accurate. After a century or so, you lose sight of life. Duty dwarfs it.

I began to wonder how I'd die. Death would probably come in fire. Maybe choking. Noxious gas. Maybe I'd simply cease to be.

Those were the only options I came up with. After a century or so, you lose your imagination.

The Crack widened in the door. Truthfully, it'd almost fallen off of its hinges. As The Crack opened, my eyes shut. We doormen, we have a saying. It goes: A doorman never has fear while his shift is still going. Sometimes our sayings are shit. After a century or so, you wonder who dreamed them up.

The last thing my predecessor did was my fondest memory of him. I barely knew the guy, but as he shook my hand, he wished me luck. He looked me right in the eyes and said that he knew I'd make him proud. Then, he was gone. Simple as that. We doormen, we have a saying. It goes: Believe in your brothers. I wonder what he'd say if he could see me now. I wonder what I'd say if I could see him now. Hell, I don't know if I remember how to talk anymore. After a century or so, you forget how to communicate.

Doormen aren't allowed to be cowards. This idea makes perfect sense. Would you want a coward guarding something as important as the door? But it's hard for anyone to be a coward when they're just watching a door. At least, that's what I tried to tell myself. In reality, my eyes were shut and I was shaking.

The Crack had almost destroyed the door. The Crack had spread throughout the door. One tap with a ficus branch, and the door would be done. I'd probably be done with it. Despite the cool temperature by the door, I was sweating. But duty calls. So does curiosity. The doormen aren't credited with penning "curiosity killed the cat." That was some other guy who obviously never sat in front of a door for centuries and was told not to open it. And so, I took a ficus branch and broke open the door. We doormen, we have a saying. It goes: Be resourceful, even if your resources are just a ficus and a fish tank.

The door splintered apart with one swift tap. I was ready for the end of my shift. I was ready for the end of my life. And so, I stared into the empty frame, wondering if centuries from now, doormen would tell stories about me.

My eyes met a brick wall. Nothing but stone and concrete. Bare, minus an inscription of a single word.

Men had watched this for centuries. Lives had been wasted on this. My predecessor's life had been wasted. My life had been wasted on this. Of course, I laughed. We doormen, we have a saying. It goes: Find humor where it exists. My predecessor's fable had been right. Bad things had happened because the door had opened. Now, I couldn't shut it. And so, I sat down. And I continued my shift. Staring at the wall this time, instead of the door. After a century or so, you forget how to do anything else.

ABOUT THE AUTHORS

MELANIE ABRAMS writes flash fiction because it forces her to make every word of her story essential. She is currently working on a novel about a fourth-grader and her malevolent imaginary friend.

GARRISON ASMA wrote his award-winning story after a trip to the northern woods of Wisconsin, where he felt a sense of complete isolation. In his next stories he wants to investigate themes such as the subconscious and social inequality. When Garrison writes, he feels he feeds a hungry monster that grows very anxious if not fed again soon.

LUISA BANCHOFF (PORTFOLIO GOLD) is a German-American writer who has spent much of her life in Arlington, Virginia, and Bonn, Germany. She believes that young writers should surround themselves with a supportive community, read the works of others, and have their work read. Her favorite book is *As I Lay Dying* by William Faulkner. In the fall she will study English and Creative Writing at Princeton University.

CELESTE BARNABY compares writing flash fiction to walking through a crowded street and deciding to peer into the window of a building. In that brief moment, "you are witness to the enthralling goings-on of another's life, but only with a tantalizingly limited view."

Usually a writer of fiction, **NACHIKETA BARU** forced himself to be more introspective and conscientious of an audience while writing this piece. "As a member of American suburbia," and therefore "one of the luckiest people on Earth," he did not want to make his essay sound like a complaint but rather a more general assessment on the nature of discontent.

The most recurrent theme in **ROBERT BEDELL'S** poetry is the beauty of nature. He's inspired by its "ability to relieve pain and suffering in our lives if only we stop to listen to it." E.E. Cummings is his favorite poet because Cummings can strip a poem to its bare essentials.

RICHA BIJLANI woke up in the middle of the night to write the first line of this essay. This sentence initiated a difficult process in which she was constantly faced with the question: "Am I doing justice to my grandfather in this memoir?" In retrospect, she regards writing this memoir as a liberating process that helped her deal with her anxiety.

BRIANNA BREAUX prefers to write early in the morning before anyone gets up or while hiding under the bleachers during gym class. The best writing advice she has received is, "We want to see them smuggling. We want to see them in the tunnels." At the moment, her favorite poet is Rita Dove.

MIRANDA CASHMAN writes to pull out a single clear voice from the world's "tangled web of noise." If she could pass a law in the United States, it would be to make the arts a mandatory area of study.

POOJA CHANDRASHEKAR writes mostly about her personal experience and finds her childhood to be an essential source of inspiration. After writing this essay, she realized how important and influential her grandmother's life has been to her own.

SERINA CHANG is greatly influenced by the prose of Ernest Hemingway. While writing, she hopes to imitate his "minimalist edge" and capture the way silences or omissions in dialogue often speak louder than the characters' words. In her future work she plans to address the difficult topic of feeling disconnected from her Asian heritage.

MCKAYLA CONAHAN likes to write about words and their history and the important connection that exists between strangers. She doesn't think the best poetry necessarily centers on the major events in one's life—successful poetry can arise from the observations made during a simple occurrence such as taking a walk to a convenience store.

AARON COOPER-LOB wrote this story after being inspired by a beautiful painting that depicted an "oblong, wood-paneled, homey-looking room with two windows opposite each other. Out one window was day, and out the other, night." His long-term plan is to keep learning.

HELEN COPP thinks of writing as a time in which she can liberate her mind. She dreams of working in theater and has been acting with a company since the age of ten. The flood and water imagery of the Studio Ghibli films *Ponyo* and *Castle* helped her write this piece.

JANAY ALEXANDREA CRANE (PORTFOLIO GOLD) feels that writing has given her an opportunity to learn about herself and share her story with others. In her future writing she wants to use her craft to explore the lives of others. In the fall she will attend Indiana-Purdue University to study English. Her life goal is to be as confident as her mother and to never go a day without doing what she loves.

ASHLEY CRUTCHER enjoys writing funny poems on random topics. While writing, she thinks it's important not to inhibit oneself or to think things over too much. She particularly enjoys the poetry of Robert Frost.

ANISHA DATTA wrote the first draft of this essay for an AP Language and Composition class. She thinks the best writing stems from honesty and that it's most enjoyable to write from the heart. She is inspired by weather, people, and photography.

According to **KATELYN DAVIS**, making people laugh is like preparing a batch of Grandma's famous cookies. If you get the formula wrong, people will be left with a dry taste in their mouth, but if you get the formula right, you'll have a room filled with happy people. If the latter happens, one should never give the secret ingredient away.

AKSHAN DEALWIS wrote this piece as an elegy to his dying grandmother, a woman who nourished her family with blessings and books. The tree in this memoir is a symbol of Akshan's cultural roots, which he came to truly appreciate after writing this essay.

ANTHONY DESANTIS (PORTFOLIO GOLD) believes writing is an act of careful consideration. "I write to take a thought in my hand like a rough little rock, and roll it . . . until it becomes a pebble," he explains. When people read his work, he wants them to lift their eyes from the page knowing that it's OK to feel passionate about something that does not fit into the context of social norms. At American University, he plans to study International Relations and hopes to become an advocate for democracy and human rights.

ALINE DOLINH writes to explore love, war, and identity. Aside from creating poetry, she writes sci-fi and fantasy. She believes it's extremely important to find time to write every day, even if it's bad writing: "You can only get better with practice."

MARY ELIZABETH DUBOIS wrote her first book at age five on messy scraps of paper. Since then, she has used writing to tackle impossible and mind-boggling subjects. "The marching man," or a man who continually strives toward a goal but does not achieve it, is a theme she would like to keep exploring in her next stories.

PARKER ELKINS loves to write about a cabin at Deer Isle, a place his family has been going to for generations. His favorite poet is Brian Turner because he writes simply and with great candor.

KATHERINE FANG'S poem is based on Stephen Crane's *In the Desert*. In her writing, she celebrates "what it means to be human"—to have limitless genius and a wellspring of flaws. Katherine writes where there is a breeze and a cup of tea.

ISABELLA GIOVANNINI (PORTFOLIO GOLD) has lived in the same apartment in Manhattan her entire life. Influenced by her parents, both journalists, she began to write at a young age. In September, she will begin her studies at Yale University, where she will take Theater, Computer Science, Arabic, and Creative Writing courses. She hopes her life will be full of travel and long philosophical discussions.

This summer, **STEFANIA GOMEZ** four other young women joined on a 45-day canoe trip in the Arctic Circle, somewhere west of the Hudson Bay. Together they hope to promote self-sufficiency and an appreciation of the natural world. In the fall, Stefania will attend Brown University.

GABRIELLA GONZALES wants other young poets to know that they are each individuals who carry information no one else does. She believes a good poet expresses his or her knowledge as precisely as possible. "It's easy to say you feel happy," she says, "everyone says that. Not many people would think to say instead that they feel as satisfied as a sun-baked tiger."

URSULA GRUNWALD wrote this story to explore the "windigo," a mythological creature that was originally human and transformed into a monster after indulging in his or her craving for human flesh. What Ursula enjoys most about writing is coming out of "the trance" and reading what she has written.

BENJAMIN HAIDT uses writing to reflect upon the things that we often take for granted in our daily lives. His favorite fictional character is Tom Sawyer because he reminds an older reader of the passion and curiosity in children.

LUKE HASS'S friends and family describe his sense of humor as eccentric, ironic, and sarcastic, but Luke deems it logical and instructional. When his friends read this, he knows they will disagree with him and label his statement as evidence of his obvious sarcasm. Besides writing, he enjoys tap-dancing and singing a cappella.

RACHEL HARGRAVE will write anytime and anywhere. She jots down poems on the margins of her class notes or in her phone if she's on the go. Tennyson and Byron are two of her favorite poets.

EMMA HATHAWAY wrote this memoir intending to illustrate an important lesson she believed she had already learned. However, while writing she discovered that the "grand transformation" she thought she had undergone "is certainly not complete." Emma is excited to keep maturing and improving herself.

After writing her memoir, ELIZABETH HEYM was able to come to terms with "the division between what I can and cannot control." She feels few aspects of life fail to inspire her but prefers to write about the simple things, which often seem ignored.

BAILEY HWA is inspired by the latest scientific and technologic advances. DNA sequencing and cloning are subjects she finds particularly fascinating. If she could have witnessed and written about any historical event, it would have been Benjamin Franklin's reaction to lightning striking his kite.

JACQUELINE KNIGHT describes her writing as casual, fun, and dependent on an audience. She strongly believes the most exciting part of a story is what is not on the page.

JAKE KUHN decided to write a profile on Edgar after he sensed "something great and alluring beneath his serene demeanor." During his free time he likes to cook food harvested in local farms. If he could have been a reporter during any time, it would have been during the Salem witch trials.

Much of HALEY LEE'S writing is inspired by snippets of overheard conversations. She loves to write because it forces her to look beyond the superficial aspects of daily life and to think in complex ways. Her English teacher gave her the best writing advice she has ever received: "A first draft is never good, and if you think it is, you're wrong."

HANA LEE has lived in four states in the United States and has moved into different houses at least eleven times. These experiences have inspired her to write stories about heroes and heroines who find themselves in disorienting and difficult situations. *Binary Switch* is the first script she has ever written.

JOHN LHOTA constructed this story by rewriting the beginning to a short story several times and finally coming to the realization that "each one of these little fragments could tell an entire story all by itself." He plans to study science and engineering and hopes that his writing will be informed and influenced by the discoveries he makes in those fields.

OLIVIA LINN writes about her friends, her body, and what it's like to be "born into a culture that makes being a woman and a feminist so difficult and necessary." She advises young writers to be honest and never hide their points of view behind rigid rhetorical techniques.

ALISON LIU writes whenever inspired. It could be at four in the morning after waking up from a wild dream or in biology class after hearing an unusual and arresting word. She prefers to write from personal experience. The ongoing process of growing up is a recurrent theme in her work.

DYLAN MAGRUDER uses sarcasm to make people laugh on a daily basis. But while writing, he enjoys describing mundane situations in an extremely objective way so as to highlight their absurdity. He mostly reads the works of Southern authors. George Singleton and Dale Ray Phillips are among his favorite.

In the future, GLORIA MARTINEZ plans to use her writing to investigate why people's morals and values so often remain intact when so much may dissuade them from acting against those values. She writes best when sitting in front of a window offering a view of the desert.

ROBYN MATHEWS writes to find an answer to the question, "What would happen if . . . ?" In her next stories, she will investigate the concept of humanity and what it takes for someone to be called inhumane.

NATHAN MEYER came up with the idea for his story while watching the clock tick during one of his classes. He decided to turn his boredom into a personal challenge to "write an interesting story where everything takes place in one room, with one character." His plan for the future is to be a writer forever.

ELIZABETH MILLER describes her writing as "freakish yet funny semirealistic fiction." Her next story will be a sequel to "Cowboys vs. Bear" featuring a Kentuckian farmer who has been digested by the Sasquatches.

INDIA NABARRO enjoys writing flash fiction because she believes it helps preserve the novelty of a brief and exceptional moment. In the future she hopes to write a story about a mundane topic in an innovative way, demonstrating to her reader the beauty of everyday life.

While writing this memoir, ALEXANDER NGUYEN came to the conclusion that he still has a lot to learn about himself. "There's so much more to me than what the world told me there was," he says. Throughout his writing process he also learned that one can write powerfully without an abundant use of adjectives.

SOLA PARK identifies herself as a social activist writing for those whose voices are dismissed and unheard. If she could implement a change in her country, it would be to revisit the Canadian Aboriginal Law so as to correct the injustices committed against the aboriginal peoples of her region.

In her future writing, ALEXIS PAYNE will keep investigating issues of discrimination and injustice. Her next story will be written in the perspective of a refugee and his or her journey to the United States. Oskar, from Jonathan Safran Foer's *Extremely Loud and Incredibly Close*, is her favorite fictional character.

KIRA PELOWITZ classifies a good poet as someone who will draw and highlight connections between things that seem unrelated. She thinks of poetry as a profound way in which strangers may communicate. She is influenced and inspired by slam poetess Andrea Gibson.

KATHLEEN RADIGAN'S (PORTFOLIO GOLD) writing portfolio, titled *Love Songs*, is an attempt to talk about love in a genuine and intelligent way. She believes that the best writing is produced by "giving the world around you your undivided attention." In the fall she will attend Connecticut College to study English and Social Science. Along with being a writer of fiction, Kathleen is a singer-songwriter with EP's available on iTunes.

CALEB RAK writes in his bedroom late at night. His favorite poet is Allen Ginsberg because even though he does not understand Ginsberg's poetry, he revels in trying to figure out its mysteries.

HOLLY RICE thinks it's important to write about contemporary and relevant issues so that large audiences can understand and connect to her work. Someday she hopes to write about her autistic sibling to give readers a further understanding of disabilities and the true ability that lies with those who have them.

MEGGIE ROYER'S favorite writing subject is love, because it's a topic she can treat uniquely in each poem. When she began to write about her vulnerabilities, she noticed that her poetry began to improve. She suggests to other writers that they use their words to explore what disturbs and frightens them.

ADAM SCHORIN wrote this story after spending a few of his lunch breaks working with special-needs students. He values writing as a cathartic experience and truly loves reading. "I can read *To Kill a Mockingbird* four, five times and still shiver when Scout says, 'Hey, Boo.' Very few other things have that sort of power over me."

REBECCA SCURLOCK'S memoir is a collection of the most vivid experiences she has had so far. Writing this essay has empowered her to reflect on her mistakes and appreciate her childhood. Sandra Cisneros' *The House on Mango Street* motivated and inspired her to complete this essay.

FRANCESCA SEDLACEK enjoys writing about the "faltering wills and ever-changing feelings" of human beings. While writing poetry she prioritizes sound, focusing particularly on the rhythm and flow of her words.

MICHAEL SUN spends several hours of his week reading articles on sports. He has found the writing on ESPN and Bleacher Report inspire him to write about an array of topics. The most important step in his writing process is brainstorming.

LYDIA SUTTLE wrote this piece late at night while taking advantage of a rush of adrenaline. She considers writing to be an act of dreaming with eyes open. Her work is stimulated by music and personal experience.

NICHOLAS TEAGUE is inspired to write whenever he hears about "the ordinary people who are able make a difference for causes that they feel passionate about." Although he is happy the Supreme Court overturned DOMA, if he could change any law in the U.S.A., it would be to legalize gay marriage in all states.

NIKLAS THEORIN wrote this story after reading through several shallow Facebook posts and asking himself, "What would these people be saying if they only had two hours to live?" He believes the best part of writing is the unmaterialistic and simplistic qualities of it. "It doesn't require any fancy equipment, just imagination and a knack for the bizarre."

MARLEY TOWNSEND characterizes her writing as "darkly whimsical." She likes to take readers' thoughts down strange and unknown pathways. Her next story will be about a young woman whose mother raises her to believe she is a mythical monster.

JACKSON TRICE'S stories are character-driven. "I started writing because I was in love with the people I made up," she explains, "and I still write for that very reason." She is currently working on a longer piece that revolves around the lives of conjoined twins and a girl addicted to Adderall.

Most of LUCY WAINGER'S writing deals with the emotional turmoils of adolescence. She will write anywhere, except in hospitals, and anytime, except when nauseated. The poetry of Sarah Manguso both fascinates and terrifies her.

MARY ROSE WEBER writes exclusively about historical events. She wants to tell all young poets of the world "to be spontaneous, because without spontaneity we simply can't be fantastic."

SAMANTHA WEST (PORTFOLIO GOLD) describes her writing style as minimalist and clear. She enjoys playing the piano and watching movies and TV shows so she can analyze the script writing. Her advice to young writers is, "Don't be afraid to start over. Even if you wrote three hundred pages, it's okay. Take time to figure out your characters and treat them like real people." She will attend Linfield College this fall.

ANNA XIE (PORTFOLIO GOLD) describes her portfolio as being full of nostalgia, soliloquy, and the observations of a wandering heart. When people read her work, she would like them to speculate and contemplate the obscurities of her writing so that in this way, her thoughts will interact with theirs. Her favorite books include *The Virgin Suicides* by Jeffrey Eugenides and *White Oleander* by Janet Fitch. In the fall she will study English and Creative Writing at the University of Massachusetts Boston.

This essay is one of the first creative pieces HANA ZERIC has ever written in English. She now believes genuine and heartfelt emotions can translate into any language. Her memories of summers spent by the Adriatic Sea served as her main source of inspiration.

A TEACHER'S GUIDE TO THE BEST TEEN WRITING OF 2013

1. Short Story
Discussion on characterization and argument

Goal: Students explain how authors use characters to make an argument in a text.

Activity: Introduce the concept of a story's "argument" by having students discuss popular folktales, stories, and movies that have a moral or special meaning behind them. Ask students to describe how the characters help the author make his or her point. Share responses with the class.

Next, choose a piece with highly engaging characterization. As you're reading out loud, have students mark any points in the text where we learn important things about the characters. After you're finished, have students discuss the following:

• What does the author wants us to know, or understand, after we read this story?

• Who are the most important characters in this story? Have them return to the text and find specific details (character appearance, action, speech, thought, and interaction with others) to illustrate the character's personality. Share student responses.

Next, ask the class:
• How does the author use these characters to make an argument in the story?

2. Short Story
Writing with focus on characterization
Goal: Students creatively interpret the way a character presents an "argument."

Activity: Ask students to write a story with two characters, each representing an opposing set of morals. Once they have completed this task, have a class discussion about their writing experience and how they individualized the characters so that each would represent certain ideals.

3. **Poetry**
Discussion with focus on sense details

Goal: Students explain how specific sense details excite the reader's imagination.

Activity: Select a poem with strong sense details from BTW and replace specific sense details with more general language. Pass the doctored poem out to the class and have them read it out loud. Ask them what they think the poem is trying to express. Next, hand out copies of the original poem. Read it aloud and have students mark the differences between the two. Ask students how they responded differently and why they think the author chose to include those details.

4. **Poetry**
Writing with focus on sense details

Goal: Students write using sense details that excite the reader's imagination.

Activity: Have students write a poem that describes their walk to or from school. They should use as many sense details as possible and be as specific as possible. Have those who would like to share read their poems to the class and discuss how the details enrich the poems.

5. **Personal Essay / Memoir—Writing with a focus on structure and pacing**

Goal: Students will write an organized and coherent memoir imitating the format of a BTW piece.

Activity: Read *Reflections* by Rebecca Scurlock out loud with your students. Talk about the format in which her memories are written. Discuss the length of each section, the way a single moment can say so much about a person, and the way in which brevity is beneficial.

Ask your students to write their own memoir modeled after hers.

The first section should be about what their names mean to them, the others may be about an important family holiday/event, a moment of hardship or sadness, and a moment in which someone told them something about themselves that they did or did not agree with. The last section can include an epiphany or an important lesson they have learned and wish to share with others.

6. **Persuasive Writing**
Discussion with a focus on Ethos, Pathos, and Logos

Goal: Students identify the types of evidence used in persuasive writing and write counterarguments.

Activity: Introduce the concept of Ethos (credibility), Pathos (sentiment), and Logos (logic) and ask students how they might use each of these concepts to get something specific that they want from their parents (extended curfew, spending money, reduced punishment, etc.). Record their responses on the board using a chart for each type of appeal.

Next, read one of the persuasive pieces from BTW aloud and have them mark examples of each of these concepts. As a class, discuss which appeals are stronger than others and why. Have students write a response to the author in which they refute at least one of each of the different types of appeals.

ABDEL SHAKUR received his M.F.A. in creative writing from Indiana University and was editor-in-chief of *Indiana Review*. His work has appeared in *2 Bridges Review, Glint Literary Journal,* and others. He teaches English at the Chicago High School for the Arts and blogs at **misstraknowitall. blogspot.com**

ACKNOWLEDGEMENTS

The Alliance for Young Artists & Writers gratefully acknowledges the thousands of educators who annually encourage students to submit their works to the Scholastic Art & Writing Awards and the remarkable students who have the courage to put their art and writing before panels of renowned jurors. We would like to especially recognize the National Writing Project for its far-reaching efforts in the writing community and its continued commitment to our program. In addition, our mission is greatly furthered through special partnerships with the National Art Education Association, the Association of Independent Colleges of Art and Design and the NAACP's ACT-SO program. As a nonprofit organization, our ability to annually recognize and honor creative teens across the country is also made possible through the generosity of our supporters: Scholastic Inc., the Maurice R. Robinson Fund, The New York Times, the Institute for Museum and Library Services, the President's Committee on the Arts and the Humanities, Command Web Offset Co., the AMD Foundation, Blick Art Materials, the National Endowment for the Arts, 3D Systems, New York Life, Bloomberg L.P., Ovation, Amazon.com, the Jacques and Natasha Gelman Trust, the Bernstein Family Foundation, Duck Tape®, the New York City Department of Cultural Affairs, and contributions from numerous other individual, foundation, and corporate funders.

REGIONAL AFFILIATE ORGANIZATIONS

The Alliance would like to thank the regional affiliates listed for coordinating the Scholastic Art & Writing Awards.

Northeast

Connecticut
Connecticut Art Region
Connecticut Art Education Association

Delaware
Delaware Art Region
Delaware State University

Delaware Writing Region
National League of American Pen Women, Diamond State Branch

District of Columbia
D.C. Metro Writing Region
Writopia Lab, *Affiliate*

Maine
Southern Maine Writing Region
Southern Maine Writing Project

Massachusetts
Massachusetts Art & Writing Region
School of the Museum of Fine Arts, Boston

New Hampshire
New Hampshire Art Region
New Hampshire Art Educators' Association

New Hampshire Writing Region
Plymouth Writing Project

New Jersey
Northeast New Jersey Art Region
Montclair Art Museum

New York
Central New York Art Region
CNY Art Council, Inc.

Hudson Valley Art Region
Hudson Valley Art Awards

Hudson-to-Housatonic Writing Region
Writopia Lab, Westchester & Fairfield

New York City Art & Writing Region
Casita Maria Center for Arts and Education

Twin Tiers Art Region
Arnot Art Museum (serving parts of New York and
Pennsylvania)

Pennsylvania
Berks, Carbon, Lehigh, and Northampton Art Region
East Central PA Scholastic Art Awards

Lancaster County Art Region
Lancaster Museum of Art

Lancaster County Writing Region
Lancaster Public Library

Northeastern Pennsylvania Art Region
The Times-Tribune

Philadelphia Art Region
Philadelphia Arts in Education Partnership at the
University of the Arts

Philadelphia Writing Region
Philadelphia Writing Project

Pittsburgh Art Region
La Roche College & North Allegheny School District

Pittsburgh Writing Region
Western PA Writing Project

South Central Pennsylvania Art & Writing Region
Commonwealth Connections Academy

Southwestern Pennsylvania Art & Writing Region
California University of Pennsylvania

Rhode Island
Rhode Island Art Region
Rhode Island Art Education Association

Vermont
Vermont Art & Writing Region
Brattleboro Museum & Art Center

Southeast

Florida
Broward Art Region
Young at Art Museum

Central Florida Writing Region
The English Teacher's Friend

Miami-Dade Art Region
Miami-Dade County Public Schools
Miami-Dade Writing Region
Miami Writes

Northeast Florida Art Region
Duval Art Teachers' Association

Palm Beach Art Region
Educational Gallery Group (Eg^2)

Pinellas County Art Region
Pinellas County Schools

Sarasota Art Region
Sarasota County Schools

Georgia
Georgia Art & Writing Region
Savannah College of Art and Design (SCAD)

Kentucky
Louisville Metropolitan Area Art Region
Jefferson County Public Schools

Northern Kentucky Writing Region
Northern Kentucky Writing Region

South Central Kentucky Art Region
Southern Kentucky Performing Arts Center

Mississippi
Mississippi Art Region
Mississippi Museum of Art

Mississippi Writing Region
The Eudora Welty Foundation

North Carolina
Eastern/Central North Carolina Art Region
Barton College

Mid-Carolina Art & Writing Region
Charlotte-Mecklenburg Schools

Western North Carolina Art Region
Asheville Art Museum

South Carolina
South Carolina Art Region
Lander University

Tennessee
Middle Tennessee Art Region
Cheekwood Botanical Garden & Museum of Art

Mid-South Art Region
Memphis Brooks Museum of Art

Virginia
Arlington County Art Region
Arlington Public Schools

Fairfax County Art Region
Fairfax County Public Schools

Richmond County Art Region
Virginia Museum of Fine Arts

Southwest Virginia Art Region
Fine Arts Center for the New River Valley

West

California
California Art Region
California Arts Project

California Writing Region
California Writing Project

Los Angeles Art Region
Armory Center for the Arts

Colorado
Colorado Art Region
Colorado Art Education Association

Hawaii
Hawaii Art Region
Hawaii State Department of Education

Idaho
Idaho Art & Writing Region
Boise State Writing Project

Nevada
Northern Nevada Art Region
Nevada Museum of Art

Northern Nevada Writing Region
Nevada Alliance for Arts Education

Southern Nevada Art & Writing Region
Springs Preserve

Oregon
Oregon Art Region—Central Oregon Area
Oregon Art Education Association

Oregon Art Region—Portland Metro Area
Oregon Art Education Association,

Oregon Art Region—Willamette Valley Art Region
Benton County Historical Society

Washington
Snohomish County Art Region
Schack Art Center

Midwest

Illinois
Chicago Writing Region
Chicago Area Writing Project

Mid-Central Illinois Art Region
The Regional Scholastic Art Awards Council of
Mid-Central Illinois

Southern Illinois Art Region
John R. and Eleanor R. Mitchell Foundation/Cedarhurst
Center for the Arts

Suburban Chicago Art Region
Downers Grove North and South High Schools

Indiana
Central/Southern Indiana Art Region
Clowes Memorial Hall of Butler University

Central/Southern Indiana Writing Region
Clowes Memorial Hall of Butler University and Hoosier
Writing Project at IUPUI

Northeast Indiana and Northwest Ohio Art & Writing Region
Fort Wayne Museum of Art

Iowa
Iowa Art & Writing Region
The Connie Belin & Jacqueline N. Blank International
Center for Gifted Education and Talent Development,
University of Iowa

Kansas
Eastern Kansas Art Region
Wichita Center for the Arts

Western Kansas Art Region
Western Kansas Scholastic Art Awards

Michigan
Southern Michigan, Macomb, St. Clair, and Lapeer Art Region
College for Creative Studies

Southeastern Michigan Thumb Art Region
College for Creative Studies

West Central Michigan Art Region
Kendall College of Art and Design of
Ferris State University

Minnesota
Minnesota Art Region
College of Visual Arts, *Affiliate*

Missouri
Missouri Writing Region
Prairie Lands Writing Project at
Missouri Western State University

Nebraska
Nebraska Art Region
Omaha Public Schools Art Department

Ohio
Central Ohio Art Region
Columbus College of Art & Design

Cuyahoga County Art & Writing Region
Cleveland Institute of Art

Lorain County Art Region
Lorain County Regional Scholastic Arts Committee

Miami Valley Art Region
TEJAS Gallery / K12

Northeast Central Ohio Art Region
Kent State University, Stark Campus

Northeastern Ohio Art Region
Youngstown State University, Art Department

Northeastern Ohio Writing Region
Ohio Writing Project at Kent State University

Southern Ohio, Northern Kentucky, and
Southeastern Indiana Art Region
Art Machine, Inc.

Wisconsin
Milwaukee Writing Region
Still Waters Collective

Southeast Wisconsin Writing Region
Harborside Academy

Wisconsin Art Region
The Milwaukee Art Museum

Southwest

Arizona
Arizona Writing Region
Arizona English Teachers Association

Louisiana
North-Central Louisiana Writing Region
Northwestern State University Writing Project

Southeast Louisiana Writing Region
Greater New Orleans Writing Project

Oklahoma
Oklahoma Art Region
Tulsa Community College Liberal Arts Department

Oklahoma Writing Region
Tulsa Community College Foundation and Oklahoma
Young Writers

Texas
Harris County Art & Writing Region
Harris County Department of Education

San Antonio Art & Writing Region
SAY Sí (San Antonio Youth Yes)

Travis County Art Region
St. Stephen's School

West Texas Art Region
Wayland Baptist University Department of Art

SUPPORT THE SCHOLASTIC ART & WRITING AWARDS

The Best Teen Writing of 2013 is made possible through the generous support of our donors.

More than 230,000 works were submitted and judged for the 2013 Awards, and upwards of 60,000 middle and high school artists and writers were recognized for their talents. Of the top national winners in the Awards' 11 writing categories, 69 works are highlighted in this publication.

The Alliance for Young Artists & Writers, which presents the Awards, is a nonprofit 501(c)(3) organization, and is supported entirely by charitable contributions from institutional partners and individuals like you. Donations underwrite the production of the Awards at the national and local levels; exhibitions, readings, and workshops; publications; and award and scholarship opportunities for creative young artists and writers in grades 7 through 12 across the country.

Help us continue to celebrate our nation's most creative teens in both writing and art. Please make your tax-deductible contribution today.

To give online: Visit **www.artandwriting.org**.
To give by check: Mail check, made payable to Alliance for Young Artists & Writers, to:

Alliance for Young Artists & Writers
Attention: Development
557 Broadway
New York, NY 10012

To make a special gift or to discuss other ways to provide your financial support, please contact Jonathan Ettinger, Director, Development & External Relations, by phone at 212-343-7773 or by e-mail at jettinger@artandwriting.org.

Made in the USA
San Bernardino, CA
03 March 2014